NO
EQUAL
JUSTICE

NO EQUAL JUSTICE

*Race and Class in the
American Criminal Justice System*

DAVID COLE

THE NEW PRESS   NEW YORK

© 1999 by David Cole.

Published in the United States by The New Press, New York
Distributed by W.W. Norton & Company, Inc., New York

The New Press was established in 1990 as a not-for-profit alternative to the large, commercial publishing houses currently dominating the book publishing industry. The New Press operates in the public interest rather than for private gain, and is committed to publishing, in innovative ways, works of educational, cultural, and community value that might be deemed insufficiently profitable.

www.thenewpress.com

Printed in the United States of America

9 8 7 6 5 4 3 2

for Nina and Aidan

—Contents

"There can be no equal justice where the kind of trial a man gets depends on the amount of money he has."

—Justice Hugo Black, *Griffin v. Illinois*, 351 U.S. 12 (1956)

—Acknowledgments

This book benefitted from discussions with many practitioners, colleagues, and students. In particular, I would like to thank Stephen Bright, Tanya Coke, Jonathan Greenberg, George Kendall, Gary Peller, and Abbe Smith for their comments on various chapters; my research assistants, A.J. Camelio, Jennifer Cannon, Dan Derechin, John Donoghue, Dan Farrington, Todd Richman, Corinne Schiff, Jeff Smagula, Stephen Warshawsky, and Ling Zeng for their invaluable research; Diane Wachtell for excellent editing; William Naugle for careful proofreading; and my agent, Ron Goldman, for helping this book see the light of day. I also received very helpful feedback from workshops at Georgetown University Law Center and Brooklyn Law School. Georgetown University Law Center supported the writing of the book with several summer writers' grants. And finally, I owe my deepest debt of gratitude to my wife, Nina Pillard, who helped me conceive, shape, and produce the book in every way imaginable, and who deserves much credit (and no blame) for the final product.

—Introduction

The mood and temper of the public in regard to the treatment of crime and criminals is one of the most unfailing tests of the civilisation of any country. A calm dispassionate recognition of the rights of the accused, and even of the convicted criminal, against the State—a constant heart-searching by all charged with the duty of punishment—a desire and eagerness to rehabilitate in the world of industry those who have paid their due in the hard coinage of punishment: tireless efforts towards discovery of curative and regenerative processes: unfailing faith that there is a treasure, if you can only find it, in the heart of every man. These are the symbols, which, in the treatment of crime and criminal, mark and measure the stored-up strength of a nation, and are sign and proof of the living virtue in it.
—Winston Churchill, House of Commons, 1910[1]

The most telling image from the most widely and closely watched criminal trial of our lifetime is itself an image of people watching television. On one half of the screen black law students at Howard Law School cheer as they watch the live coverage of a Los Angeles jury acquitting O.J. Simpson of the double murder of his ex-wife and her friend. On the other half of the screen, white students at George Washington University Law School sit shocked in silence as they watch the same scene. The split-screen image captures in a moment the division between white and black Americans on the question of O.J. Simpson's guilt. And that division in turn reflects an even deeper divide on the issue of the fairness and legitimacy of American criminal justice.

Before, during, and after the trial, about three-quarters of black citizens maintained that Simpson was not guilty, while an equal fraction of white citizens deemed him guilty. More people paid attention to this trial than any other in world history, but neither the DNA evidence nor the dubious reliability of Los Angeles detective Mark Fuhrman altered either group's views on guilt or innocence.

In some respects, the racially divided response to the verdict was understandable. For many black citizens, the acquittal was a sign of hope, or at least payback. For much of our history, the mere allegation that a black man had murdered two white people would have been sufficient grounds for his lynching. Until very recently, the jury rendering judgment on O.J. Simpson would likely have been all white; Simpson's jury, by contrast, consisted of nine blacks, two whites, and an Hispanic. And the prosecution was poisoned by the racism of the central witness, Detective Mark Fuhrman, who had, among other things, called blacks "niggers" on tape and then lied about it on the stand. To many blacks, the jury's "not guilty" verdict demonstrated that the system is not *always* rigged against the black defendant, and that was worth cheering.

The white law students' shock was also understandable. The evidence against Simpson was overwhelming. Simpson's blood had been found at the scene of the murders. The victims' blood had been found in Simpson's white Bronco and on a sock in Simpson's bedroom. And a glove found at Simpson's home had, as prosecutor Marcia Clark put it in her closing argument to the jury, "all of the evidence on it: Ron Goldman, fibres from his shirt; Ron Goldman's hair; Nicole's hair; the defendant's blood; Ron Goldman's blood; Nicole's blood; and the Bronco fibre."[2] The defense's suggestion that the Los Angeles Police Department somehow planted all of this evidence ran directly contrary to their simultaneous (and quite effective) demonstration of the LAPD's "keystone cops" incompetence. To many whites, it appeared that a predominantly black jury had voted for one of their own, and had simply ignored the overwhelming evidence that Simpson was a brutal double murderer.

But there is a deep irony in these reactions. Simpson, of course, was atypical in every way. The very factors that played to his advantage at trial generally work to the disadvantage of the vast majority of black defendants. Simpson had virtually unlimited resources, a jury that identified with him along racial grounds, and celebrity status. Most black defendants, by contrast, cannot afford any attorney, much less a "dream team." Their fate is usually decided by predominantly or exclusively white juries. And most black defendants find that their image is linked in America's mind not with celebrity, but with criminality.

At the same time, the features that worked to Simpson's advantage, and that occasioned such outrage among whites, generally benefit whites. Whites have a disproportionate share of the wealth in our society, and are more likely to be able to buy a good defense; white defendants generally face juries composed of members of their own race; and a white person's face is not stereotypically associated with crime. Thus, what dismayed whites in Simpson's case is precisely what generally works to their advantage, while what blacks cheered is what most often works to their disadvantage.

Had Simpson been poor and unknown, as most black (and white) criminal defendants are, everything would have been different. The case would have garnered no national attention. Simpson would have been represented by an overworked and underpaid public defender who would not have been able to afford experts to examine and challenge the government's evidence. No one would have conducted polls on the case, and the trial would not have been televised. In all likelihood, Simpson would have been convicted in short order, without serious testing of the evidence against him or the methods by which it was obtained. Whites would have expressed no outrage that a poor black defendant had been convicted, and blacks would have had nothing to cheer about. That, not *California v. O.J. Simpson*, is the reality in American courtrooms across the country today.

In other words, it took an atypical case, one in which minority race and lower socioeconomic class did *not* coincide, in which the defense outperformed the prosecution, and in which the jury was predominantly black, for white people to pay attention to the role that race and class play in criminal justice. Yet the issues of race and class are present in every criminal case, and in the vast majority of cases they play out no more fairly. Of course, they generally work in the opposite direction: the prosecution outspends and outperforms the defense, the jury is predominantly white, and the defendant is poor and a member of a racial minority. In an odd way, then, the Simpson case brought to the foreground issues that lurk beneath the entire system of criminal justice. The system's legitimacy turns on equality before the law, but the system's reality could not be further from that ideal. As Justice Hugo Black wrote over forty years ago: "There can be no equal justice where the kind of trial a man gets depends on the amount of money he has." He might well have added, "or the color of his skin." Where race and class affect outcomes, we cannot maintain that the criminal law is just.

Equality, however, is a difficult and elusive goal. In our nation, it has been the cause of a civil war, powerful political movements, and countless violent uprisings. Yet the gap between the rich and the poor is larger in the United States today than in any other Western industrialized nation,[3] and has been steadily widening since 1968.[4] In 1989, the wealthiest 1 percent of U.S. households owned nearly 40 percent of the nation's wealth. The wealthiest 20 percent owned more than 80 percent of the nation's wealth. That leaves precious little for the rest.[5] The income and wealth gap correlates closely with race. Minorities' median net worth is less than 7 percent that of whites.[6] Nine percent of white families had incomes below the poverty level in 1992, while more than 30 percent of black families and 26.5 percent of Hispanic families fell below that level.[7] The consequences of the country's race and class divisions are felt in every aspect of American life, from infant mortality and unemployment, where black rates are double white rates;[8] to public education, where the proportion of black children educated in segregated schools is increasing;[9] to housing, where racial segregation is the norm, integration the rare exception.[10] Racial inequality, which Alexis de Tocqueville long ago recognized as "the most formidable evil threatening the future of the United States,"[11] remains to this day the most formidable of our social problems.

This inequality is in turn reflected in statistics on crime and the criminal justice system. The vast majority of those behind bars are poor; 40 percent of state prisoners can't even read; and 67 percent of prison inmates did not have full-time employment when they were arrested. The per capita incarceration rate among blacks is seven times that among whites. African Americans make up about 12 percent of the general population, but more than half of the prison population. They serve longer sentences, have higher arrest and conviction rates, face higher bail amounts, and are more often the victims of police use of deadly force than white citizens. In 1995, one in three young black men between the ages of twenty and twenty-nine was imprisoned or on parole or probation. If incarceration rates continue their current trends, one in four young black males born today will serve time in prison during his lifetime (meaning that he will be convicted and sentenced to more than one year of incarceration). Nationally, for every one black man who graduates from college, 100 are arrested.[12]

In addition, poor and minority citizens are disproportionately victimized by crime. Poorer and less educated persons are the victims of violent crime at significantly higher rates than wealthy and more educated persons.[13] African Americans are victimized by robbery at a rate 150 percent higher than whites; they are the victims of rape, aggravated assault, and armed robbery 25 percent more often than whites.[14] Homicide is the leading cause of death among young black men.[15] Because we live in segregated communities, most crime is intraracial; the more black crime there is, the more black victims there are. But at the same time, the more law enforcement resources we direct toward protecting the black community from crime, the more often black citizens, especially those living in the inner city, will find their friends, relatives, and neighbors behind bars.

This book argues that while our criminal justice system is explicitly based on the premise and promise of equality before the law, the administration of criminal law—whether by the officer on the beat, the legislature, or the Supreme Court—is in fact predicated on the exploitation of inequality. My claim is not simply that we have ignored inequality's effects within the criminal justice system, nor that we have tried but failed to achieve equality there. Rather, I contend that *our criminal justice system affirmatively depends on inequality*. Absent race and class disparities, the privileged among us could not enjoy as much constitutional protection of our liberties as we do; and without those disparities, we could not afford the policy of mass incarceration that we have pursued over the past two decades.

White Americans are not likely to want to believe this claim. The principle that all are equal before the law is perhaps the most basic in American law; it is that maxim, after all, that stands etched atop the Supreme Court's magnificent edifice. The two most well-known Supreme Court decisions on criminal justice stand for equality before the law, and that is why they are so well known. In *Gideon v. Wainwright*, the Court in 1963 held that states must provide a lawyer at state expense to all defendants charged with a serious crime who cannot afford to hire their own lawyer. The story became a best-selling book and an award-winning motion picture. Three years later, in *Miranda v. Arizona*, the Court required the police to provide poor suspects with an attorney at state expense and to inform all suspects of their rights before questioning them in custody. In these landmark decisions, the Court sought to ameliorate societal inequalities—both among suspects and between suspects and the state—that undermined the criminal justice system's promise of equality. As the Court stated in *Miranda*, "[w]hile authorities are not required to relieve the accused of his poverty, they have the obligation not to take advantage of indigence in the administration of justice."

The prominence of these decisions, however, is misleading. They were both decided by the Supreme Court under Chief Justice Earl Warren, at a time when the Court was solidly liberal and strongly committed to racial and economic equality. At virtually every juncture since *Gideon* and *Miranda*, the Supreme Court has undercut the principle of equality reflected in those decisions, and has itself "take[n] advantage of indigence in the administration of justice." Today, those decisions stand out as anomalies. *Gideon* is a symbol of equality unrealized in practice; poor defendants are nominally entitled to the assistance of counsel at trial, but the Supreme Court has failed to demand that the assistance be meaningful. Lawyers who have slept through testimony or appeared in court drunk have nonetheless been deemed to have provided their indigent clients "effective assistance of counsel." And today's Court has so diluted *Miranda* that the decision has had little effect on actual police interrogation practices.

The exploitation of inequality in criminal justice is driven by the need to balance two fundamental and competing interests: the protection of constitutional rights, and the protection of law-abiding citizens from crime. Virtually all constitutional protections in criminal justice have a cost: they make the identification and prosecution of suspected criminals more difficult. Without a constitutional requirement that police have probable cause and a warrant before they conduct searches, for example, police officers would be far more effective in rooting out and stopping crime. Without jury trials, criminal justice administration would be much more efficient. But if police could enter our homes whenever they pleased, we would live in a police state, with no meaningful privacy protection. And absent jury trials, the community would have little check on overzealous prosecutors. Much of the public and academic debate about criminal justice focuses on where we should draw the line between law enforcement interests and constitutional protections. Liberals tend to argue for more rights-protective rules, while conservatives tend to advocate rules that give law enforcement more leeway. But both sides agree, at least in principle, that the line should be drawn in the same place for everyone.

In fact, however, we have repeatedly mediated the tension not by picking one point on the continuum, but in effect by picking two points—one for the more privileged and educated, the other for the poor and less educated. For example, the Supreme Court has ruled that the Fourth Amendment bars police from searching luggage, purses, or wallets without a warrant that is based on probable cause to believe evidence of crime will be found. But at the same time, the Court permits police officers to approach any citizen—without any basis for suspicion—and request "consent" to search. The officer need not inform the suspect that he has a right to say no. This tactic, not surprisingly, is popular among the police, and is disproportionately targeted at young black men, who are less likely to assert their right to say no. In this way, the privacy of the privileged is guaranteed, but the police still get their evidence, and society does not have to pay the cost in increased crime of extending to everyone the right to privacy that the privileged enjoy. This pattern is repeated throughout the criminal justice system: the Court affirms a constitutional right, but in a manner that effectively protects the right only for the privileged few, while as a practical matter denying the right to those who are less privileged. By exploiting society's "background" inequality, the Court sidesteps the difficult question of how much constitutional protection we could afford if we were willing to ensure that it was enjoyed equally by all people.

Nor is the Supreme Court alone in exploiting inequality in this way. If there is a common theme in criminal justice policy in

America, it is that we consistently seek to avoid difficult trade-offs by exploiting inequality. Politicians impose the most serious criminal sanctions on conduct in which they and their constituents are least likely to engage. Thus, a predominantly white Congress has mandated prison sentences for the possession and distribution of crack cocaine one hundred times more severe than the penalties for powder cocaine. African Americans comprise more than 90 percent of those found guilty of crack cocaine crimes, but only 20 percent of those found guilty of powder cocaine crimes. By contrast, when white youth began smoking marijuana in large numbers in the 1960s and 1970s, state legislatures responded by reducing penalties and in some states effectively decriminalizing marijuana possession. More broadly, it is unimaginable that our country's heavy reliance on incarceration would be tolerated if the black/white incarceration rates were reversed, and whites were incarcerated at seven times the rate that blacks are. The white majority can "afford" the costs associated with mass incarceration because the incarcerated mass is disproportionately nonwhite.

Similarly, police officers routinely use methods of investigation and interrogation against members of racial minorities and the poor that would be deemed unacceptable if applied to more privileged members of the community. "Consent" searches, pretextual traffic stops, and "quality of life" policing are all disproportionately used against black citizens. Courts assign attorneys to defend the poor in serious criminal trials whom the wealthy would not hire to represent them in traffic court. And jury commissioners and lawyers have long engaged in discriminatory practices that result in disproportionately white juries.

These double standards are not, of course, explicit; on the face of it, the criminal law is color-blind and class-blind. But in a sense, this only makes the problem worse. The rhetoric of the criminal justice system sends the message that our society carefully protects everyone's constitutional rights, but in practice the rules assure that law enforcement prerogatives will generally prevail over the rights of minorities and the poor. By affording criminal suspects substantial constitutional protections in theory, the Supreme Court validates the results of the criminal justice system as fair. That formal fairness obscures the systemic concerns that ought to be raised by the fact that the prison population is overwhelmingly poor and disproportionately black.

I am not suggesting that the disproportionate results of the criminal justice system are wholly attributable to racism, nor that the double standards are intentionally designed to harm members of minority groups and the poor. Intent and motive are notoriously difficult to fathom, particularly where there are multiple actors and decisionmakers, and this book does not set out to prove intentional discrimination. In fact, I think it more likely that the double standards have developed because they are convenient mechanisms for avoiding hard questions about competing interests, and it is human nature to avoid hard questions. But whatever the reasons, we have established two systems of criminal justice: one for the privileged, and another for the less privileged. Some of the distinctions are based on race, others on class, but in no true sense can it be said that all are equal before the criminal law. Thus, I take issue with those, like Professor Randall Kennedy, who argue that as long as we can rid the criminal justice system of *explicit* and *intentional* considerations of race, we will have solved the problem of inequality in criminal justice.[16] The problems canvassed in this book for the most part do not stem from explicit and intentional race or class discrimination, but they are problems of inequality nonetheless. To suggest that a "color-blind" set of rules is sufficient is to ignore the lion's share of inequality that pervades the criminal justice system today. The disparities I discuss are built into the very structure and doctrine of our criminal justice system, and unless and until we acknowledge and remedy them, we will have "no equal justice."

Equality in criminal justice does not necessarily mean more rights for the criminally accused. Indeed, I think it likely that were we to commit ourselves to equality, the substantive scope of constitutional protections accorded to the accused would be reduced, not expanded. If we had to pay full cost, in law enforcement terms, for the constitutional rights we now claim to protect, the scope of those constitutional rights would probably be cut back for all. But at least we would then strike the balance between law enforcement and constitutional rights honestly.

Much of this book will be dedicated to demonstrating how the double standards in criminal justice operate. Some readers will need more convincing than others on this score. By a detailed description of the problem, I hope to shake the confidence of those who believe the system is fair. But I also hope to demonstrate to those more skeptical of the system that the problems cannot be explained by simple charges of racism, and cannot be solved by banning intentional racism from the system. I discuss in turn the constitutional rules governing police practices, the provision of legal representation to those who cannot afford it, jury discrimination, disparities in sentencing, and legal challenges to discrimination in the criminal justice system. In each of these areas, we have "used" inequality to forge an illegitimate compromise between law enforcement needs and constitutional rights. Sometimes the double standard is achieved by exploiting ignorance, as in the Supreme Court's refusal to require police officers to inform suspects of their right to say no when they are asked to "consent" to a search. Sometimes the double standard stems from the different resources that rich and poor defendants have at their disposal for their defense. And sometimes the double standard is integral to the criminal justice policy set by legislators; politicians can afford to be "tough on crime" because society has already written off most of those on whom we will be "tough."

No one disputes that the criminal justice system's legitimacy depends on equality before the law, so demonstrating that we have not lived up to that promise—this book's first purpose—should be a sufficient argument for demanding a remedy. It should require little argument to maintain that as a moral matter we must take Justice Black's dictate about equal justice much more seriously if we are to remain true to the first principle of criminal justice. We should do it because it is the right thing to do. But my second task in writing this book is to demonstrate that there are also strong pragmatic reasons for responding to inequality in criminal justice, because a criminal justice system based on double standards both fuels racial enmity and encourages crime.

The racially polarized reactions to the Simpson case illustrate a deep and longstanding racial divide on issues of criminal justice: blacks are consistently more skeptical of the criminal justice system than whites. A long history of racially discriminatory practices in criminal law enforcement has much to do with this skepticism, but it is not just a matter of history: the double standards we rely on today in drawing the lines between rights and law enforcement re-inforce black alienation and distrust. Because criminal law governs the most serious sanctions that a society can impose on its members, inequity in its administration has especially corrosive conse-quences. Perceptions of race and class disparities in the criminal justice system are at the core of the race and class divisions in our society.

The perception and reality of double standards also contribute to the crime problem by eroding the legitimacy of the criminal law and undermining a cohesive sense of community. As any wise ruler knows (and many ineffective despots learn), the most effective way to govern is not through brute force or terror, but by fostering broad social acceptance for one's policies. Where a community accepts the social rules as legitimate, the rules will be largely self-enforcing. Studies have found that most people obey the law not because they fear formal punishment—the risk of actually being apprehended and punished is infinitesimal for all crimes other than murder—but because they and their peers have accepted and internalized the rules, and because they do not want to let their community down. The rules will be accepted, and community pressure to conform will be effective, only to the extent that "the community" believes that the rules are just and that the authority behind them is legiti-mate. Thus, although the double standards I discuss in this book were adopted for the purpose of *reducing* the costs of crime associ-ated with protecting constitutional rights, I argue that in the end they undermine the criminal justice system's legitimacy, and thereby *increase* crime and its attendant costs.

When significant sectors of a community view the system as un-just, law enforcement is compromised in at least two ways. First, people feel less willing to cooperate with the system, whether by offering leads to police officers, testifying as witnesses for the prosecution, or entering guilty verdicts as jurors. Second, and more importantly, people are more likely to commit crimes, precisely because the laws forbidding such behavior have lost much of their moral force. When the law loses its moral force, the only deterrents that remain are the strong-arm methods of conviction and imprisonment. We should not be surprised, then, that the United States has the second highest incarceration rate of all developed nations. And it should be no wonder that black America, which has been most victimized by the inequalities built into the criminal justice system, is simultaneously most plagued by crime and most distrustful of criminal law enforcement.

What is to be done? In the book's final chapter, I suggest a series of responses. The first step, of course, is to recognize the scope of the problem. Although African Americans are generally skeptical of the criminal justice system's fairness, their skepticism is not shared by the white majority, nor apparently by the courts. Until now, the courts and legislatures have been extremely reluctant even to allow the issue of inequality in criminal justice to be aired, and have instead impermissibly exploited inequality to make the hard choices of criminal justice seem easier. This book argues that a realistic response to crime, and in the end our society's survival as a cohesive community, depend on a candid assessment of the uses of inequality in criminal justice.

The second step is to eliminate the double standards. This turns out to be rather straightforward in some instances, but difficult if not impossible in others. We could certainly require, for example, that police officers seeking consent to search inform citizens that they have the right to say no. But wealthy defendants will always be able to outspend poor defendants; not everyone can afford Johnny Cochran. Even an *attempt* to limit such disparities would be a reversal of the current approach, however, which affirmatively exploits them. Such reforms are necessary if the criminal justice system is to regain the legitimacy so critical to effective law enforcement.

But restoring legitimacy through adjusting the rules that govern criminal law enforcement will not be nearly enough. The double standards have also had a devastating impact on black communities, particularly in poor, inner-city enclaves. The racial divide fostered and furthered by inequality in criminal justice has contributed to a spiral of crime and decay in the inner city, corroding the sense of belonging that encourages compliance with the criminal law. Therefore, we cannot limit ourselves to restoring the criminal law's legitimacy, but must also seek to restore the communities that have been doubly ravaged by crime and the criminal justice system. To accomplish this, we must both reinforce and support community-building organizations in the inner cities, and change the way we respond to crime itself.

These remedies go hand in hand. In order to adopt a more effective approach to criminal punishment, we must rebuild communities. In order to rebuild communities, we must forgo our reliance on mass incarceration—a policy that has robbed inner-city neighborhoods of whole generations of young men. We respond to crime today in a self-defeating way, by stigmatizing criminals, cutting them off from their communities, and fostering criminal subcultures that encourage further criminal behavior. In doing so, we undermine one of the most important deterrents to crime: a sense of belonging to a law-abiding community. By the same token, to the extent that we reinforce and reify divisions between individuals and communities, and between the law-enforcing and law-breaking communities, we encourage continuing criminal behavior. If we are to reduce criminal recidivism, we must adopt measures that seek to reintegrate offenders into the community, and that reinforce social ties within and across communities.

This is an ambitious agenda. But unless all Americans begin to see the problem of inequality in criminal justice as their own, and unless we take responsible measures to respond to it, America's crime problem and racial divide will only get worse.

ENDNOTES

1. Robert James, ed., *Winston S. Churchill: His Complete Speeches, 1897–1903*, 1598 (New York: Chelsea House Publishers, 1974).
2. Jeffrey Toobin, "A Horrible Human Event," *The New Yorker*, 23 October 1995, 40, 46.

3. Keith Bradsher, "Gap in Wealth in U.S. Called Widest in West," *N.Y. Times*, 17 April 1995, A1; Keith Bradsher, "Low Ranking for Poor American Children," *N.Y. Times*, 14 August 1995, A9 (reporting that gap between rich and poor children is larger in United States than any other Western industrialized nation).

4. Steven A. Holmes, "Income Disparity Between Poorest and Richest Rises," *N.Y. Times*, 20 June 1996, A1.

5. Elmer W. Johnson, "Corporate Soulcraft in the Age of Brutal Markets," *Business Ethics Quarterly*, vol. 7, no. 4, October 1997.

6. Bureau of the Census, U.S. Dept of Commerce, *Statistical Abstract of the United States — 1993*, 477 (Table 753).

7. Id. at 47 (Table 50), 471 (Table 741), 473 (Table 743).

8. In 1993, the infant mortality rate among whites was 6.8 deaths per 1,000 live births, while the rate among blacks was 16.5 deaths per 1,000 births. U.S. Dept. of Commerce, *Statistical Abstract of the United States — 1996*, 93 (Table 127) (Infant Mortality Rates, by Race). From 1980 to 1995, the unemployment rate among blacks has always been at least twice that among whites. In 1995, unemployment among blacks was 10.4 percent, and among whites was 4.9 percent. Id. at 413 (Table 644) (Unemployed Workers — Summary: 1980 to 1995).

9. Gary Orfield, Mark D. Bachmeier, David R. James, and Tamela Eitle, "Deepening Segregation in American Public Schools" (Harvard Project on School Desegregation, 5 April 1997).

10. Douglas Massey and Nancy Denton, *American Apartheid: Segregation and the Making of the Underclass* (Cambridge, MA: Harvard Univ. Press, 1993).

11. Alexis de Tocqueville, *Democracy in America*, 340 (trans. George Lawrence, ed. J.P. Mayer) (New York: Harper & Row, 1969).

12. David C. Lewen, "Curing America's Addiction to Prisons," 20 Fordham Urb. L.J. 641, 646 (1993) (socioeconomic characteristics of prisoners); Michael Tonry, *Malign Neglect — Race, Crime and Punishment in America*, 4 (New York: Oxford Univ. Press, 1995) (white and black incarceration rates). In 1996, there were 526,200 black men and 510,900 white men in prison. Fox Butterfield, "Prison Population Growing Although Crime Rate Drops," *N.Y. Times*, 9 August 1998, 18. The average sentence imposed on black offenders sentenced to incarceration in U.S. district courts in 1992 was 84.1 months, while the average sentence for white offenders was 56.8 months. Bureau of Justice Statistics, *Sourcebook of Criminal Justice Statistics — 1995*, 474 (Table 5.25) (1996). Although they are only 12 percent of the population, blacks make up 31.3 percent of those arrested. Id. at 408 (Table 4.10). Among convicted offenders, 80 percent of black defendants and 75 percent of whites are sentenced to incarceration. Id. at 471 (Table 5.22). See also Ian Ayres and Joel Waldfogel, "A Market Test for Race Discrimination in Bail Setting," 46 Stan. L. Rev. 987 (1994) (finding that judges impose higher bail amounts on black defendants); Marc Mauer and Tracy Huling, *Young Black Americans and the Criminal Justice System: Five Years Later* (The Sentencing Project, 1 October 1995) (young black men under criminal justice supervision); Henry Louis Gates, Jr., "The Charmer," *The New Yorker*, 29 April/6 May 1996, 116 (100 black men arrested for every one in college); David B. Mustard, "Racial, Ethnic and Gender Disparities in Sentencing: Evidence from the US Federal Courts," Univ. of Georgia Economics Working Paper, 97–458 (1997) (finding

that even under federal sentencing guidelines, and controlling for offense level and criminal history, blacks receive sentences six months longer on average than whites).

13. Ronet Bachman, U.S. Dept. of Justice, Bureau of Justice Statistics, *Crime Victimization in City, Suburban, and Rural Areas: A National Crime Victimization Survey Report,* 6 (June 1992).

14. John Hagan and Ruth Peterson, "Criminal Inequality in America," in J. Hagan & R. Peterson, *Crime and Inequality,* 25 (Stanford: Stanford Univ. Press, 1995).

15. Id. at 16.

16. Randall Kennedy, *Race, Crime and the Law* (New York: Pantheon, 1997).

1—Policing Race and Class

Miami to Atlanta is 663 miles. If you had a choice, you'd fly. Those who can't afford air travel often make the trip by bus, a grueling nineteen-hour ride. On August 27, 1985, Terrance Bostick, a twenty-eight-year-old black man, was sleeping in the back seat of a Greyhound bus, on his way from Miami to Atlanta, when he awoke to find two police officers standing over him. They were wearing bright green "raid" jackets bearing the Broward County Sheriff's Office insignia and displaying their badges; one held a gun in a plastic gun pouch. The bus was stopped at a brief layover in Fort Lauderdale, and the officers were "working the bus," looking for persons who might be carrying drugs.

Upon waking Bostick, the officers asked for his identification and ticket. He complied. They then asked to search his bag. Again, Bostick complied, somewhat inexplicably, because upon opening the bag, the officers found a pound of cocaine. The officers admitted that at no time prior to the search did they have any basis for suspecting Bostick of any criminal activity.

Bus and train sweeps of this kind are a common method of drug enforcement investigations. Police board buses or trains at intermediate stops to exploit the fact that the traveler has nowhere to go. In theory, passengers have a constitutional right to refuse to answer any questions, and to say no when a police officer asks to search their luggage. In practice, virtually everybody talks and consents. One officer testified that he had searched 3,000 bags without once being refused consent.[1] The tactic works. In West Palm Beach alone, bus sweeps over a thirteen-month period netted 300 pounds of cocaine, 800 pounds of marijuana, 24 handguns, and 75 suspected drug "mules."[2] But whether it should be constitutional raises fundamental questions about the role of race in law enforcement decisionmaking, and about the courts' responsibility to police the police.

REASONABLE PEOPLE

When prosecutors charged Bostick with drug possession, he challenged the police officer's conduct, and the Florida Supreme Court held it unconstitutional. The court reasoned that Bostick had effectively been "seized" when the officers cornered him at the back of the bus, because at that moment he was not free to leave. The Fourth Amendment forbids the police from seizing individuals without some individualized suspicion that they have committed or are committing a crime, and the police admitted they had none for Bostick. The remedy for such a violation—under the Fourth Amendment's "exclusionary rule"—is that the prosecution may not use evidence obtained by the encounter to establish its case. In addition to holding the evidence inadmissible against Bostick, the Florida Supreme Court broadly condemned "bus sweeps," likening them to methods used by totalitarian states:

> [T]he evidence in this case has evoked images of other days, under other flags, when no man traveled his nation's roads or railways without fear of unwarranted interruption, by individuals who had temporary power in the Government . . . This is not Hitler's Berlin, nor Stalin's Moscow, nor is it white supremacist South Africa. Yet in Broward County, Florida, these police officers approach every person on board buses and trains ("that time permits") and check identification, tickets, ask to search luggage—all in the name of "voluntary cooperation" with law enforcement.[3]

Florida's Attorney General appealed to the U.S. Supreme Court, which agreed to hear the case. In the Supreme Court, Bostick was represented by Donald Ayer, a highly respected Washington lawyer with impeccable conservative credentials. A Republican, Ayer had clerked for Chief Justice William Rehnquist. Shortly before taking Bostick's case, he had stepped down from a position as the Deputy Solicitor General, where he had represented the Reagan administration in some of its most politically charged cases before the Supreme Court. Ayer felt that this was a case of law enforcement going too far, and offered to handle Bostick's case pro bono before the Supreme Court. Ayer convinced Americans for Effective Law Enforcement, a pro-law-enforcement organization that had previously filed eighty-five amicus briefs in the Supreme Court, all supporting the police, to file an amicus brief on Bostick's behalf urging the Court to find an unreasonable seizure in this case.[4]

The principles at stake were fairly basic. The Fourth Amendment prohibits "unreasonable searches and seizures," and the Supreme Court had previously held that a "seizure" is unreasonable without some articulable reason, specific to the individual, for suspecting crime. Seizures come in two varieties: full-scale arrests, which require probable cause that the individual has committed a crime; and brief "stops," which require only a reasonable suspicion that crime is afoot. But all seizures require at least some degree of *individualized* suspicion, and the police had admitted that they had none when they approached Bostick.

Not every encounter between a citizen and a police officer, however, is a "seizure" that must be justified under the Fourth Amendment. Otherwise, police officers would not be able to approach anyone on the street without first having grounds to suspect criminal conduct. In prior cases, the Court had ruled that a police officer "seizes" an individual when "by means of physical force or show of authority, [the officer] has restrained [the citizen's] liberty,"[5] and that the relevant question is whether a reasonable person in the citizen's shoes would feel "free to disregard the [officer's] questions and walk away."[6]

Few of us, awakened in the middle of a marathon bus ride by armed police officers standing over us, asking for our identification and requesting to search our bags, would feel free to tell the officers to mind their own business. But the Supreme Court's "reasonable person" apparently has a lot more mettle than the average Joe. The Court had previously ruled, for example, that a traveler approached by police in an airport and asked to show his identification and ticket was not "seized" by the encounter,[7] because a "reasonable person" would feel free to walk away. As long as the police do not convey a message that their requests must be obeyed, the Court ruled, they can approach citizens without any basis for suspicion, interrogate them, ask to see their identification, and request to search their luggage.

But even accepting the dubious proposition that a passenger walking through an airport will feel free to ignore an approaching police officer, Ayer argued, it is quite another thing to say that a reasonable person *in Bostick's place* would have felt free to ignore the two officers who stood above him in the bus aisle, blocking the only way out. Even if Bostick had been able to push his way around the officers and get off the bus, he would have found himself in the middle of rural Florida, far from his destination, and separated from any luggage he'd checked. If he chose to remain on the bus but to refuse to cooperate, he might reasonably have predicted that his conduct would raise police suspicion, and lead to their searching his bags anyway, or worse. The encounter was not truly consensual, as Bostick's conduct demonstrated. Indeed, Ayer argued, no "reasonable person" would agree to a search of a bag that contained a pound of cocaine if he really believed he was free to say no without adverse consequences.

The Supreme Court rejected Ayer's arguments, and reversed the Florida Supreme Court. The proper test, the Court explained, was not whether a reasonable person in Bostick's shoes would have felt free *to leave* — the test the Court had used until Bostick's case — but *to terminate the encounter.* The Court posited that even if he didn't feel free to leave, a "reasonable person" would have felt free to sit there and adamantly refuse to answer the police officer's questions. That Bostick was on a bus may well have restricted his freedom to walk away, but, the Court reasoned, that wasn't the police's fault. The police did not make him get on the bus. They merely found him there. Bostick would have to point to something extraordinary in the *police officer's conduct* to establish that he had been "seized." The mere fact that they had boarded the bus en route, were standing over him, blocking his exit, displaying badges and a gun, and directing questions at him was not enough.

The consequence of *Florida v. Bostick* is that police are free to engage in dragnet-like searches of buses and trains, in settings where it is extremely difficult for any citizen to refuse to cooperate. As long as the police do not effect a "seizure," there are no Fourth Amendment limits whatsoever on whom they approach or what questions they ask. They could routinely direct such inquiries at every person on every bus, train, and for that matter, airplane in America.

By adopting a "reasonable person" standard that is patently fictional, this ruling allows the police to engage in substantial coercion under the rubric of "consent," without any limits on the persons to whom that coercion can be applied. As federal judge Prentice Marshall explained in a separate case, "[i]mplicit in the introduction of the [officer] and the initial questioning is a show of authority to which the average person encountered will feel obliged to stop and respond. Few will feel that they can walk away or refuse an answer."[8] The Court's test assumes the opposite, and finds coercion only where police engage in some coercive conduct above and beyond their inherent authority. For all practical purposes, the Court's test erases the inherently coercive nature of *all* police encounters from the legal calculus for determining whether a Fourth Amendment "seizure" has occurred.[9] As long as police officers use *only* the inherent coercion of their own official identity, they are free to seek citizens' "cooperation" for questioning and searches. In *Bostick* the Court went still further, permitting the police to exploit circumstances that independently constrain citizens' freedom to escape an encounter with the police.

The Court's reasonable person fiction has its benefits. It substantially reduces the law enforcement costs that would result were the Fourth Amendment applied to all nonconsensual encounters. By adopting a standard that ignores the coercion inherent even in a situation such as Bostick's, the Court permits the police to engage in a wide range of nonconsensual, coercive intrusions on privacy without any basis for individualized suspicion.

At first glance, this fiction deprives all of us of our Fourth Amendment rights; it equally ignores the coerciveness of police encounters with rich white businessmen and unemployed black teenagers. But this standard will have very different effects on the poor and the wealthy, and on minority and white citizens. First, the police are far more likely to use this unfettered discretion against black teenagers than white executives. In practice, the police are selective about their targets. This is partly a matter of resources; the personnel required to confront all travelers would be extraordinary, and the yield would likely be small, because the vast majority of travelers presumably are not carrying contraband. Selective enforcement may also, however, reflect a savvy political judgment; if the police did in fact inflict such suspicionless treatment on everyone, there would likely be sufficient political will to curtail the practice politically, either by legislation or by community pressure on police departments.

So the police "work the buses" selectively, and because in the Court's view no "seizure" takes place, they need not explain *how* they select their targets. Targets could be selected at random, on the basis of unadulterated hunches, or, more likely, on the basis of unspoken stereotypes and assumptions about the kind of traveler likely to be carrying contraband. There is good reason to believe that minorities in general, and young black men in particular (such as Terrance Bostick), are disproportionately targeted. This tactic is practiced not on airplanes, but on buses and trains, modes of transportation more frequently used by poor and minority travelers.[10] Once on the train, few officers will choose to approach an elderly white woman or a well-dressed businessman over a young black man "roughly dressed."[11] There are few available statistics on the racial breakdown of police stops. Where reported cases discuss bus and train sweeps, however, the defendants are virtually always black or Hispanic. A search of all reported federal bus and train sweep cases from January 1, 1993, to August 22, 1995, found that, of fifty-five cases in which the defendant's race could be identified, thirty-six were black, eleven were Hispanic, one was Asian, one was Filipino, and six were white.[12] As Justice Thurgood Marshall stated in dissent in *Bostick*, "the basis of the decision to single out particular passengers during a suspicionless sweep is less likely to be inarticulable than unspeakable."[13]

Thus, although the doctrine leaves the police free to target whomever they please, the targets will not be random; by and large they will be young black men. All relevant data—from arrest rates to conviction rates to victim reporting—suggest that young people are more likely to commit crime than old people, men more likely than women, and black people more likely than white people. The disproportionate numbers of young black men in prison and jail— disparities that cannot be explained by discriminatory policing or prosecuting alone—suggest that if police are going to be guided not by individualized suspicion but by more general characteristics, the odds of discovering some evidence of crime will be greater if they stop young black men. By permitting the police to use what is actually quite coercive behavior without any articulable basis for individualized suspicion, the Court's standard encourages the police to act on race-based judgments.

Second, the Court's "objective," one-size-fits-all reasonable person standard fails to take into account that citizens may be differently situated with respect to encounters with the police. It would seem noncontroversial, for example, that a fourteen-year-old child would feel less free to terminate an encounter with a police officer than a fifty-year-old member of Congress, even if the encounters were identical in all other respects. Yet the Supreme Court has held that the reasonable person standard "does not vary with the state of mind of the particular individual being approached," and "calls for consistent application from one police encounter to the next, regardless of the particular individual's response to the actions of the police."[14] Applying that ruling, the District of Columbia Court of Appeals held that the same reasonable person standard applies to a fourteen-year-old child as to an adult.[15]

A citizen's prior experiences with the police are also likely to play a part in how coercive an encounter seems. As the acquittal of O.J. Simpson dramatically illustrated, there is little love lost between the black community and the police in many areas of the nation. A survey of the Los Angeles Police Department found that one-quarter of the 650 *officers* responding agreed that "racial bias (prejudice) on the part of officers toward minority citizens currently exists and contributes to a negative interaction between police and the community," and that "an officer's prejudice toward the suspect's race may lead to the use of excessive force."[16] For a host of reasons, from the disproportionate number of blacks behind bars today, to the historical use of the criminal justice system to maintain racial subordination, to the contemporary treatment of blacks on the streets by many police, the black community has a low level of trust for the criminal justice system, and for the police in particular.[17]

The videotaped beating of Rodney King by officers of the Los Angeles Police Department encapsulated for many blacks the treatment they expect and fear from the police.[18] As California Assemblyman Curtis Tucker was quoted as saying at a subsequent hearing on LAPD practices, "When black people in Los Angeles see a police car approaching, 'They don't know whether justice will be meted out or whether judge, jury and executioner is pulling up behind them.'"[19] Similarly, a black man encountering a police officer in the Bronx today cannot help being affected by the knowledge that police officers there have engaged in a practice of indiscriminate beatings of minority citizens in order to establish their authority. In 1994, the Mollen Commission reported on widespread police corruption and brutality in the Bronx. One officer testified that he was called "the Mechanic," because "I used to tune people up," a "police word for beatin' up people."[20] He testified that the beating was widespread:

Q. Did you beat people up who you arrested?
A. No. We just beat people up in general. If they're on the street, hanging around drug locations. Just—It was a show of force.
Q. Why were these beatings done?
A. To show who was in charge. We were in charge, the police.[21]

The officer admitted that most of the victims were black and Hispanic, although he denied that the attacks were racially motivated. He conceded that the neighborhood residents hated the police, saying, "You'd hate the police too, if you lived there."[22]

The Mollen Commission found that police corruption, brutality, and violence were present in every high-crime precinct with an active narcotics trade that it studied, all of which have predominantly minority populations.[23] It found disturbing patterns of police corruption and brutality, including stealing from drug dealers, engaging in unlawful searches, seizures, and car stops, dealing and using drugs, lying in order to justify unlawful searches and arrests and to forestall complaints of abuse, and indiscriminate beating of innocent and guilty alike.[24] The commission found that police officers and supervisors often accepted lying and brutality as necessary aspects of the job, in part because of what they perceived to be unrealistic legal constraints, and in part because of the police officers' "Us vs. Them" mentality, particularly in minority communities.[25]

Similar practices were ongoing in Philadelphia, as Arthur Colbert, a black college student from Michigan, learned first-hand in 1991 when he made the mistake of getting lost in North Philadelphia while looking for his date. Two police officers looking for a drug dealer named Hakim pulled Colbert over, put him in a police van, and took him to an abandoned house, where they repeatedly accused him of being Hakim. Colbert showed them his Temple University ID and his driver's license, but they were not deterred. The officers hit him with their flashlights and a two-by-four. When Colbert still would not admit to being Hakim, one officer put his gun to Colbert's head and said, "If you don't tell us what we want to know, I'm going to blow your head away. You have three seconds." He cocked the gun's hammer and began to count down: "Three . . . two . . . one." But there wasn't anything Colbert could tell them, because he wasn't Hakim, and had never even heard of Hakim. The officers ultimately let him go without charges.

This was only one of many such stories uncovered in a corruption investigation in Philadelphia, which found a pattern of misconduct directed at the predominantly poor black neighborhood of North Philadelphia. In the early 1990s, a group of police officers there engaged in a widespread practice of beating and robbing citizens, planting evidence, and lying to support false convictions. The investigation's disclosures led to several criminal convictions of the police officers, and reversals of over fifty criminal convictions obtained on the strength of the officers' testimony.[26]

Stories of black men being stopped by the police for no apparent reason other than the color of their skin are so common that they are not even considered news, and often get reported only when the victims happen to be celebrities or the confrontation is captured on film. In 1988, Joe Morgan, former All-Star second baseman for the Cincinatti Reds, was at Los Angeles International Airport waiting for a flight to Tucson. According to Morgan and an eyewitness, a police officer approached Morgan while he was making a phone call, said he was conducting a drug investigation, asked for his identification, and accused him of traveling with another person suspected of dealing drugs. Morgan objected, and turned to get his identification from his luggage, forty feet away. The officer grabbed him from behind, forced him to the floor, handcuffed him, put his hand over Morgan's mouth and nose, and led him off to a small room, where the police ascertained that Morgan was not traveling with the suspected drug dealer after all. The police maintained that Morgan had been hostile throughout the encounter, and that he had been forced to the floor only after he started swinging his arms. Even by the police officer's own account, however, the only basis for approaching Morgan in the first place was that another black man, stopped as a suspected drug dealer, had told the officers that he was traveling with a man that "locked like himself." As a result, the officers were on the lookout for a black man, and Joe Morgan fit that description.[27]

In 1989, former police officer Don Jackson was doing a news story about police abuse against black men in Long Beach, California, when he was pulled over by the police on Martin Luther King, Jr., Boulevard, allegedly for straddling lanes. When he asked why he was being stopped, an officer pushed him through a plate glass store window. NBC captured the incident on film.[28] In 1992, the ABC newsmagazine "20/20" conducted an experiment, sending out two groups of young men—one white, the other black—on successive evenings in Los Angeles. They drove in identical cars and took identical routes at identical times. The black group was stopped and questioned by police on several occasions in one evening, while the white group saw police cars pass them by sixteen times without showing any interest.[29]

In 1990, the Massachusetts Attorney General's Civil Rights Division issued a report condemning the Boston Police Department for a practice of subjecting black citizens to unconstitutional stops and searches.[30] The report recounted more than fifty such incidents in 1989 and 1990. The incidents followed the Boston Police Department's announcement of a policy of searching on sight "known gang members" in Roxbury, a predominantly black neighborhood in Boston. A deputy superintendent admitted that he had instructed his officers to "stop and frisk any known gang members in a gang location where there has been high-crime problems . . . , and if there are other kids with the gangs that are not known to us, that we will search them too for the protection of my officers."[31] The report also discussed widespread complaints that the Boston Police Department had responded to the killing of a white woman, Carol Stuart, by engaging in unconstitutional stops, searches, and interrogations of young black men. Carol Stuart was in fact killed by her husband, Charles Stuart, a white man, who then falsely claimed that a black man had killed his wife.[32]

As a result of such experiences, and the recounting of these and countless similar tales within the black community, black citizens, and particularly young black men, are likely to feel considerably less comfortable than members of other demographic groups in their encounters with police officers.[33] Those practices were the backdrop for the encounter between the Broward County officials and Terrance Bostick, just as they are the backdrop for any encounter between a police officer and a black citizen. As Judge Julia Cooper Mack of the District of Columbia Court of Appeals put it in another case, "no reasonable innocent black male (with any knowledge of American history) would feel free to ignore or walk away from a drug interdiction team."[34] Yet the Supreme Court did not even mention Bostick's race.[35]

The Court's use of a uniform reasonable-person standard effectively sanctions *greater* coercion against those more vulnerable to police authority. By failing to consider the citizen's prior experiences with the police in determining whether a "seizure" has occurred, the Court permits the police to employ, on average, more coercion against black persons than against whites. The history of police practices against black citizens means that the same police conduct will be more threatening when directed against a black man than when directed against a white man. The objective standard builds that inequality into the criminal justice system, and sanctions it under the rubric of applying the same standard to all.

The effect is to tolerate a double standard. Most citizens will not be approached by a police officer for questioning unless the officer has some objective grounds for suspecting that they are involved in criminal activity. Our freedom to walk the streets is protected, in other words, by the constitutional requirement of probable cause. But young black men will routinely be subjected to police stops, not rising to the legal formality of "seizures," simply because they are young black men. At the same time, the police will be able to apply more coercion to black citizens than to whites in such "noncoercive" encounters, because the Court's legal standard presumes that we all have the same set of experiences vis-à-vis the police, and that none of us has any reason to feel coerced by an "ordinary" police encounter. As a result, the Court has it both ways—it protects the rights of some, but avoids the cost of extending the same protections equally to all.

CONSENT SEARCHES

Terrance Bostick had a choice. The police officers *asked* him whether they could search his bag. They did so because they had no legal authority to *demand* that he submit to such a search. The Supreme Court has held that the police generally cannot conduct a search without obtaining a warrant, which must be based on probable cause that evidence of a crime is likely to be found in the area to be searched. Because the police had no reason to suspect Bostick was carrying drugs or anything else unlawful, they could not have searched or seized his bag. So they asked his permission.

According to the police's story, they even told Bostick he had the right to say no. Yet knowing that his bag contained a pound of cocaine, Bostick agreed to let the police open it. Had an attorney been at Bostick's side, his advice would have been simple: "Just say no." The Fourth Amendment guarantees the right to refuse to consent to such a request. And a citizen's exercise of that right does not authorize the police to take more intrusive steps. Had Bostick known and believed this, he would certainly have said no. He had everything to lose and nothing to gain by saying "yes." Yet, like thousands of others in similar circumstances, he said yes.

The Supreme Court has held that "consent searches" satisfy the Constitution so long as the government demonstrates that the consent was "voluntary." But as with the test for identifying a seizure, the Court has created a standard for consent that effectively countenances the coercion of unknowing and involuntary consents. And as with bus and train sweeps, those who are coerced into giving their consent are most likely to be the young, the poor, the uneducated, and the nonwhite.

In theory it makes good sense to say that a search conducted by consent of the party searched is constitutional. Like other constitutional rights, the Fourth Amendment right to be free of unreasonable searches and seizures is "waivable"; that is, a person is free to choose not to exercise the right. Where an individual has made such a choice, there is no benefit to barring the search, and there may be some benefit to permitting it—either the police will find what they are looking for, or they won't and can focus their investigation elsewhere, allowing the individual to continue on his way.

But the Supreme Court is usually skeptical of claims that citizens have waived their constitutional rights (because it is so rarely in one's interest to do so). Thus, in every other setting the Supreme Court has held that the goverment bears the burden of demonstrating that a waiver was "knowing, intelligent, and voluntary."[36] When a defendant pleads guilty to a criminal charge, for example, the judge must first inform him of the consequences of his actions, and must ensure that he is acting voluntarily and knowingly.[37] Similarly, when a citizen takes action that by statute has the effect of surrendering his citizenship—such as enlisting in a foreign army—the government cannot in fact revoke his citizenship absent a showing that he took the action voluntarily and with full knowledge of the consequences.[38] This strict waiver standard also applies to *Miranda* rights in a custodial interrogation,[39] and to the right to have an attorney present at an identification lineup.[40]

Yet consent searches, the Supreme Court held, do not require such a showing. In this setting, the Court merely requires that consent be "voluntary," not that it be knowing and intelligent. As a result, the police officers who approached Bostick did not have to tell him that he had a right to say no. In 1973, the Supreme Court explicitly rejected such a requirement. In *Schneckloth v. Bustamonte*,[41] police officers pulled over a car at 2:40 A.M. for driving with a burnt-out headlight and license-plate light. They ordered all six occupants out of the car, and then asked the owner, Robert Bustamonte, if they could search the car. He consented, and in the ensuing search the officers found three stolen checks. Bustamonte argued that the evidence should be suppressed because the police never told him he had the right to decline their request to search. How could he have meaningfully waived his constitutional right, he asked, without knowing that he had the right in the first place?

Bustamonte's argument was not without strong precedent. Only seven years earlier, the Supreme Court had held, in *Miranda v. Arizona*, that police officers must give a warning and establish a knowing, intelligent, and voluntary waiver of rights before obtaining a confession from a person in custody. Although the "*Miranda* warning" was formally based on the Fifth Amendment's privilege against compelled self-incrimination, it was driven by equality concerns: the Court thought that requiring that every suspect be read his rights and provided an attorney on request would put all interrogation suspects on relatively equal footing.[42] In addition, such warnings would help to dissipate the coercion otherwise inherent in such encounters.

Bustamonte argued that requiring a warning in the consent search setting would similarly give every citizen a roughly equal opportunity to assert her rights, and offset some of the coercion inherent in a police-citizen encounter. Yet in a 6-3 decision, the Supreme Court declined to extend *Miranda*'s reasoning to consent searches. The Court held that the "waiver" line of cases was limited to rights closely associated with trial rights. It reasoned that unlike waiver of a trial right, consent to a search is generally obtained in a fluid situation not susceptible to the strict showings required in the highly structured setting of a trial. But that contention does not adequately distinguish the Court's application of the waiver standard to other nontrial constitutional rights, such as *Miranda* rights, rights of citizenship, and the right to be represented during a police lineup.

The real reason the Court rejected a warning requirement is found elsewhere in its opinion. The Court stressed that consent searches are an important investigative tool, and that the Court must balance the "legitimate need for such searches and the equally important requirement of assuring the absence of coercion."[43] The most important consideration in that balance was the Court's view that "the community has a real interest in encouraging consent."[44] Requiring a knowing, intelligent, and voluntary waiver would "in practice, create serious doubt whether consent searches could continue to be conducted."[45] And requiring a warning would be "thoroughly impractical,"[46] the Court reasoned, despite the fact that federal agents were already in the practice of giving such warnings.[47] In other words, the Court declined to require a warning because warnings would undermine the community's interest in "encouraging consent." But of course warnings would only discourage consent if individuals were saying yes because they did not know they had the right to say no.

The consent-search doctrine thus intentionally exploits the ignorance of the citizenry to reduce the law enforcement costs of the Fourth Amendment. It creates a constitutional loophole, by which police can and do routinely search people's bags without any articulable basis for suspecting that they are carrying contraband. Requiring warnings would, the Court feared, close that loophole. It would seriously hamper investigative efforts used in bus and train sweeps, airport drug-courier investigations, and car stops.

The Supreme Court recently reaffirmed its desire not to discourage consent by providing citizens with information about their rights. *Ohio v. Robinette*[48] arose out of a routine traffic stop in Ohio, when a police officer pulled over Robert Robinette for speeding. After checking Robinette's license and issuing a warning, but before telling Robinette that he could leave, the officer ordered him out of the car, turned on a video camera in the officer's car, and returned to ask Robinette whether he was carrying any drugs and whether he would consent to a search of his car. Robinette testified that he "automatically" consented. The police officer found a small amount of marijuana and a pill that turned out to be methamphetamine. The Ohio Supreme Court ruled that the officer had extended the stop beyond its legitimate traffic law enforcement purpose and had exploited the coercive setting of the traffic stop to wrest consent to search from Robinette. Noting that traffic stops were increasingly being used for such "consent" searches, and reasoning that "a 'consensual encounter' immediately following a detention is likely to be imbued with the authoritative aura of the detention," the Ohio Supreme Court adopted a bright-line rule requiring police officers to tell drivers they are free to leave *before* asking for consent to search.[49] The United States Supreme Court reversed, holding that it would be "unrealistic" to require such a warning. Thus, police are free to use not only the confines of a bus or train to "encourage" consent, but also the coercive setting of a traffic stop.

Such reliance on ignorance and thinly veiled coercion is deeply troubling. As a very different Supreme Court said in 1964, "no system of criminal justice can, or should survive if it comes to depend for its continued effectiveness on the citizens' abdication through unawareness of their constitutional rights."[50] The current system creates two Fourth Amendments—one for people who are aware of their right to say no and confident enough to assert that right against a police officer, and another for those who do not know their rights or are afraid to assert them.

This double standard would be problematic even if it did not closely parallel race and class lines. But like the "reasonable person" standard, the consent doctrine in application is likely to reflect race and class divisions. Because a consent search requires no objective individualized suspicion, it is more likely to be directed at poor young black men than wealthy white elderly women. In addition, those who are white and wealthy are more likely to know their rights and to feel secure in asserting them.

In *Schneckloth v. Bustamonte*, the Court dismissed the concern that its rule would "relegate the Fourth Amendment to the special province of 'the sophisticated, the knowledgeable, and the privileged.'"[51] It cautioned that the "voluntariness" inquiry "has always taken into account evidence of minimal schooling, low intelligence, and the lack of any effective warnings to a person of his rights."[52] In theory, the voluntariness inquiry—unlike the reasonable person standard used to tell whether someone has been "seized"—does allow for consideration of the different situations of each individual approached. In practice, however, the courts find consent to be voluntary in all but the most extreme circumstances. Ray O'Brien, a Georgetown University Law Center student, reviewed all cases involving consent searches decided by the United States Court of Appeals for the D.C. Circuit from January 1, 1989, to April 15, 1995.[53] In every case in which the validity of consent was challenged, the court found the consent voluntary.[54]

In most of the cases, the courts did not even discuss the subjective factors that the Supreme Court in *Schneckloth* said would be relevant in determining voluntariness. When they did mention them, the courts turned a blind eye to factors strongly suggesting a less than voluntary encounter. In one case, for example, the police obtained consent to search an eighteen-year-old woman at 3:40 A.M. outside a bus station.[55] An expert witness testified that the woman had an IQ only six points above mild retardation, had been in special-education classes before she dropped out of school in ninth grade, read at a second-grade level and wrote at a third-grade level, and was suffering from a borderline personality disorder. Yet the court found her consent voluntary, stressing the absence of threatening behavior by the police officers.

In another case, the court found voluntary consent where a twenty-four-year-old defendant with only a tenth-grade education had on four previous occasions refused consent to police requests to search, only to be searched anyway each time.[56] And in still another, the court noted that the defendant was young, foreign born, poorly educated, not fluent in English, and ignorant of his rights, only to hold that the trial court had not erroneously found his consent voluntary.[57] If these factors do not support a finding that consent is involuntary, it is difficult to imagine what set of circumstances *would* invalidate consent.

Instead of focusing on the subjective characteristics of the defendant, courts generally focus on the conduct of the police. On that question, it will virtually always be a matter of the police officer's word against that of the defendant, who has by definition been found to be carrying contraband (because cases in which no contraband is found will rarely reach the courts). The difficulty of determining the truth concerning such encounters has long been recognized in the interrogation setting. Indeed, it was largely for that reason that the Supreme Court shifted from a case-by-case analysis of whether confessions were "voluntary" to the across-the-board requirement of the *Miranda* rules.[58] Yet in the consent-search context, the courts have continued to engage in precisely the case-by-case inquiry that they recognized as deeply problematic in the interrogation setting.[59]

Whether an individual's consent to search can ever be truly voluntary is also rendered doubtful by the courts' failure to protect the right to say no. The courts have never clearly answered a basic question: can the police use an individual's exercise of her right to say no as a basis for developing suspicion justifying a nonconsensual search? If the police can use a citizen's negative answer against her, then she is not truly free to say no. The Supreme Court has said that the refusal to consent, "without more," does not justify a search,[60] but has not ruled on whether a refusal can be one factor among many contributing to the justification for a nonconsensual stop or search. Some courts have allowed the police to rely at least in part on a suspect's refusal to consent to search to justify further police action.[61] The U.S. Court of Appeals for the D.C. Circuit has ruled that the *manner* in which a defendant withdraws consent to a search may be considered as a factor supporting reasonable suspicion.[62] Other courts have held that a refusal cannot be considered at all.[63] The very fact that the law is unclear on this point means that a citizen confronted by the police cannot know whether her choice to say no will be held against her.

The situation on the ground may even be worse: one of my students reports that when she attempted to teach the consent doctrine to prisoners at a federal prison in Virginia, her predominantly black and Hispanic students ridiculed the notion. They maintained that although it might be true that she, a white woman, had the right not to consent, if they declined consent, the police would either beat them or go ahead and search anyway, and then testify that they had consented. It is of course difficult to verify such statements, but that perception itself will factor into a citizen's decision to assert her rights.

The foreseeable impact of a rule that does not require the police in inherently coercive settings to inform people of their rights is that those who do not know their rights, and those who lack the assurance to assert their rights, will not in fact enjoy the protection of those rights. In *Schneckloth* itself, the Court admitted that informing citizens of their rights would be costly because it would discourage consent. But if that is the case, then the Court has consciously created a regime designed to coerce the less well educated and the less self-assured among us to surrender their constitutional rights.

PRETEXT STOPS

Robert Wilkins is highly educated and self-assured. He is also a young black man. A soft-spoken Harvard Law School graduate in his thirties, he doesn't earn the six-figure income that many of his fellow Harvard alums do, but that's his choice. He's a lawyer with the Public Defender Service in Washington, D.C., nationally renowned as one of the best public defender offices in the country. He makes his living knowing his rights. So when a Maryland state trooper stopped him on Highway 68 just outside Cumberland, Maryland, early one May morning in 1992, he knew what the officers could and could not do.

Wilkins was returning from a family funeral in Chicago that morning, with his aunt, uncle, and cousin. Maryland State Trooper Bryan Hughes signaled Wilkins' rental car to pull over. Hughes told the driver, Wilkins' cousin, Norman Scott El-Amin, that he had been doing sixty miles an hour in a forty-mile-per-hour zone. Within minutes the officer asked El-Amin if he would sign a consent form authorizing a search of the car. Even if they had been speeding, of course, that would provide no reason to search the car. But as we have seen, a police officer need not have a reason to seek consent to a search.

With Wilkins by his side, El-Amin asserted his right to say no. The officer then held them there for thirty minutes so that he could have a drug-sniffing dog brought to the scene. Wilkins explained to the officer that he had no right to detain them without a basis for suspicion, and even cited the Supreme Court case establishing that principle, but the officer was not deterred. The dog arrived, and Hughes ordered the Wilkins family out of the car and made them stand in the rain as the German shepherd sniffed all around the car. When the dog showed no positive reaction for drugs, Hughes wrote out a speeding ticket. Earlier in the encounter, he had told El-Amin that he would issue only a warning, but evidently something during the forty-five-minute encounter had changed his mind. Could it have been the family's assertion of their rights?

Had the passenger been anyone other than Robert Wilkins, that would probably have been the end of the matter — another small piece of evidence in the black community's case against the police. But Wilkins immediately contacted the American Civil Liberties Union (ACLU) of Maryland. Deborah Jeon, a staff attorney there, filed a civil suit on behalf of Wilkins and his family against the Maryland State Police. They suspected that the encounter was a "pretext" stop, and that the officer's real motive was not the asserted speeding violation, but his race-based suspicion that the passengers were transporting drugs. How else could one explain the immediate request for consent to search? How else to explain the drug-sniffing German shepherd? The Maryland ACLU had received a number of similar complaints about traffic stops by the Maryland State Police in the past, the only common feature of which was that the drivers were black or Hispanic. In particular, they suspected that the police were using a "drug-courier profile" that targeted blacks. So they brought the suit as a class action, on behalf of "all African Americans who have been in the past, or who will be in the future, unconstitutionally stopped, detained and searched on Maryland highways by

Maryland State Troopers pursuant to a race-based drug courier profile."[64]

In fact, only a week before the Wilkins incident, the Maryland State Police had distributed a memo alerting all officers to be on the lookout for dealers and couriers, "predominantly black males and black females," who were bringing crack cocaine into Cumberland, Maryland. Because they were black and driving in the vicinity of Cumberland, the Wilkins family fit the profile.

Apparently realizing that they had been caught red-handed, the Maryland State Police settled, agreeing to pay the Wilkins family money damages and attorneys' fees, to issue a written policy barring stops based on race, and to include that policy in all officers' training. In addition, Maryland agreed to future monitoring of its stops: the police would provide the ACLU with a racial breakdown of all car stops in which either a consent search or a dog-sniff search was done, and the ACLU could seek further relief if the monitoring demonstrated a continuing problem.[65]

One would expect that having been put on notice that their every stop was being monitored, Maryland state troopers would be careful not to allow racial factors to influence their actions. Yet the state police continued to stop black drivers in wildly disproportionate numbers. From January 1995 through December 1997, 70 percent of the drivers stopped on Interstate 95 were African Americans, while according to an ACLU survey, only about 17.5 percent of the traffic and speeders on that road were black.[66]

The use of traffic stops as a pretext for investigating other crimes, particularly drug offenses, is extremely common, and blacks and Hispanics are disproportionately targeted by the practice. Indeed, the phenomenon has become so commonplace that it is known in the black community as DWB, or driving while black.[67] Many black professionals tell of being stopped simply because they were black and driving a fancy car; in fact, some have taken to choosing bland over fancy rental cars to minimize the possibility of a police stop.[68]

In Volusia County, Florida, the practice was caught on videotape. Police officers there routinely videotape automobile stops with a camera mounted on the police car's dashboard. In 1992, the *Orlando Sentinel* obtained the tapes under Florida's public records law, and reviewed 148 hours of videotape involving more than 1,000 stops on an interstate highway. They found that while about 5 percent of drivers on that highway were dark-skinned,[69] nearly 70 percent of those stopped were black or Hispanic, and more than 80 percent of cars searched were driven by blacks and Hispanics.[70] Stops of black and Hispanic drivers on average lasted more than twice as long as stops of white drivers. The vast majority of the stops were for petty traffic violations, such as following too closely, having a burned-out license-plate light, or making an unsafe lane change. Only 9 of the more than 1,000 stops, or less than 1 percent, resulted in a traffic ticket.

Tapes of individual stops reinforced the statistics. In one, a bewildered black man explained to the state troopers that this was the seventh time he'd been stopped; in another, a black man shakes his head because it's the second time in minutes that he's been stopped. In one of the relatively rare stops of a white driver, Sergeant Dale Anderson asks the motorist how he is doing. When the man answers, "Not very good," Anderson replies, "Could be worse— could be black."[71]

Sergeant James Perry of the Eagle County Sheriff's Department in Colorado was a convert to the traffic stop technique. A member of the High Country Drug Task Force, Perry initially used a drug-courier profile to stop and search cars driving through Eagle County. That a driver was black or Hispanic was an explicit factor in the profile.[72] In December 1988, however, Perry learned the hard way that a driver's race is not a permissible ground to stop and search. The district attorney had to throw out a case against three black men found carrying twenty pounds of cocaine because Perry's stop, based only on the drug-courier profile factors of race and out-of-state plates, was plainly unconstitutional. Perry's response was not to refine the profile, but to switch—at least in name—to using traffic violations as a basis for stopping vehicles. Before the December incident, Perry's logs consistently cited "criminal investigation" for his stops; after that date, the logs just as consistently cited "traffic enforcement." But Perry almost never issued a traffic ticket. He continued to stop the same number of cars and a disproportionate number of minority drivers. As a district court judge reviewing Perry's records stated, "If Perry's own records are to be construed literally, Perry went from being a Drug Task Force officer who went for days at a time without ever concerning himself with any traffic violations, to a drug enforcement officer obsessed with traffic enforcement."[73] A subsequent lawsuit identified over 400 people whose vehicles had been pulled over based solely on Eagle County's drug-courier profile targeted at blacks and Hispanics. Not one of the 400 persons was charged with a traffic offense or arrested for drugs. In November 1995, Eagle County agreed to pay $800,000 to the drivers to settle the lawsuit.[74]

In New Jersey, similar police tactics led to the dismissal in 1996 of nineteen cases against black motorists. In *State v. Pedro Soto*, defense attorneys showed that New Jersey State Police officers patrolling the New Jersey Turnpike disproportionately stopped black motorists. They conducted a "windshield survey" of over 40,000 turnpike drivers, and found that about 13.5 percent were black. They then conducted a "violator" survey, in which a defense attorney drove on the highway at sixty miles per hour and noted the race of the drivers who passed him (and were therefore speeding in a fifty-five-mile-per-hour zone). Fifteen percent of the violators were black. Yet black drivers made up more than 46 percent of the drivers stopped by the New Jersey State Police—a disparity of more than three to one.

Thus, the available evidence suggests that traffic stops are routinely used as a "pretext" to stop minority drivers. The sheer scope of traffic regulations makes it easy for an officer to construct a legal basis for investigating virtually anyone in a vehicle. Following a car too closely, failing to pay sufficient attention to one's driving, a burned-out license-plate light, or having a piece of string hanging from one's rearview mirror may all be grounds for traffic stops. An officer who suspects an individual but has no justifiable basis for stopping him need only follow his car until he inevitably violates one or another traffic code provision. Once the car is stopped, the officer can look into the windows of the vehicle. If he develops reasonable suspicion that the car may contain a weapon, he can search the passenger compartment for weapons. If he develops probable cause that the car contains contraband, he can search the entire car. And where the officer upon approaching the car finds nothing to justify a further search, he can simply ask the driver for permission to search, a request that, as we have seen, is rarely denied.

Successful legal challenges to this practice are extremely rare. Most often the courts look the other way. In 1996, the Supreme Court formally sanctioned that approach in *Whren v. United States*.[75] The encounter that sparked the case should by now be familiar. Plainclothes officers in an unmarked vehicle patrolling a high-crime area noticed two young black men driving a brand-new Nissan Pathfinder. The car was stopped at a stop sign. Under D.C. traffic law, it is a violation to stop *too long* at a stop sign. Under D.C. police regulations, however, plainclothes officers in unmarked cars are barred from enforcing traffic laws unless the violation poses an immediate safety threat. Nonetheless, suspecting that the Pathfinder's occupants might have drugs, the officers used the pretext of the traffic violation to pursue and stop the car. They admitted in court that they had no interest in enforcing the traffic law, which in any event they had no authority to enforce under the department's regulations.

The Supreme Court unanimously upheld the stop, ruling that as long as an officer observes a traffic violation, a stop is constitutional, even if the officer has no authority to make the stop and no intention to enforce the law violated. The decision gives a green light to dishonest police work. It permits officers who lack probable cause or reasonable suspicion to manufacture a pretextual basis for intervention. And that allows officers who have no more basis for suspicion than the color of a driver's skin to make a constitutional stop. Under *Whren,* a racially motivated pretextual stop is "reasonable" under the Fourth Amendment.

The Court in *Whren* did state that the Equal Protection Clause might be violated were it established that a stop had in fact been motivated by race. But the very nature of a "pretext" stop makes it extremely difficult to establish such a motivation. If the officer follows a driver until there is a traffic violation, the violation itself will inevitably be advanced as the reason for the stop, and *Whren* makes any traffic violation, no matter how petty and pretextual, a legitimate rationale. Police officers are not likely to admit that they made the stop because the driver was black, and absent such an admission, it will be nearly impossible for minority defendants to challenge the stop. As one federal judge complained, the standard "frees a police officer to target members of minority groups for selective enforcement."[76]

A computer search of all published federal court of appeals decisions involving allegedly pretextual stops from August 1993 to February 1996 and of all published federal district court cases on the same issue from February 1992 to January 1996 in which race could be identified found that 80 percent of the stops involved minority drivers.[77] In many of these cases, defendants argued that the stop was motivated by race. Such claims invariably failed. In several cases, the courts simply accepted the officer's testimony that he did not notice the race of the occupants until *after* he had stopped the car.[78] In other cases, courts declined to look at evidence of an officer's past record of racially disproportionate traffic stops, finding such evidence irrelevant as long as there was a traffic violation to justify the stop.[79] In one case, the court of appeals rejected a claim that three black drivers had been stopped because of their race where the officer testified that he had pulled them over for driving without having their headlights on, even though the officer did not mention headlights during the stop and did not issue a citation for that asserted infraction.[80]

Finally, consider the court's treatment of Theophilis Bell, an African American stopped in a high-crime neighborhood of Des Moines, Iowa, for riding his bicycle without a headlamp after sunset. The officers admitted the stop was pretextual, stating that they stopped Bell because they knew him to be a gang member and suspected he might be transporting drugs. They arrested him for the bicycle infraction, conducted a search incident to lawful arrest, and found a package of crack cocaine. Bell challenged his arrest on equal protection grounds, and offered evidence showing that 98 percent of bicycles in Des Moines had no headlamps, that the Des Moines population was predominantly white, and that every person arrested for riding a bike without a headlamp in the month before his stop was black. The court dismissed the claim on the ground that Bell had failed to prove that white people rode their bikes after sunset in Des Moines.[81] With this kind of judicial oversight, it is perhaps not surprising that the Louisiana State Police Department's training film explicitly exhorts officers to use traffic stops to conduct narcotics searches of "males of foreign nationalities, mainly Cubans, Colombians, Puerto Ricans, or other swarthy outlanders."[82]

Like consent searches, pretext stops reduce the "cost" of the Fourth Amendment right against search and seizure. They permit police officers to conduct criminal investigations by "manufacturing" probable cause through a petty traffic violation. The net of traffic regulations is so wide that everyone will fall within it, and as a result police officers have virtually unfettered discretion to decide whom to stop. That discretion will often be guided by the same prejudices and stereotypes that guide bus and train sweeps. And as a result, minority drivers on the nation's highways simply do not have the same Fourth Amendment rights as whites.

THE COLOR OF REASONABLE SUSPICION AND QUALITY-OF-LIFE POLICING

In 1993, Reverend Jesse Jackson told a Chicago audience, "There is nothing more painful to me at this stage in my life than to walk down the street and hear footsteps and start thinking about robbery — then look around and see somebody white and feel relieved."[83] Jackson is not alone: a 1990 University of Chicago study found that over 56 percent of Americans believe that blacks are "violence prone."[84] As Professor Jody Armour has put it, "it is unrealistic to dispute the depressing conclusion that, for many Americans, crime has a black face."[85]

If this is true of a majority of Americans, is there any reason to believe that it is less true of American police officers? A police officer who considers the racial makeup of the prison population might rationally conclude that blacks are more likely to commit crime than whites. Although one cannot simplistically equate prison demographics with the demographics of criminal behavior, most criminologists who have studied the matter have concluded that blacks (and men and young people) do in fact commit crime at a higher per capita rate than whites (and women and older people). Thus, all other things being equal, it is rational to be more suspicious of a young black man than an elderly white woman.

But that it may be rational does not make it right. First, the correlation of race and crime remains a stereotype, and most blacks will not conform to the stereotype. Even though blacks are arrested and convicted for a disproportionate amount of violent crime, it is nonetheless true that in any given year only about 2 percent of black citizens are arrested for committing any crime; the vast majority, or 98 percent, of black citizens are not even charged with crime.[86] A police officer who relies on race in stopping and questioning individuals is therefore likely to stop many more innocent than guilty individuals. Second, our nation's historical reliance on race for invidious discrimination renders suspect such consideration of race today, even if it might be "rational" in some sense. Indeed, the history of racial discrimination has led the Supreme Court to subject even expressly benign considerations of race, such as affirmative action programs, to strict scrutiny. Under strict scrutiny, it is not enough to prove that it is "rational" to rely on race; the government must demonstrate that the consideration of race is "necessary" to further a "compelling state interest," a test the police officer relying on a racial generalization could not meet.

What then should the criminal justice system do about the likelihood that police officers will associate black skin with suspicion of crime? One familiar method for checking race-based suspicion is to impose strict requirements of probable cause on police officers' actions. "Probable cause" requires an officer to articulate objective facts, attributable to reliable sources, to support the suspicion that a particular individual has or is engaged in crime. Because probable cause requires officers to point to objective facts about specific individuals rather than group-based probabilities, it precludes reliance on race. Until 1968, police were not permitted to seize an individual without such "probable cause."

In 1968, however, in a closely watched case, the Court faced the question whether brief investigative stops should be permissible without probable cause. In *Terry v. Ohio*,[87] a police officer observed two men pacing up and down a city street, repeatedly peering into a jewelry store window. Suspecting that they were casing the store for an armed robbery, but lacking probable cause to believe a crime had occurred, he approached, stopped the men, asked some questions, and frisked them for weapons. The frisk revealed a pistol, and Terry maintained that the evidence had been obtained in violation of the Fourth Amendment.

Ohio argued that because the stop was not a full-scale arrest, it did not require any justification under the Fourth Amendment. Civil rights advocates and criminal defense attorneys responded that Terry had been forcibly detained, and that any forcible detention required probable cause. The Court split the difference. It held that the detention was a "seizure" triggering Fourth Amendment requirements, but that brief investigatory stops could be justified by something less than probable cause: "reasonable suspicion that crime is afoot."[88] And it further ruled that where there were specific reasons for fearing that the individual stopped might be armed, a frisk for weapons—although not a search for evidence—was also justified.

Like the doctrines governing seizure, consent searches, and pretext stops, the "stop-and-frisk" rule is in theory color-blind, but has in practice created a double standard. It does so principally by extending a wide degree of discretion to police officers in settings where race and class considerations frequently play a significant role. "Reasonable suspicion" is an extremely open-ended standard. The Court initially placed some limits on the concept, ruling that reasonable suspicion was not satisfied merely by the observation that an individual was in a high-crime area,[89] or had associated with known drug users.[90] However, the Court has also held that even an anonymous tip, with no indicia of reliability, can support reasonable suspicion, and lower courts have increasingly deferred to the police on questions of reasonable suspicion.

Professor David Harris has found that courts routinely find reasonable suspicion established by factors very close to those the Supreme Court initially found insufficient.[91] For example, courts will generally find a stop justified where an individual in a high-crime area takes measures to avoid an encounter with the police. In Professor Harris's terms, "location plus evasion" equals reasonable suspicion. "High-crime areas" tend to be inner-city neighborhoods populated by the black or Hispanic underclass. Simply by living in such neighborhoods, black and Hispanic citizens already have one "reasonable suspicion" strike against them.[92] For reasons set forth above, black and Hispanic citizens are more likely to avoid the police. Yet under the "location plus evasion" theory, any attempt to avoid the police in the inner city is likely to create the grounds for a forcible stop. And although *Terry* initially limited "frisks" to those settings in which the police had reason to believe the individual might be armed, the courts have effectively adopted a presumption that where drug activity is suspected, there is reason to suspect that arms may be involved, thus automatically justifying a frisk.[93]

Some would argue that the police should be authorized to engage in routine investigatory stops in high-crime areas, as such policing may be an effective tool for deterring and preventing crime before it occurs. This thinking underlies the recent trend toward "quality of life" policing, which depends on the aggressive use of stop-and-frisk tactics, pretext stops, and arrests for minor quality-of-life infractions, such as drinking or urinating in public, panhandling, littering, or sleeping on park benches. The theory of quality-of-life policing is that subjecting people to regular frisks and reducing the incidence of quality-of-life crimes will also prevent more serious crime by promoting a sense of law and order, making it more costly to carry weapons in public, and using arrests for minor infractions to detect, detain and deter more serious criminals. This strategy relies heavily on inherently discretionary police judgments about which communities to target, which individuals to stop, and whether to use heavy-handed or light-handed treatment for routine infractions.

According to law enforcement officials, quality-of-life policing works. Its introduction in New York City, for example, coincided with a 50 percent drop from 1990 to 1996 in the seven categories of serious crime measured by the FBI's Uniform Crime Reports. In 1990, New York City had 2,246 homicides and 6,000 shooting victims. In 1996, it had fewer than 1,000 homicides and about 3,000 shooting victims. In one especially violent precinct in northwest Harlem, there were eighteen murders and forty shootings in the first five months of 1995. In June of that year, the police increased *Terry* stops by 150 percent, and the number of shootings dropped to zero. As one street vendor explained, "With all the police vigilance, nobody dares carry their guns."[94] Because this practice is targeted at inner-city high-crime neighborhoods, its *beneficiaries*, too, are likely to be disproportionately the disadvantaged.

It is never easy to identify causes for change in the crime rate. So many factors have been found to correlate with crime rates, from unemployment to age demographics to the incidence of broken homes to drug problems to the role of gangs, that it is difficult if not impossible to say what role quality-of-life policing in particular has played in the recent downward trend. On the one hand, New York City has experienced greater drops than much of the rest of the country, and it is the most prominent locus of the new policing. On the other hand, the crime rate began dropping in New York City *before* quality-of-life policing was instituted.[95] Nevertheless, many experts agree that quality-of-life policing seems to be having some significant beneficial effects on crime rates. That success raises a fundamental question: do the reduced crime rates justify subjecting inner-city residents to more frequent and intrusive searches and seizures?

It is easy for liberals living in the comfort of more privileged neighborhoods to argue that constitutional rights should not be sacrificed for safety; their safety is not at issue. But it is just as easy for conservatives living in the comfort of more privileged neighborhoods to argue that the reduction in crime outweighs the intrusions on citizens' constitutional rights; their rights are not threatened. The privileged, whether liberal or conservative, do not have to bear the costs of their positions, so long as they do not live in the inner city. Residents of the inner city, by contrast, face a no-win situation—either they are preyed on by crime, or they are preyed on by the police. Not surprisingly, reactions in the inner city to quality-of-life policing are mixed. Complaints about police abuse are up dramatically in New York City since the institution of quality-of-life policing in 1994. From 1993 to 1996, complaints increased by more than 55 percent. Complaints from Manhattan north of 59th Street, which includes the predominantly minority neighborhoods of Harlem, East Harlem, and Washington Heights, rose by 38 percent from 1993 to 1996, while complaints south of 59th Street rose by only 8 percent.[96] As Diane Saarinen, a Manhattan resident who initially cheered the arrival of quality-of-life policing in her neighborhood, told Newsweek, "In the beginning we all wanted the police to bomb the crack houses. But now it's backfiring at the cost of the community. I think the cops have been given free rein to intimidate people at large."[97]

These reactions raise doubts about whether quality-of-life policing will produce long-term benefits. This method of policing is ultimately premised on restoring the legitimacy of law and the strength of community. The police's vigorous enforcement of quality-of-life crimes is designed to forestall a perception that the neighborhood is lawless, and to foster a stronger sense of a safe and stable community. But the stop-and-frisk and pretext-stop tactics that are the lifeblood of quality-of-life policing give police the discretion to be abusive. If it means that innocent citizens in the inner city will routinely be subjected to forcible stops and intrusive frisks, the practice is likely to engender hostility and distrust toward police officers.[98] The Supreme Court explicitly acknowledged that danger in the *Terry* opinion, noting that "in many communities, field interrogations are a major source of friction between the police and minority groups."[99] The routine stopping of black citizens, particularly young black men, is a consistent complaint in black communities across the country, and no doubt contributes to the pervasive sense among African Americans that the criminal justice system is biased against them.[100] As Charles Ogletree, a black professor at Harvard Law School summed it up, "If I'm dressed in a knit cap and hooded jacket, I'm probable cause."[101] That perception is ultimately very corrosive, and if quality-of-life policing alienates a substantial segment of minority communities, it may in the long term encourage more criminal behavior than it deters by undermining the very sense of legal legitimacy that it is designed to foster.

DRUG-COURIER PROFILES

The selective impact on minority citizens of the tactics described earlier is not limited to high-crime neighborhoods. One of the most common rationales for stopping and questioning citizens is the "drug-courier profile." Used to select suspects in airports, bus terminals, train stations, and on the nation's roads and highways, the drug-courier profile is a set of characteristics designed to guide law enforcement officials in deciding whom to target for investigatory stops. In theory, it simply compiles the collective wisdom and judgment of a given agency's officials. Instead of requiring each officer to rely on his or her own limited experience in detecting suspicious behavior, the drug-courier profile gives every officer the advantage of the agency's collective experience.

But in practice, the drug-courier profile is a scattershot hodge-podge of traits and characteristics so expansive that it potentially justifies stopping anybody and everybody. Law enforcement agencies do not publicize their profiles, out of concern that savvy drug couriers might then avoid detection by fitting their behavior into unsuspicious categories. Where the constitutionality of a stop is challenged, however, police officers often justify their actions by claiming that the suspect fit the drug-courier profile, and as a result enterprising researchers have pieced together a drug-courier profile by compiling the traits identified in reported cases. Federal agents have asserted all of the following traits as parts of a drug-courier profile:

- arrived late at night
- arrived early in the morning
- arrived in afternoon
- one of first to deplane
- one of last to deplane
- deplaned in the middle
- purchased ticket at airport
- made reservation on short notice
- bought coach ticket
- bought first-class ticket
- used one-way ticket
- used round-trip ticket
- paid for ticket with cash
- paid for ticket with small denomination currency
- paid for ticket with large denomination currency
- made local telephone call after deplaning
- made long-distance telephone call after deplaning
- pretended to make telephone call
- traveled from New York to Los Angeles
- traveled to Houston
- carried no luggage
- carried brand-new luggage
- carried a small bag
- carried a medium-sized bag
- carried two bulky garment bags
- carried two heavy suitcases
- carried four pieces of luggage
- overly protective of luggage
- disassociated self from luggage
- traveled alone
- traveled with a companion
- acted too nervous
- acted too calm
- made eye contact with officer
- avoided making eye contact with officer
- wore expensive clothing and gold jewelry
- dressed casually
- went to restroom after deplaning
- walked quickly through airport
- walked slowly through airport
- walked aimlessly through airport
- left airport by taxi
- left airport by limousine
- left airport by private car

- left airport by hotel courtesy van
- suspect was Hispanic
- suspect was black female[102]

Needless to say, it would be extremely difficult for anybody *not* to come within such a profile. Such profiles do not so much focus an investigation as provide law enforcement officials a ready-made excuse for stopping whomever they please. The Supreme Court has warned that the mere fact that someone fits a drug-courier profile does not automatically constitute reasonable suspicion justifying a stop.[103] In practice, however, courts frequently defer to the profile and equate it with reasonable suspicion. As one judge said after conducting a comprehensive review of drug-courier profile decisions, "[m]any courts have accepted the profile, as well as the Drug Enforcement Agency's scattershot enforcement efforts, unquestioningly, mechanistically, and dispositively."[104] To invoke a "profile" sounds much more professional and scientific than a single officer's hunch, but it may do nothing more than provide a cover for such hunches. To that extent, the profile expands the already wide swath of discretion accorded police officers in deciding whom to stop and frisk. And as we have seen, unguided discretion invites stereotyped judgments.

Some profiles appear to take race explicitly into account. In one case, a DEA agent testified in the late 1970s that blacks prefer heroin and whites cocaine, so that "a black arriving from a major heroin distribution point arouses greater suspicion, *ceteris paribus* [all other things being equal], than one arriving from a major cocaine distribution point."[105] The same agent testified in another case that most drug couriers are black females.[106] Another agent testified that "being Hispanic was part of the profile."[107] Still another admitted that his profile included the fact that the defendant was an African American.[108] A DEA drug profile used to detect drug couriers on Florida highways in the 1980s listed, as types to watch out for, Colombian males, aged twenty-five to thirty years; black males, aged twenty to fifty years; white males, aged twenty to thirty years; blacks and Colombians wearing "lots of gold"; and "whites wear[ing] boots."[109]

Even without explicitly referring to race, the drug-courier profile is likely to encourage reliance on racial characteristics. A New York State judge, reviewing a drug interdiction program at the Port Authority bus terminal, reported that none of the three judges who arraigned felony cases in New York County could recall a single Port Authority drug interdiction case where the defendant was not black or Hispanic.[110] A police officer working at the Memphis International Airport testified that at least 75 percent of those followed and questioned at the airport were black.[111] A Lexis review of all federal court decisions from January 1, 1990, to August 2, 1995, in which drug-courier profiles were used and the race of the suspect was discernible revealed that of sixty-three such cases, all but three suspects were minorities: thirty-four were black, twenty-five were Hispanic, one was Asian, and three were white.[112] Although this is not a scientific sampling—it does not include cases in which the race of the suspect could not be discerned, and it does not include cases that did not result in judicial decisions (either because there was no arrest or indictment, because a decision was unpublished, or because the defendant pleaded guilty)—the statistics are so one-sided as to raise serious questions about racial targeting even where profiles are race-neutral.

Professor Randall Kennedy has argued that race should never be a legitimate factor in profiles, and I agree.[113] Although racial identity, like hair color or attire, is an appropriate consideration in identifying suspects where an eyewitness has described a specific perpetrator of a particular crime, profiles serve a different function altogether. They identify characteristics that should *generally* be deemed suspicious, and race should never be a permissible basis for such generalized suspicion. But to say that race should not be a permissible factor does not go far enough. Indeed, most courts already agree that explicit racial factors are impermissible in profiles. Thus, the U.S. Court of Appeals for the Sixth Circuit stated in 1992 that a racial component in a drug-courier profile would have "due process and equal protection implications."[114]

Even where race is not an explicit factor, it will often be an unstated one, and toleration of loose, race-neutral profiles will therefore have the effect of tolerating race-based stops. In other words, it is not enough to declare, as Professor Kennedy does, that race-based stops should not be permitted. Courts consistently look the other way when this issue arises. In one case, for example, where police stopped an automobile for driving three miles above the speed limit, and where the officer admitted that the race of the driver was a factor, the court held that as long as there is probable cause to stop the car—and exceeding the speed limit is probable cause—the inquiry goes no further. In a footnote, it observed that although the officer admitted that race had been a factor, there was no evidence that it was the determinative, "but for," reason for the stop.[115] In another case in which it appeared that officers singled out a black airline passenger in part because of his race, the court reasoned that because the ultimate encounter was consensual, there was no seizure, and therefore no need to consider the claim that the police had improperly considered the suspect's race in deciding to approach him in the first place.[116] And in several cases addressing the issue of race-based stops, the Sixth Circuit has repeatedly stated that stops based *solely* on race would violate equal protection, suggesting that as long as the police can identify a neutral factor in addition to race, the stop will be upheld.[117]

These cases are plainly inconsistent with established equal protection doctrine. Where the police point to a number of factors that caused them to approach a particular traveler, and race is one of them, the case presents what the courts call a "mixed motive." In such cases, the prosecution should have to demonstrate that the police would have engaged in the same conduct even if the defendant's race were not considered.[118] Where race has been identified as a factor, it will be difficult for the police to establish that they would have taken the same action absent consideration of race. Thus, under traditional equal protection analysis, the police should be barred from considering race in singling out whom to follow, approach, or question, whether or not the encounter reaches the level of a seizure for Fourth Amendment purposes, and whether or not other factors were also at play. But traditional equal protection analysis is triggered only by a showing of intentional or explicit discrimination, and most drug-courier-profile stops will not meet that initial threshold showing.

The drug-courier profile, like each of the tactics discussed previously, has the advantage of making it easier to detect crime without diminishing the constitutional rights of the privileged. Drug-courier profiles are seldom invoked to justify a search of a rich white businessman; they are used to justify searches of people who "look like criminals." Because in our society crime so often has the face of a racial minority, the drug-courier profile will be used disproportionately against minorities, whether or not it explicitly refers to race. At the same time, the deference profiles receive from many courts means that in effect the profile grants police officers a free hand in whom they target. It is difficult even to imagine a drug-courier profile that singled out characteristics of well-off travelers, but one can be sure that if such a profile existed, either political pressure or judicial review would quickly bring its demise. Here, as elsewhere in the regulation of police practices, intrusive law enforcement tactics are tolerated precisely because the intrusion is not likely to affect the privileged among us.

ELIMINATING DOUBLE STANDARDS

In many situations, the police use a combination of the above tactics. It is common, for example, for the police to use the drug-courier profile to approach an individual and ask for identification, tickets, and destination. Because the courts do not treat such an encounter as a "seizure," there are no Fourth Amendment constraints on whom the police select for such treatment. The encounter often includes a request to search the individual's luggage; here, too, the Fourth Amendment places no limit on whom the police can target. Most people consent to the search, and the only Fourth Amendment rule regarding that decision is the largely pro forma "voluntariness" test. And if the individual refuses to consent, courts often uphold a brief stop and frisk based on the suspect's "nervous" responses to the police questioning.[119]

In effect, then, the Supreme Court has immunized a wide range of law enforcement from any Fourth Amendment review. All these tactics are disproportionately directed at persons of color. The Court's removal of meaningful Fourth Amendment review allows the police to rely on unparticularized discretion, unsubstantiated hunches, and nonindividualized suspicion. Racial prejudice and stereotypes linking racial minorities to crime rush to fill the void. As a result, many innocent minorities are stopped, questioned, and searched on a routine basis, reinforcing a sense among members of minority communities that the police are their enemy, and that they have been singled out for suspicion because of the color of their skin.

None of this is necessary. Were the Supreme Court so inclined, it could adopt rules that would demand equal protection rather than rules that invite racial targeting and discrimination. For example, it should require police officers to inform suspects that they have the right to say no when they seek consent to a search, instead of permitting the police to exploit ignorance and fear. And it should apply the usual waiver standards, requiring the police to establish that consent was "knowing, intelligent, and voluntary." If the Supreme Court is unwilling to impose such a requirement, legislatures and police departments should do so of their own accord. The FBI, for example, has long required its agents to inform suspects of their right to refuse a search. There is no reason why all police officers should not be required to do so.

Similarly, the Court should be more demanding in the justifications it requires for forcible stops and arrests. At a minimum, it should adopt a "reasonable person" standard that is more sensitive to the inherent coercion of most police-citizen encounters. This would subject more encounters to the constitutional requirement of individualized suspicion. At the same time, the Court should increase the level of suspicion required for a stop and frisk. It has now been so reduced that it effectively no longer requires individualized suspicion. But the requirement that stops be based on *individualized* grounds for suspicion is all that stands in the way of racial stereotyping. Courts should be particularly skeptical of bases for suspicion that seem to be manufactured by police conduct—such as "location plus evasion"— and of drug-courier profiles, which often do little more than legitimate generalized prejudices.

We should also require police officers to keep public records of the race of those whom they stop, question, and subject to consent searches. As we have seen, encounters short of arrest are largely a matter of police discretion, and there is a sound basis for believing that such discretion may be driven by racial stereotypes and prejudices. Requiring public recording of the racial character of such stops might lead the police to evaluate more carefully and critically their own bases for action, and might also identify where supervisory action is needed to redress imbalances. So that enforcement is not left to the police themselves, citizen commissions should be empowered to review these records and to demand explanations from the police when racial disparities become evident. If necessary, federal judicial oversight might be obtained by bringing discrimination suits under Title VI of the Civil Rights Act, which makes unlawful practices that have a disparate racial impact, does not require a showing of intent, and applies to all entities that receive federal funding, including most state and local police departments.

If we restored equality to the policing process, it would become more "self-policing." If well-to-do white people were routinely stopped, questioned, and searched, there would likely be more community pressure on the police to regulate themselves. We would likely find more sympathy within the legislative, executive, and judicial branches for protecting those subjected to such tactics. Restrictions on police behavior would soon develop. If those restrictions turned out to impede law enforcement too greatly, we would be forced as a community to reach a consensus on where the appropriate line should be drawn—*for everyone*—between crime control and privacy interests.

But under the law as it stands, wealthy white people are not subject to such treatment; black and Hispanic people are, and especially poor black and Hispanic people living in the inner city. These groups are underrepresented in all branches of government. The fact that these tactics are for the most part targeted along race and class lines means that coalitions between the powerful and the powerless are unlikely. The association of blacks and Hispanics with crime that appears to pervade much of the white community makes it likely that whites will perceive their interests to be at odds with those of minority groups on these issues. Because they do not bear the costs of law enforcement, white people have less reason to be concerned about discretionary law enforcement. So it should not be surprising that crime bills are a growth industry in Congress, and only the Black and Hispanic Caucus introduces measures responsive to equality concerns.

What is perhaps most troubling about all of this is that it is entirely foreseeable. At rare moments, such as in *Miranda v. Arizona*, the Supreme Court has explicitly acknowleged and sought to counteract the effects of social inequality on criminal justice. But *Miranda* is the exception that proves the rule. As this chapter shows, far more common are decisions that balance the competing interests in protecting rights and preventing crime by striking two balances, one for the well-to-do, and the other for the disadvantaged. In the area of police practices, at least, we have come to rely on social disparity to mediate the central tension in criminal justice.

ENDNOTES

1. Joseph P. Kahn, "The Right to Be Secure," *Boston Globe Magazine*, 7 April 1991, 18. A District of Columbia detective testified that in 85 bus and train encounters, he could recall only three or four passengers who refused to be interviewed. He also testified that when passengers appeared nervous and refused to talk, detectives would sometimes notify authorities at the next stop down the line, who would target that person for another approach. *United States v. Felder*, 732 F. Supp. 204, 205 (D.D.C. 1990).

2. Kahn, *supra* note 1 at 18.

3. *Bostick v. State*, 554 So.2d 1153, 1158 (Fla. 1989) (quoting *State v. Kerwick*, 512 So.2d 347, 348–49 (Fla. 4th DCA 1987)).

4. See Brief of Respondent at 17–18 in *Florida v. Bostick*, 501 U.S. 429 (1991); Amicus Curiae Brief of Americans for Effective Law Enforcement in *Florida v. Bostick*.

5. *Terry v. Ohio*, 392 U.S. 1, 19 n.16 (1968).

6. *United States v. Mendenhall*, 446 U.S. 544, 554 (1980).

7. *Mendenhall*, 446 U.S. at 555.

8. *Illinois Migrant Council v. Pilliod*, 398 F. Supp. 882, 899 (N.D. Ill. 1975). Professor Tracey Maclin put it more bluntly: "Common sense teaches that most of us do not have the chutzpah or stupidity to tell a police officer to 'get lost' after he has

stopped us and asked for identification or questioned us about possible criminal conduct." Tracey Maclin, "Black and Blue Encounters — Some Preliminary Thoughts about Fourth Amendent Seizures: Should Race Matter?," 26 Valparaiso U.L. Rev. 243, 249–50 (1991).

9. See Wayne R. LaFave, "Pinguitudinous Police, Pachydermatous Prey: Whence Fourth Amendment 'Seizures'?," 3 U. Ill. L. Rev. 729, 740–41 (1991).

10. As one court stated regarding bus sweeps, "such means of transportation are utilized largely by the underclass of this nation who, because of greater concerns (such as being able to survive), do not often complain about such deprivations." *United States v. Lewis*, 728 F. Supp. 784, 789 (D.D.C. 1990). See also J. Bolt, "Greyhound Takes to Radio for Summer Ad Campaign," *Associated Press*, 3 May 1990 ("Greyhound says its passsengers tend to be students or from low-income families"); L. Cunningham and K. Thompson, "The Intercity Bus Tour Market," J. Travel Res., fall 1986, 8 ("[Intercity bus r]idership typically includes a disproportionate number of low-income individuals"); Interstate Commerce Comm'n Bureau of Economics, *Intercity Bus Industry: A Preliminary Study* 32 (1978) (finding that majority of intercity bus travelers have low household income, and that largest proportion of intercity bus riders are nonwhite).

11. *United States v. Weaver*, 966 F.2d 391, 396 (8th Cir. 1992) (upholding stop of a "roughly dressed black male").

12. In twenty-nine cases the decisions themselves indicated the race of the defendants. In another twenty-six cases, I identified the race of the defendant by contacting the defense attorney. See also *United States v. Lewis*, 728 F. Supp. at 786; *United States v. Felder*, 732 F. Supp. 204, 206 (D.D.C. 1990); *People v. Evans*, 556 N.Y.S.2d 794 (Sup.Ct. 1990).

13. *Florida v. Bostick*, 501 U.S. at 441 n.1 (Marshall, J., dissenting) (noting that "at least one officer who routinely confronts interstate travelers candidly admitted that race is a factor influencing his decision whom to approach").

14. *Michigan v. Chesternut*, 486 U.S. 567, 573–74 (1988).

15. *In re J.M.*, 619 A.2d 497, 501–2 (D.C.App. 1992); see also *State ex rel. Juvenile Dept. of Multnomah County v. Fikes*, 842 P.2d 807, 809–10 (Or. App. 1992) (interpreting Fourth Amendment and Oregon State Constitution).

16. *Report of the Independent Commission on the Los Angeles Police Department*, 69 (1991).

17. See, e.g., Stephen Braun, "Black Men, LAPD — A Mix of Bitterness and Suspicion," *L.A. Times*, 16 December 1991, A1 (recounting frequency with which young black men are stopped by police, and resulting distrust for police officers among black community).

18. Don Terry, "Badge Tarnishes on Los Angeles Streets, Police Say," *N.Y. Times*, 25 March 1991, A1 (chronicling suspicion toward police among black community after Rodney King beating).

19. Richard W. Stevenson, "Los Angeles Chief Taunted at Hearing," *N.Y. Times*, 15 March 1991, A16.

20. "Ex-Officer's Account of Brutal Police Fraternity," *N.Y. Times*, 30 September 1993, B3 (quoting excerpts from testimony of Bernard Cawley before the Mollen Commission).

21. Id.
22. Id.
23. City of New York, Comm'n to Investigate Allegations of Police Corruption and the Anti-Corruption Procedures of the Police Department, *Commission Report*, 11, 45 (July 7, 1994). The Commission focused on five precincts in particular, all of them disproportionately minority: one in the South Bronx, two in Brooklyn, one in Harlem, and one on Manhattan's Lower East Side.
24. Id. at 21–50.
25. Id. at 36, 38, 49, 58.
26. Don Terry, "Philadelphia Shaken by Criminal Police Officers," *N.Y. Times*, 28 August 1995, A1.
27. *Morgan v. Woessner*, 975 F.2d 629, 631–34 (9th Cir. 1992).
28. See William Raspberry, "Finding Trouble Was Easy," *Wash. Post*, 20 January 1989, A27; Chris Woodyard, "Citizen Review of Police Urged After Taped 'Sting,'" *L.A. Times*, 17 January 1989, metro section, 2.
29. Elizabeth A. Gaynes, "The Urban Criminal Justice System: Where Young + Black + Male = Probable Cause," 20 Ford. Urb. L.J. 621, 625 n.18 (1993) (describing Nov. 6, 1992 broadcast, of "20/20").
30. *Report of the Attorney General's Civil Rights Division on Boston Police Department Practices* (Dec. 18, 1990).
31. Id. at 13.
32. Id. at 4–5, 46–59.
33. As Justice Stevens has recognized,

    > [T]hose who have found — by reason of prejudice or misfortune — that encounters with the police may become adversarial or unpleasant without good cause will have grounds for worrying at any stop designed to elicit signs of suspicious behavior.

    Michigan Dept. of State Police v. Sitz, 496 U.S. 444, 465 (1990) (Stevens, J., dissenting).
34. *In re J.M.*, 619 A.2d at 513 (Mack, J., dissenting).
35. Neither did the Florida courts. See William R. O'Shields, "The Exodus of Minorities' Fourth Amendment Rights into Oblivion: Florida v. Bostick and the Merits of Adopting a Per Se Rule Against Random, Suspicionless Bus Searches in the Minority Community," 77 Iowa L. Rev. 1875, 1904 n. 235 (1992).
36. *Johnson v. Zerbst*, 304 U.S. 458, 464 (1938).
37. *McCarthy v. United States*, 394 U.S. 459 (1969); *Boykin v. Alabama*, 395 U.S. 238 (1969).
38. *Afroyim v. Rusk*, 387 U.S. 253 (1967); *Vance v. Terrazas*, 444 U.S. 252 (1980).
39. *Miranda v. Arizona*, 384 U.S. 436 (1966).
40. *United States v. Wade*, 388 U.S. 218, 237 (1967).
41. *Schneckloth v. Bustamonte*, 412 U.S. 218 (1973).
42. *Miranda*, 384 U.S. at 472 ("While authorities are not required to relieve the accused of his poverty, they have the obligation not to take advantage of indigence in the administration of justice"); see generally A. Kenneth Pye, "The Warren Court and Criminal Procedure," 67 Mich. L. Rev. 249 (1968) (characterizing Warren

Court's criminal procedure jurisprudence, including *Miranda*, as an "attempt[] to make the rich and poor substantially equal before our criminal courts").

43. *Schneckloth*, 412 U.S. at 227.

44. Id. at 243.

45. Id. at 229.

46. Id. at 231.

47. Id. at 287 (Marshall, J., dissenting) (noting that the FBI had for many years routinely informed subjects of their right to refuse consent). One DEA agent customarily read the following from a warning card when asking suspects for consent to search:

> You have the right to allow, or refuse to allow a search to be made of your peron and the personal property that you have with you. You have the right to consult an attorney before deciding whether you wish to allow or refuse to allow the search. If you consent to the search any illegal objects found can be used against you in court proceedings. Do you understand?

United States v. Williams, 647 F.2d 588, 590 (5th Cir. 1981).

48. *Ohio v. Robinette*, 117 S. Ct. 417 (1996).

49. *State v. Robinette*, 653 N.E.2d 695, 699 (Oh. S.Ct. 1995).

50. *Escobedo v. Illinois*, 378 U.S. 478, 490 (1964).

51. 412 U.S. at 248.

52. Id.

53. Ray O'Brien, "Consent Search Abuse in Poor and Minority Communities" (May 17, 1995), paper on file with author.

54. Id. at 36.

55. *United States v. Hall*, 969 F.2d 1102, 1107 (D.C. Cir. 1992).

56. *United States v. Rodney*, 956 F.2d 295, 297 (D.C. Cir. 1992).

57. *United States v. Ferreira*, No. 89–3101, 1990 WL 93381 (D.C. Cir. June 27, 1990).

58. Louis Michael Seidman, "Brown and Miranda," 80 Calif. L. Rev. 673, 744 (1992). As a technical matter, the Court did not substitute the *Miranda* rules for the Court's prior "voluntariness" inquiry, and the voluntariness of a confession is still theoretically an issue even where *Miranda* warnings have been given and waiver has been established. However, as a practical matter the Court has shifted the focus of the legal inquiry to the *Miranda* warnings, and has rarely reviewed the voluntariness of a confession since *Miranda*.

59. Although the subjective focus of the consent test at least in theory offers more opportunity to consider matters of inequality than the objective "reasonable person" test used for seizures, it comes at a cost. Whether a particular individual consented voluntarily is a question of fact, and therefore the test gives substantial leeway to trial judges. Once a trial judge has found consent to be voluntary, a reviewing court can reverse only if the trial court's judgment was "clearly erroneous," a very difficult standard to meet. *In re J.M.*, 619 A.2d at 500. Thus, for all practical purposes, the only chance most defendants get to challenge the validity of their consent is before a state trial court, where the need to stand for re-election often biases judges against ruling for criminal defendants on constitutional issues. Stephen Bright and Patrick J. Keenan, "Judges and the Politics of Death: Deciding Between

the Bill of Rights and the Next Election in Capital Cases," 75 B.U. L. Rev. 759 (1995).

60. *Bostick*, 501 U.S. at 437.

61. *United States v. Withers*, 972 F.2d 837, 843 (7th Cir. 1992). In an earlier case, however, the Seventh Circuit held that refusal to consent could not be the "single additional event that ripens preexisting concerns to the 'founded suspicion' that a *Terry* stop requires." *United States v. Sterling*, 909 F.2d 1078, 1082 (7th Cir. 1990).

62. *United States v. Carter*, 985 F.2d 1095, 1097 (D.C. Cir. 1993)

63. *United States v. White*, 890 F.2d 1413 (8th Cir. 1989); *United States v. Wilson*, 953 F.2d 116, 126 (4th Cir. 1991).

64. Complaint in *Wilkins v. Maryland State Police*, C.A. No. MJG-93–468 (D. Md.)

65. Settlement Agreement in *Wilkins v. Maryland State Police*.

66. Complaint in *Northern Division Maryland State Conference of NAACP Branches v. Dept. of Maryland State Police*, Civ. Action No. CCB-98-1098 (D.Md), 30–32.

67. Michael A. Fletcher, "Driven to Extremes; Black Men Take Steps to Avoid Police Stops," *Wash. Post*, 29 March 1996, A1.

68. Id.

69. Henry Pierson Curtis, "Statistics Show Pattern of Discrimination," *Orlando Sentinel*, 23 August 1992, A11.

70. Jeff Brazil & Steve Berry, "Color of Driver Is Key to Stops in I-95 Videos," *Orlando Sentinel*, 23 August 1992, A1.

71. Id.

72. *United States v. Laymon*, 730 F. Supp. 332, 337 (D. Colo. 1990).

73. Id.

74. *Whitfield v. Bd. of County Commissioners of Eagle County*, 837 F. Supp. 338 (D. Co. 1993); Robert Jackson, "Eagle County must pay for stopping motorists; ACLU wins $800,000 settlement for drivers stopped because they fit drug courier profile," *Rocky Mountain News*, 10 November 1995, 4A (available on NEXIS).

75. *Whren v. United States*, 116 S. Ct. 1769 (1996).

76. *United States v. Botero-Ospina*, 71 F.3d 783, 790 (10th Cir. 1995) (en banc) (Seymour, J., dissenting).

77. Of thirty-four cases in which the race of the defendant or defendants was mentioned in the decision, only two involved white defendants, while thirty-two involved minority defendants. By contacting defense counsel in the cases where race was not mentioned, I identified the race of the defendant in thirteen more cases, and found that nine were white and four were black. Thus, thirty-six of forty-seven federal pretext-stop cases in which race could be identified involved minority defendants.

78. See, e.g., *United States v. Dirden*, 38 F.3d 1131 (10th Cir. 1994); *United States v. Perez*, 37 F.3d 510 (9th Cir. 1994); *United States v. Perez*, 37 F.3d 510 (9th Cir. 1994) (evidence of racial pattern of prior stops irrelevant because officers testified they couldn't see driver's race until he was stopped); *United States v. Torres-Soria*, 1993 U.S. App. LEXIS 30481 (9th Cir. 1993).

79. *United States v. Goodman*, 1993 U.S. App. LEXIS 33664, *11 (4th Cir. 1993); *United States v. Ceballes-Gamez*, 1995 U.S. App. LEXIS 7957 (9th Cir. 1995); *United States v. Dirden*, 38 F.3d at 1139 n.11 (fact that 50 percent of police officers'

stops for drugs over prior year involved minorities irrelevant because traffic violation was an objective basis for stop).

80. *United States v. Cure*, 996 F.2d 1136 (11th Cir. 1993).

81. *United States v. Bell*, 86 F.3d 820 (8th Cir. 1996).

82. *United States v. Thomas*, 787 F. Supp. 663, 676 (E.D. Tex. 1992).

83. "Perspectives," *Newsweek*, 13 December 1993, 17 (quoting Jesse Jackson).

84. Tom W. Smith, *Ethnic Images*, 9, 16 (Dec. 1990) (General Social Survey Topical
Report No. 19), quoted in Jody D. Armour, "Race Ipsa Loquitor: Of Reasonable
Racists, Intelligent Bayesians, and Involuntary Negrophobes," 46 Stan. L. Rev.
781, 787 (1994).

85. Armour, *supra* note 84 at 787.

86. "Developments in the Law: Race and the Criminal Process," 101 Harv. L. Rev.
1472, 1508 (1988) (noting that 97.9 percent of blacks and 99.5 percent of whites in
any given year are not arrested for committing a crime).

87. 392 U.S. 1 (1968).

88. 392 U.S. at 30.

89. *Brown v. Texas*, 443 U.S. 47 (1979).

90. *Sibron v. New York*, 392 U.S. 40 (1968).

91. David A. Harris, "Factors for Reasonable Suspicion: When Black and Poor Means
Stopped and Frisked," 69 Ind. L.J. 659, 672–75 (1994).

92. Id. at 677–78.

93. Id. at 676.

94. Clifford Krauss, "Shootings Fall as More Guns Stay at Home," *N.Y. Times*, 30 July
1995, 29.

95. Even before New York instituted quality-of-life policies in 1992, its murder rate had
dropped from 2,246 in 1990 to 1,995 in 1992. Jerome H. Skolnick, "Making Sense
of the Crime Decline," *Newsday*, 2 February 1997, G6; William Bratton, "Cutting
Crime and Restoring Order: What America Can Learn from New York's Finest,"
The Heritage Lectures, No. 573 (Washington, D.C.: Heritage Foundation Reports, 1997).

96. Jane Lii, "When the Saviors Are Seen as Sinners," *N.Y. Times*, 18 May 1997, Section 13, 1.

97. Larry Reibstein, "NYPD Black and Blue," *Newsweek*, 2 June 1997, 66.

98. See, e.g., Brent Staples, "Growing Up to Fear the Law," *N.Y. Times*, 28 March
1991, A24 (arguing that African Americans "tend to grow up believing that the law
is the enemy, because those who are sworn to uphold the law so often enforce it in
a biased way"); Stephen Braun, *supra* note 17 (describing black citizens' description of "routine" stops by the police and resulting hostility).

99. 392 U.S. at 14 n.11 (quoting President's Commission on Law Enforcement and
Administration of Justice, *Task Force Report: The Police*, 183 (1967)).

100. See, e.g., Sean Murphy, "5 File Lawsuit Challenging Boston Police on Search
Policy," *Boston Globe*, 22 November 1989, 17 (describing suit challenging police
practice of indiscriminately stopping and searching blacks in Roxbury); "Toledo is
Sued Over Random Stopping of Blacks," *N.Y. Times*, 14 August 1988, section 1,
part 1, 31 (describing federal civil rights suit challenging policy of randomly stop-

ping and questioning black teenagers in racially mixed neighborhood of Old West End).

101. Ellen Goodman, "Simpson Case Divides Us by Race," *Boston Globe*, 10 July 1994, 73 (quoting Charles Ogletree).

102. "Fluid Drug Courier Profiles See Everyone as Suspicious," 5 Crim. Prac. Man. (BNA) *333*, *334*–35 (July 10, 1991) (citing cases); *U.S. v. §129,727.00 U.S. Currency*, 129 F.3d 486, 490 (9th Cir. 1997); *U.S. v. Armstead*, 112 F.3d 320, 321 (8th Cir. 1997); *U.S. v. Small*, 74 F.3d 1276, 1282 (D.C.Cir. 1996); *U.S. v. $13,570.00 U.S. Currency*, 1997 U.S. Dist. LEXIS 18351, *8–*12 (E.D. La. 1997); Charles L. Becton, "The Drug Courier Profile: All Seems Infected That Th' Infected Spy, As All Looks Yellow To The Jaundic'd Eye," 65 N.C.L.Rev. 417, 438–54, 474–80 (1987) (listing and discussing drug-courier profile characteristics from reported decisions).

103. *Reid v. Georgia*, 448 U.S. 438, 440–41 (1980) (per curiam); *United States v. Mendenhall*, 446 U.S. 544, 565 n.6 (1980) (Powell, J., concurring).

104. Becton, "Drug Courier Profile," *supra* note 102, at 444–45.

105. *United States v. Coleman*, 450 F. Supp. 433, 439 n.7 (E.D. Mich. 1978).

106. *United States v. McClain*, 452 F. Supp. 195, 199 (E.D. Mich. 1977).

107. *United States v. Westerbann-Martinez*, 435 F. Supp. 690, 698 (E.D.N.Y. 1977). See also *United States v. Vasquez*, 612 F.2d 1338, 1353 n.10 (2d Cir. 1979) (Oakes, J., dissenting) (DEA agent admitted that Hispanic appearance was part of reason for stopping defendant).

108. *United States v. Harvey*, 16 F.3d 109, 112 n.3 (6th Cir. 1994).

109. See Joseph P. D'Ambrosio, "The Drug Courier Profile and Airport Stops: Reasonable Intrusions or Suspicionless Seizures?," 12 Nova L.Rev. 273, 289 n. 120 (1987) (quoting from discontinued drug-courier profile received from Miami office of the DEA).

110. *People v. Evans*, 556 N.Y.S.2d 794, 796 (Sup. Ct. 1990); id. at 799 (New York police officer testified that 65 percent to 75 percent of people stopped for drug interdiction questioning are black or Hispanic).

111. *United States v. Taylor*, 917 F.2d 1402, 1409 (6th Cir. 1990) (Memphis police officer testified that 75 percent of the people followed as result of drug-courier profile in Memphis airport are black); *United States v. Taylor*, 956 F.2d 572, 581 n.1 (6th Cir. 1992) (en banc) (Keith, J., dissenting).

112. Hispanic identity was discerned either by identification in the opinion itself or by a Hispanic surname.

113. Randall Kennedy, *Race, Crime and the Law*, 136–67 (New York: Pantheon, 1997).

114. *United States v. Taylor*, 956 F.2d at 578.

115. *United States v. Harvey*, 16 F.3d at 111, 112 n.3.

116. *United States v. Taylor*, 956 F.2d at 578.

117. *United States v. Avery*, 128 F.3d 974 (6th Cir. 1997); *United States v. Travis*, 62 F.3d 170 (6th Cir. 1995).

118. *Mt. Healthy School District Bd. of Education v. Doyle*, 429 U.S. 274 (1977) (holding that where government acts for "mixed motives," a plaintiff challenging the decision need only demonstrate that an impermissible factor, such as race, was "a motivating factor," and then the burden shifts to the defendant to demonstrate that it

would have taken the same action absent consideration of the impermissible factor).

119. In *United States v. Bloomfield*, 40 F.3d 910, 918 (8th Cir. 1994), for example, the court relied in part on the officer's testimony that a driver pulled over for a traffic stop was unusually "fidget[ing]" to justify reasonable suspicion. In *United States v. Weaver*, 966 F.2d 391, 396 (8th Cir. 1992), the court cited, among other factors giving rise to reasonable suspicion, the defendant's "nervousness, as manifested by his unsteady, rapid speech, his tremulous hands, and his swaying body."

2—A Muted Trumpet

Anthony Lewis's *Gideon's Trumpet* is one of the most widely read law books in our nation's history. And for good reason: it tells a classic American story. Clarence Earl Gideon, a penniless Florida man, down on his luck and charged with breaking and entering a poolroom, claims that although he can't afford a lawyer, he has a constitutional right to have a lawyer appointed by the state to defend him. When the Florida trial court denies his request, he represents himself, and is convicted. From prison, he sends a hand-written note to the Supreme Court asking it to hear his case. The Supreme Court appoints Abe Fortas, one of the most highly respected lawyers in the country, to argue Gideon's case, and then rules that the Sixth Amendment guarantees indigent defendants the assistance of a lawyer in all serious criminal trials. On retrial, with a lawyer paid for by the state, Gideon is acquitted.

What makes the story so peculiarly American—so much so that Henry Fonda played Gideon in the movie version—is its dramatic illustration of the principle of equal opportunity. With a handwritten note, a poor prisoner in Florida set the wheels of justice in motion, gained the attention of the Supreme Court, and won a victory that established the right of every American, no matter how poor, to have the assistance of counsel when charged with a crime. The right Gideon established is central to realizing equality before the law—without a lawyer, a criminal defendant has virtually no chance to vindicate his constitutional rights and obtain a fair trial, and a large proportion of criminal defendants cannot afford lawyers. So Gideon's right makes the promise of equality in the criminal justice system possible. It's a great story, with a great lesson, and for that reason it is widely taught in American high schools, colleges, and law schools.

What isn't taught, however, is our utter failure to realize the promise represented by Gideon's case. Lewis's book, published in 1964, one year after the *Gideon* decision was handed down, bears the mark of optimistic faith in progress that so characterized the period. But even Lewis predicted that it would be "an enormous social task to bring to life the dream of *Gideon v. Wainwright*—the dream of a vast, diverse country in which every man charged with crime will be capably defended, no matter what his economic circumstances, and in which the lawyer representing him will do so proudly, without resentment at an unfair burden, sure of the support needed to make an adequate defense."[1] Much like Dr. Martin Luther King, Jr.'s dream of the same year, the dream of *Gideon* has not been realized. The most troubling lesson of the more than thirty-five years since *Gideon v. Wainwright* is that neither the Supreme Court nor the public appears to have any interest in making the constitutional right announced in *Gideon* a reality.

This is not to suggest that *Gideon* has made no difference. Whenever the state seeks to impose prison time on an indigent criminal defendant, *Gideon* requires that the government provide the defendant with a lawyer; failure to do so is constitutional error requiring reversal of the conviction. But as long as the state provides a warm body with a law degree and a bar admission, little else matters. Indigent defense counsel are generally underpaid, overworked, and given insufficient resources to conduct an adequate investigation and defense. Although the Supreme Court formally requires that defense counsel provide "effective assistance," it has set the standard for effectiveness so low that even lawyers who are drunk or asleep in court have been deemed "effective."

These shortcomings in indigent representation have been long assailed. At least every five years since *Gideon* was decided, a major study has been released finding that indigent defense is inadequate.[2] Yet society has done next to nothing about the problem. We are unwilling to commit the resources necessary to provide effective legal assistance for accused criminals. Nationwide, we spend more than $97.5 billion annually on criminal justice.[3] More than half of that goes to the police and prosecution, who together investigate, develop, and prosecute criminal cases. Indigent defense, by contrast, receives only 1.3 percent of annual federal criminal justice expenditures, and only 2 percent of total state and federal criminal justice expenditures.[4] The national average per capita spending on state and local indigent defense in 1990, the latest year for which figures are available, was $5.37; Arkansas spent eighty-eight cents per capita on indigent defense that year, and Louisiana spent only eleven cents.[5] In 1990, Kentucky spent an average of only $162 on each indigent criminal case.[6] That came to a total of $11.4 million, approximately 1/1000 of the state budget, and four million dollars less than the University of Kentucky's athletic budget.[7]

Why have we been unwilling to make *Gideon* a reality? Why has the Supreme Court allowed the dream to remain nothing more than a dream? After all, providing lawyers is something that ought to be relatively easy for courts to accomplish; constitutional reform in this setting does not pose the problems of judicial intrusion into the workings of other institutions that prison or school reform might. Yet the Court has not only been unwilling to adopt rules that would guarantee adequate counsel for the poor; its rules virtually ensure that the poor will get inadequate representation, and then be punished for the inadequacy of the lawyers the state has provided. The story of the enforcement of the right to counsel suggests that our failure to make good on *Gideon*'s promise is no mere mistake. Rather, it is the single most significant mechanism by which the courts and society ensure a double standard in constitutional rights protection in the criminal law.

THE BIRTH OF A RIGHT

One of the most remarkable facts about the constitutional right declared in *Gideon v. Wainwright* is that it was not a constitutional right for the first 184 years of our Constitution. The Sixth Amendment guarantees that "In all criminal prosecutions, the accused shall enjoy the right . . . to have the Assistance of Counsel for his defence." But for most of our history, this right applied only to the approximately 10 percent of criminal trials that take place in federal court, and even there it meant only that defendants who had the money to do so could hire an attorney to defend them.

The Sixth Amendment's original purpose was to bar the federal courts from adopting the English common-law practice, in which defendants facing felony charges were affirmatively *precluded* from having a lawyer, even if they were willing and able to hire one. Twelve of the thirteen colonies had rejected that common-law rule as a matter of state law.[8] The Sixth Amendment merely required the federal courts to do the same.

But the constitutional right to an attorney in federal criminal trials did not initially include the right of an indigent defendant to have the government pay for an attorney. The Constitution generally does not obligate the government to provide affirmative assistance to those seeking to exercise constitutional rights. It says what the government *cannot* do, but does not generally tell the government what it *must* do. For example, while the First Amendment guarantees the right to read pornography in the privacy of one's home,[9] it certainly does not require the government to purchase pornography for those who cannot otherwise afford it. Similarly, parents have a constitutional right to send their children to private schools,[10] but indigent parents have no federal constitutional right to make the government pay the tuition.

There are, of course, good practical and policy arguments for treating the right to counsel in a criminal trial differently from other rights. The vast majority of criminal defendants are too poor to hire an attorney. In 1992, about 80 percent of defendants charged with felonies in the country's seventy-five largest counties were indigent.[11] Approximately three-quarters of all inmates in state prisons were represented by public defenders or some other publicly provided attorney.[12] Without such assistance, most criminal defendants would go unrepresented. The adversarial process, in theory at least, is predicated on an even fight—the truth is supposed to emerge from a fair struggle. Moreover, the criminal justice system is predicated on the proposition that all are equal before the law, and that claim is impossible to sustain where only wealthy defendants have the help of a lawyer.

Over the years, attorneys arguing for the right to appointed counsel for the poor made all these arguments. They contended that the Sixth Amendment guaranteed a right to appointed counsel paid for by the government. They objected that a trial without defense counsel was fundamentally unfair, in violation of the Fourteenth Amendment's Due Process Clause. And they claimed that allowing a criminal defendant's rights to turn on whether he had enough money to hire a lawyer contravened the Fourteenth

Amendment's Equal Protection Clause. The right to counsel that the courts recognize today has roots in all three arguments.

The Supreme Court did not recognize a right to counsel for the indigent under any provision of the Constitution until 1932. It did so then in *Powell v. Alabama,* a notorious case from Scottsboro, Alabama, in which nine young black men, aged thirteen to twenty, were charged with raping two young white women on a freight train traveling from Chattanooga to Memphis. The defendants, taken off the train at Scottsboro, narrowly escaped a lynch mob, but were then tried and sentenced to death within a matter of days, as thousands stood outside the courthouse door and cheered. The defendants could not afford counsel, so the judge appointed the whole bar of Scottsboro (six men) to represent them. Only one attorney agreed to serve, and he did so only on the morning of trial. Needless to say, he had no time to prepare or investigate the case. A group of concerned citizens from Chattanooga hired a Tennessee lawyer to assist the defendants, but he was unschooled in Alabama law, and met the defendants only moments before the trials began. After all eight defendants were sentenced to death by an all-white jury, the Communist Party took up the defendants' appeals, retained one of the nation's premier civil rights lawyers, Walter H. Pollak, to argue their case before the Supreme Court, and transformed the Scottsboro case into a national and international cause célèbre.

The Supreme Court reversed the convictions on the ground that the defendants had been denied assistance of counsel. The Court relied on the Fourteenth Amendment, which prohibits states from depriving any person of life, liberty, or property without due process of law. It ruled that the Due Process Clause requires that a criminal trial be fundamentally fair, and that at least in the circumstances presented, fundamental fairness required appointment of counsel. Although the judge had formally appointed counsel, the Court found that the manner in which counsel had been appointed was a charade. Thus, the first time the Court ruled that the Constitution required appointment of counsel for an indigent defendant, it also effectively held that the legal assistance must be meaningful.

The Scottsboro case was unique, however, and the Court made clear that its decision was limited to the especially strong facts presented: "All that it is necessary now to decide, as we do decide, is that in a capital case, where the defendant is unable to employ counsel, and is incapable adequately of making his own defense because of ignorance, feeble mindedness, illiteracy, or the like, it is the duty of the court, whether requested or not, to assign counsel for him as a necessary requisite of due process of law."[13] *Powell v. Alabama* left unresolved, for example, whether appointed counsel would be required in noncapital cases, or in cases where the defendants were not "feeble minded."

Six years later, in *Johnson v. Zerbst*,[14] the Court held that, in all federal criminal trials, the Sixth Amendment requires the government to pay for a lawyer where the defendant cannot afford one. The Court reasoned that the Sixth Amendment right to counsel "embodies a realistic recognition of the obvious truth that the average defendant does not have the professional legal skill to protect himself when brought before a tribunal with power to take his life and liberty."[15] However, because about 90 percent of criminal prosecutions are tried in state court, the *Johnson* decision, which applied only to *federal* trials, had limited effect. Only four years later, in 1942, the Court refused to extend the right to state criminal trials. The Sixth Amendment, like the rest of the original Bill of Rights, by its terms applies only to the federal government. Over time, the Court has interpreted the Fourteenth Amendment's Due Process Clause to "incorporate" and apply against the states those protections in the Bill of Rights that are "fundamental to ordered liberty." In *Betts v. Brady*,[16] however, the Court held that the right to appointed counsel for the poor was not a "fundamental right," and therefore did not apply to the states. The states remained free, therefore, to prosecute and convict indigent defendants in one-sided proceedings in which the state was represented by a lawyer and the defendant was left to fend for himself.

This left the law in a schizophrenic state. An indigent criminal defendant in federal court was always entitled to a lawyer. But in state courts, appointment of counsel for the poor was required only where the trial would otherwise be "fundamentally unfair" under the case-by-case approach set out in *Powell v. Alabama*, which initially limited the right to capital cases in which defendants were not only poor but "feeble minded."

At the same time, criminal defendants were also challenging the denial of access to the courts on equal protection grounds. In 1956, the Supreme Court ruled for Judson Griffin, an indigent man convicted of armed robbery, who had been precluded from appealing his conviction because he could not afford to pay the fee to obtain the transcript from his trial. Stating that "there can be no equal justice where the kind of trial a man gets depends on the amount of money he has," the Supreme Court held that the state denied equal protection when it barred the defendant from appealing simply because he could not afford to pay the trial transcript fee.[17]

Like *Gideon v. Wainwright*, *Griffin v. Illinois* cut sharply against the grain of the Constitution, which generally treats economic differences as inevitable and beyond constitutional purview. Every day our system offers opportunities and privileges to those who can afford them while denying them to those who cannot. Any public good that is available at a price effectively discriminates against the poor, yet we do not generally consider such fees a denial of equal protection. The University of Michigan, for example, does not violate equal protection by charging tuition, even though some students will not be able to afford to attend. Yet in *Griffin*, the Court held that charging a fee to take an appeal in a criminal case violates equal protection because it treats rich and poor people differently based on their ability to pay. The Court's decision in *Griffin* underscores the special importance of equality in the criminal justice system. In this arena, it suggests, we are unwilling to tolerate the inequities that we otherwise take for granted in a free-market economy.

By the time Clarence Gideon's case reached the Supreme Court in 1963, the Court had already addressed the problem of assistance for indigent defendants from the standpoint of the Sixth Amendment, the Due Process Clause, and the Equal Protection Clause. The technical question presented by Gideon's case was whether the Court should overrule *Betts v. Brady*, which had held that the Sixth Amendment right to assistance of counsel for the indigent did not apply to state trials. At bottom, the very legitimacy of criminal justice was on the line.

In some respects, the result in *Gideon* was foreordained. Under the "fundamental fairness" analysis it had used in the Scottsboro case, the Supreme Court had found that an increasingly wide range of criminal trials without appointed counsel violated due process. Such case-by-case review was inefficient and time-consuming, however, and the Court could review only a handful of the thousands of criminal cases tried each year. Most defendants' cases never reached the Supreme Court. And because fundamental fairness was such an open-ended standard, it failed to establish clear guidelines for lower courts or state legislatures regarding when appointment of counsel was required. In *Gideon*, the Court put an end to such case-by-case analysis, and instead imposed a much more easily administered across-the-board rule, reiterating the "obvious truth" it had previously recognized only for federal criminal trials: "that in our adversary system of criminal justice, any person haled into court, who is too poor to hire a lawyer, cannot be assured a fair trial unless counsel is provided for him."

The same day that it decided *Gideon*, the Supreme Court also ruled, in *Douglas v. California*, that the Fourteenth Amendment's Equal Protection Clause required states to provide appointed counsel for indigent defendants on their first appeal of a conviction.[18] Expanding the right announced earlier in *Griffin*, the Court said that "there is lacking that equality demanded by the Fourteenth Amendment where the rich man, who appeals as of right, enjoys the benefit of counsel's examination into the record, research of the law, and marshalling of arguments on his behalf, while the indigent . . . is forced to shift for himself."

That day, March 18, 1963, was the highwater mark for the right to counsel. In *Gideon* and *Douglas*, the Court guaranteed indigent defendants an appointed attorney for their initial trial and first appeal. The Court's rationale in *Gideon* acknowledged the fundamental importance of an attorney to *any* fair criminal proceeding. Its reasoning in *Douglas* suggested that equality principles would require the state to appoint counsel for the poor through all stages of appeal. It was in the wake of these decisions that Anthony Lewis's celebratory book was written. Had Lewis waited ten years, *Gideon's Trumpet* would have been substantially muted. Today, after thirty-six years, Gideon's horn sounds only a distant, and increasingly hollow, echo.

THE DEMISE OF A RIGHT

In the 1970s and 1980s, the Court took three steps that radically undermined the rights announced in *Gideon* and *Douglas*. First, the Court denied the right to counsel when many defendants most needed it—*before* they were indicted, but after the state had singled them out for investigation and arrest. Second, the Court retreated from the equality principle reflected in *Griffin* and *Douglas*, holding that the state need not provide appointed counsel for most appeals. Third, and most significantly, the Court adopted an "effective assistance of counsel" standard so low that as a practical matter states need not ensure that defendants are appointed *competent* attorneys, and also developed a "procedural default" rule that visits the sins and errors of those attorneys on the defendant himself.

The Disappearing "Critical Stage"

A wealthy individual who is called in by the police, or who even suspects that he may be under investigation, will immediately consult his attorney. Former President Ronald Reagan, for example, spent half a million dollars on legal advice to respond to an investigation of his activities in connection with the Iran-Contra affair, even though the investigation never led to criminal charges against him.[19] Advice before indictment is often critical to protecting one's rights, particularly since, as we have seen, the police are generally not required to inform people of their rights.

The Sixth Amendment says that a person has a right to the assistance of counsel "in all criminal prosecutions." One might interpret that language to limit the right to representation *during* a criminal trial. The Supreme Court has rejected that reading, however, because it fails to reflect the modern-day reality of criminal prosecutions. When the Sixth Amendment was adopted, there were no organized police forces, and the trial was truly the "main event." "In contrast," the Supreme Court has noted, "today's law enforcement machinery involves critical confrontations of the accused by the prosecution at pretrial proceedings where the results might well settle the accused's fate and reduce the trial itself to a mere formality."[20] The vast majority of criminal cases are resolved without a trial. Accordingly, the Court has ruled, the Sixth Amendment right to counsel applies to all "critical stages" of a criminal proceeding.

But that simply raises the question of what amounts to a critical stage. In the Warren Court years, the Court interpreted that term functionally, and demanded that counsel be appointed wherever necessary to preserve the accused's right to a fair trial. It required counsel at identification lineups,[21] interrogations,[22] and preliminary hearings.[23] In the 1970s, however, the Court shifted to a more formalistic approach, limiting the right to counsel to those confrontations with law enforcement personnel that occur *after* adversary proceedings have been formally initiated.[24] On this view, a defendant has no right to an attorney at a lineup that takes place before the initiation of formal proceedings,[25] even though the Court had previously treated a lineup as a "critical stage" requiring assistance of counsel. Whether a lineup occurs before or after indictment does not affect its "critical" character for a defendant, but is now determinative of whether or not he has a right to counsel. The functional critical-stage analysis, which was initially used to extend the right to counsel to pretrial settings, has more recently been used to restrict the right to counsel even *after* criminal proceedings have formally begun — a defendant must now show *both* that formal proceedings have begun *and* that the encounter is a "critical stage." For example, defendant's counsel need not be present when the prosecution, after initiating criminal proceedings, shows a witness an array of photographs for purposes of identifying the defendant at trial, because the Court treats that as a noncritical stage of the prosecution.[26]

Under these rules, prosecutors can often obtain information from a defendant without the "interference" of defense counsel. Although these rules technically apply to the rich and poor alike, in practice they have a much greater impact on those who must depend on the state for legal help. Where an individual has the resources to hire her own attorney, she will generally be able to have counsel at her side during all encounters with the police. She is not dependent on the constitutional right. As a practical matter, then, only the poor will be denied the benefit of legal advice before proceedings begin.

Limiting Appeal

The Supreme Court has also curtailed the right to counsel at the back end of the criminal process. In *Douglas v. California*, as we have seen, the Court said that the state must provide counsel for the indigent's first appeal, because otherwise the rich have a distinct advantage over the poor. But in many state criminal cases, there are nine stages of review *after* the initial appeal, including two separate sets of appeals through the state system, and a separate review process known as habeas corpus, in which defendants are allowed to present their constitutional claims to the federal courts. If equal protection requires that a poor defendant be given roughly the same opportunity as a rich defendant, as *Douglas* suggested, the government should be required to provide appointed counsel to indigent defendants for every stage of review in which a rich defendant could hire a lawyer. Yet in 1974, the Supreme Court rejected that reasoning, and held that the right recognized in *Douglas* stops abruptly at the first appeal.[27] From that point on, as a constitutional matter, an indigent prisoner is on her own.

To reach that result, the Court abandoned the equality principle that had guided *Griffin* and *Douglas*, and substituted a kind of due process inquiry. From the standpoint of equality, there is no difference between the first appeal and subsequent review. In both instances, poor defendants who must proceed without a lawyer are denied an opportunity available to rich defendants. In 1974, however, in *Ross v. Moffitt*,[28] the Court reasoned that once a defendant has had the assistance of counsel at trial and in handling the initial appeal, subsequent courts can provide fair consideration based on the trial record and the initial appellate briefs. Instead of asking whether poor defendants were treated equally, the Court in *Moffitt* asked whether poor defendants really needed an attorney to make further appeals meaningful, and found that they did not. The Court later used the same reasoning to hold that indigent defendants have no right to counsel at any stage of post-conviction proceedings, even when facing the death penalty.[29]

In fact, it is at least as important to be represented by an attorney at the nine subsequent stages of appeal as it is on a first appeal. It is often very difficult to obtain discretionary review from the state's highest court, and it is next to impossible to do so from the U.S. Supreme Court. The U.S. Supreme Court receives more than 6,000 petitions for certiorari seeking its review every year, and grants fewer than 100 of those petitions. The odds of getting the Court's attention are long, and the assistance of an attorney experienced in Supreme Court practice is often essential. In 1994, the Supreme Court granted review in 92 of 2,130 petitions filed by paid attorneys, but granted review in only 13 of 4,514 petitions filed in forma pauperis.[30] Nobody with the money to afford an attorney would choose to file a petition for certiorari without legal assistance, yet indigent defendants have no choice.

Assistance of counsel may be even more critical for "post-conviction review." The purpose of these proceedings is to address matters beyond the scope of the initial trial and direct appeal, and therefore the issues raised may never have been previously addressed with the assistance of an attorney. Many of these matters, such as the effectiveness of trial and appellate counsel, the prosecutor's failure to turn over exculpatory material, or the significance of newly discovered evidence, require the development of an evidentiary hearing. Because such matters involve new facts, an indigent defendant cannot rely on the trial record or the initial appeal briefs to present his claims. He must somehow seek to conduct investigations, present evidence, and advance legal arguments without an attorney.

Exzavious Gibson, a man sentenced to death in Georgia, found himself in this situation in attempting to pursue a state habeas corpus petition in 1996. Gibson, who has an IQ below 80, could not afford a lawyer, and therefore had to proceed in a hearing concerning the "effectiveness" of his prior appointed counsel without the assistance of new counsel. When Butts County Superior Court Judge J. Carlisle Overstreet began the hearing, he asked Gibson if he was ready to proceed:

THE COURT: Okay, Mr. Gibson, do you want to proceed?
MR. GIBSON: I don't have an attorney.
THE COURT: I understand that.
MR. GIBSON: I am not waiving any rights.
THE COURT: I understand that. Do you have any evidence you want to put on?
MR. GIBSON: I don't know what to plead.
THE COURT: Huh?
MR. GIBSON: I don't know what to plead.
THE COURT: I am not asking you to plead to anything, I am just asking you if you have anything you want to put up, anything you want to introduce to this Court.
MR. GIBSON: But, I don't have an attorney.[31]

The state's attorney then pointed out that Gibson was not entitled to any assistance of counsel, and the judge directed the state to proceed. When an observer objected that Gibson did not even have anything to write with, Gibson was given a legal pad and a pen. The state's attorney then put on her witness, Dennis Mullis, who had been Gibson's appointed attorney at trial and on his first appeal, and whose effectiveness Gibson was challenging. As she conducted direct examination of Mullis, she sought to introduce various documents. At each point, the judge asked Gibson if he objected, but he could only reply that he didn't know what to say without an attorney.[32] At the close of the direct testimony, the judge asked Gibson if he wanted to cross-examine Mullis:

THE COURT: Mr. Gibson, would you like to ask Mr. Mullis any questions?
MR. MIBSON: I don't have any counsel.
THE COURT: I understand that, but I am just asking, can you tell me yes or no whether you want to ask him any questions or not?
MR. GIBSON: I'm not my own counsel. . . .
THE COURT: I understand that, but do you want, do you, yourself, individually, want to ask him anything?
MR. GIBSON: I don't know.
THE COURT: Okay, sir. Okay, thank you, Mr. Mullis, you can go down.[33]

This hearing took place more than thirty years after the Supreme Court recognized the "obvious truth" that Clarence Earl Gideon could not get a fair hearing without a lawyer. Exzavious Gibson faced a much more severe sanction—the death penalty—and was borderline retarded. Yet because he was in a post-conviction hearing, not a trial or direct appeal, he was not entitled to any legal assistance. That an attorney had been appointed to represent Gibson at the trial and appellate stages was no help at all when it came to conducting a habeas corpus hearing that attacked that very attorney's assistance.

Only a handful of states guarantee indigent prisoners legal assistance for post-conviction proceedings.[34] Most states allow judges to appoint counsel at the state's expense, but leave that decision wholly to the judge's discretion. Some states provide no right to assistance at all.[35] In federal habeas corpus proceedings, Congress provides appointed counsel only for those defendants sentenced to death.[36]

Thus, virtually the only defendants assured of legal representation through all stages of the criminal review process are those who can afford to hire a private attorney. As a result, indigent defendants' rights will be systematically underenforced, while wealthy defendants will receive the best constitutional protection that money can buy.

Effective Assistance?

When a rich person hires an attorney, she does not hire the first lawyer who comes along. Rather, she seeks referrals for someone skilled in the particular kind of lawyering she needs, much as she would in looking for a medical specialist. She may interview several attorneys and check references before choosing one to represent her. The poor person facing criminal charges, by contrast, not only has no choice in the matter, but has no right to be represented by a lawyer experienced in his kind of case, in criminal law generally, or even in trial work. For all practical purposes, he has only the right to be represented by an individual admitted to the bar. Defendants facing the death penalty have found themselves represented by attorneys who have never tried a criminal case before in their lives, who are fresh out of law school, and who are wholly unaware of the complex law governing death penalty trials. Too often, assistance of counsel for the poor can be like getting brain surgery from a podiatrist.

The blame for this state of affairs must be laid in large part at the Supreme Court's door. Although the Court acknowledged in the 1932 Scottsboro case that ineffective counsel violates an indigent defendant's constitutional rights,[37] it did not get around to defining what it means for a lawyer to be ineffective for over fifty years. In a pair of cases decided in 1984, *Strickland v. Washington*[38] and *United States v. Cronic*,[39] the Supreme Court finally established a uniform standard for judging the effectiveness of counsel. In *Strickland*, a capital murder case, David Leroy Washington's appointed lawyer engaged in minimal investigation, in part, he later explained, because Washington had confessed to the murders. But although the existence of a confession may make it difficult to dispute guilt, it should not affect the separate penalty phase of a capital trial, where the jury decides whether the defendant should be executed or sentenced to some lesser punishment. At the sentencing stage, a defendant is allowed to introduce any evidence whatsoever that might support a decision not to execute, and accordingly, a defense attorney preparing for a sentencing hearing must exhaustively review not only the circumstances of the crime, but the defendant's life history, reputation, level of intelligence, and psychological profile. Washington's lawyer merely talked by phone to Washington, his wife, and mother, never met with any of them in person before trial, and pursued no other character witnesses. He did not request a psychiatric examination, nor even a presentence investigation report.

Harrison Cronic did not face the death penalty, but his case was nonetheless quite complex. He was charged with fraudulent check kiting involving over nine million dollars. The government had spent four and one-half years investigating and preparing its case against Cronic. When Cronic's retained counsel withdrew from the case, the judge appointed counsel for him: a real estate lawyer who had never before tried a case to a jury. The judge gave the newly appointed lawyer less than one month to prepare a defense. Cronic was convicted, and sentenced to twenty-five years in prison.

The courts of appeals in both *Strickland* and *Cronic* found ineffective assistance of counsel. In *Strickland*, the court ruled that

Washington's attorney had failed to satisfy minimal standards of representation requiring that the lawyer at least *investigate* plausible lines of defense. In *Cronic*, the court found that the court's last-minute appointment precluded effective representation, irrespective of any particular errors identifiable in the trial record.

The Supreme Court reversed both decisions. To establish ineffective assistance of counsel, the Court held, a defendant must show both deficient performance and prejudice. On the issue of deficient performance, the Court stressed that reviewing courts "must indulge a strong presumption that counsel's conduct falls within the wide range of reasonable professional assistance," and mandated a "highly deferential" standard. Insisting that the Sixth Amendment was not designed to "improve the quality of legal representation," the Court held that a defendant must show that his attorney's performance was "outside the wide range of professionally competent assistance."

Even if a defendant is able to defeat the strong presumption that his lawyer was competent, he must also show he suffered prejudice, which the Court defined in *Strickland* as a "reasonable probability that the result would have been different." Ordinarily, where a defendant shows that a constitutional violation occurred, the burden shifts to the government to prove that the error was "harmless beyond a reasonable doubt." For ineffectiveness claims, however, the Court placed the burden on the defendant to show both that his attorney performed deficiently, and that the deficiency probably affected the outcome. Who should shoulder the burden of proof is no technical matter. Indeed, where the burden lies will often be determinative when the question is the necessarily speculative one of whether an error, often an omission, affected the result of a trial.

The *Strickland* standard has proved virtually impossible to meet. Courts have declined to find ineffective assistance where defense counsel slept during portions of the trial,[40] where counsel used heroin and cocaine throughout the trial,[41] where counsel allowed his client to wear the same sweatshirt and shoes in court that the perpetrator was alleged to have worn on the day of the crime,[42] where counsel stated prior to trial that he was not prepared on the law or facts of the case,[43] and where counsel appointed in a capital case could not name a single Supreme Court decision on the death penalty.[44] In one case, a capital murder defendant's attorney was found effective even though he "consumed large amounts of alcohol each day of the trial . . . drank in the morning, during court recess, and throughout the evening . . . [and] was arrested [during jury selection] for driving to the courthouse with a .27 blood-alcohol content."[45]

Consider Gregory Wilson, on death row in Kentucky. Kentucky pays so little to lawyers defending indigents in capital punishment cases that the judge responsible for appointing a lawyer for Wilson hung a notice on the courthouse door that read, in capital letters, "PLEASE HELP — DESPERATE."[46] Local lawyer William Hagedorn responded. Wilson might well have been better off without him. Hagedorn had never tried a death penalty case before. He had no office, and only a few out-of-date law books. He worked out of a room in his house that prominently featured a lighted "Budweiser" sign. A prosecution witness described Hagedorn as "a well-known drunk." Hagedorn filed only one pretrial motion, made no closing argument, didn't interview any of the other side's witnesses, and hired no experts. During the most crucial testimony in the case — that of the pathologist — Hagedorn wasn't even in the courtroom. Yet to date the courts have found Hagedorn's representation "effective."

How do courts ratify such woefully deficient representation? In *Strickland*, the Supreme Court stressed that attorneys must have wide leeway to make "tactical" decisions, and that the ineffectiveness test should not be an occasion for second-guessing such judgments. As *Strickland* itself illustrated, however, almost any deficiency in performance can in hindsight be described as "tactical"; Strickland's attorney justified his failure to investigate Strickland's background thoroughly as a strategic decision not to invite negative counter-evidence from the state. In another case, the defendant's lawyer made no opening statement to the jury, and did not object when the prosecutor introduced evidence of the defendant's prior criminal convictions, which are generally inadmissible. Although the attorney was suffering from Alzheimer's disease during the trial, the court held that these lapses were not ineffective assistance, but "tactical decisions."[47] As one court has explained, "Even if many reasonable lawyers would not have done as defense counsel did at trial, no relief can be granted on ineffectiveness grounds unless it is shown that *no* reasonable lawyer, in the circumstances, would have done so."[48]

Courts also routinely deny ineffectiveness claims by finding that the defendant failed to demonstrate "prejudice." Assessing the damage that an incompetent attorney has done is extremely difficult, because the damage often will not show up on a cold record. The consequences of an attorney's failure to pursue a line of investigation, argument, or cross-examination are by definition speculative. And as capital defense attorney Stephen Bright has argued, the difference a good lawyer makes often shows up in such things as rapport with a defendant's family and witnesses, negotiating skills that may bring a favorable plea agreement, skilled judgments about prospective jurors, and pursuit of investigative leads—none of which will be apparent from the trial record.[49] It is particularly difficult to demonstrate prejudice where juries apply open-ended standards, as they do when they balance "mitigating" against "aggravating" evidence in deciding whether to impose a death sentence. How is a court to determine whether the jury might have struck a different balance if the attorney had introduced a particular piece of mitigating evidence? As Justice Alan Handler of the New Jersey Supreme Court has noted, "as a judgment becomes more subjective, the task of assessing the extent to which that judgment might have been influenced by more competent representation becomes more difficult."[50] Courts routinely reject ineffectiveness claims by finding no prejudice where a capital defendant's attorney failed to investigate or present mitigating evidence at sentencing.[51]

Ineffective assistance claims rarely succeed. Of 103 reported cases raising such claims in the California Supreme Court from January 1, 1989, through April 21, 1996, 94 were denied, 3 were remanded for further factual development, and only 6 were granted. Of 158 reported cases raising such claims in the United States Court of Appeals for the Fifth Circuit during the same period, 142 were denied, 10 remanded, and 6 granted.[52] In the end, the ineffectiveness standard does less to protect defendants from bad lawyers than it does to legitimate the poor quality of representation generally provided to criminal defendants. That so few lawyers are deemed ineffective sends the message that the bulk of representation is effective. That in turn gives a thin patina of fairness to the skewed results of the criminal justice system, in which those who cannot afford to buy good representation are not likely to get it, and are therefore unlikely to have their constitutional claims effectively litigated.

Having an incompetent but not constitutionally "ineffective" attorney will often mean not only that a defendant's rights are less vigorously defended, but forfeited altogether. This is because of a related doctrine, labeled "procedural default," which visits the sins and omissions of attorneys on their clients. Under this doctrine, if a lawyer fails to raise an objection or argument in a timely fashion, the client is barred from having *any* court rule on it, absent extraordinary circumstances. Thus, for example, Roger Keith Coleman was executed without obtaining appellate review of several potentially life-saving legal arguments because his attorney misinterpreted the local court rules, and filed his notice of appeal three days late.[53]

"Procedural default" rules penalize those who cannot afford competent counsel. Given the inadequate system of indigent defense that we maintain and tolerate, mistakes are entirely foreseeable. Society is unwilling to pay for, and the Supreme Court is unwilling to require, lawyers who would make fewer mistakes. The ultimate cause of most mistakes, then, has nothing to do with defendants, and everything to do with our collective failure as a community—and the Court's failure as guardian of the process—to ensure that the indigent are adequately represented. The Supreme Court's "procedural default" rule imposes the burden of those mistakes not on society, but on the indigent defendant. As a result, indigent defendants spend years in jail, and even lose their lives, because we are unwilling to provide them with adequate representation.

THE STATE OF INDIGENT DEFENSE TODAY

What these legal rules mean in practice for poor defendants is perhaps best exemplified by the case of Leonard Peart. At age twenty, he faced charges of armed robbery, aggravated rape, aggravated burglary, attempted armed robbery, and first-degree murder, in connection with the death of Tulane University undergraduate Karen Knupp. Without the resources to hire his own counsel, Peart sought appointed counsel. In a sense, he was luckier than most; he was assigned Rick Teissier, an experienced thirty-year-old public defender who hadn't lost a felony case in the prior year. There was only one problem—Teissier was otherwise engaged.

At the time he was appointed, Teissier was handling seventy active felony cases. From January to August of that year, he had represented 418 defendants. He often wasn't even able to conduct an initial interview with his clients until they had been incarcerated for thirty to seventy days; at that point, the best thing to do was often to plead guilty in exchange for a sentence of the time they had already served. He entered 130 guilty pleas in the first eight months of 1991, a number that John Kramer, the Dean of Tulane Law School, said violated ethical rules requiring diligent investigation of a client's claims before pleading guilty.[54] But Teissier had little time to investigate. He had at least one serious felony case set for trial for every trial date during 1991, and his office had only three investigators to cover some 7,000 cases a year. The Orleans Indigent Defender Program had a worse library than many prisons have, and no money to hire experts.

Everyone in Teissier's office was similarly overworked, as the local government sought to stretch as far as possible the limited dollars it was willing to spend on indigent defense. The public defender program was funded by receipts from traffic tickets, and when ticket collecting fell, so did the program's funding. Peart's case was the straw that finally broke Teissier's back. He took the unusual step of filing a pretrial motion asking the judge to declare his own legal assistance ineffective before trial. He argued that under these conditions it was simply impossible to provide Peart an effective defense. The trial judge agreed, finding that "Not even a lawyer with an 'S' on his chest could effectively handle this docket."[55] He declared the entire Orleans public defender system unconstitutional, and ordered the legislature to come up with sufficient resources to bring it up to constitutional standards.

On appeal, the Louisiana Supreme Court agreed that "because

of excessive caseloads and insufficient support, indigent defendants are generally not provided effective assistance in New Orleans."[56] It declined to find the entire defender system unconstitutional, reasoning that each case must be examined individually on its facts. But the court did hold that, absent a change in workloads and resources, it would apply a rebuttable presumption that indigent defendants represented by the Orleans public defender office were receiving ineffective assistance of counsel. And it authorized judges to halt criminal trials until the state allocated reasonable resources to indigent defense.

Peart and Teissier's story is unusual only in their success in the courts. Across the country, indigent defendants are routinely assigned attorneys who, for systemic and foreseeable reasons, are incapable of providing effective representation. Indigent defense comes in a variety of forms, but the fundamental problem facing all systems is the public's unwillingness to allocate the resources necessary to the task. Public defenders in Albuquerque, New Mexico, for example, handle as many as 1,000 to 1,200 misdemeanor cases a year.[57] In Fulton County, Georgia, public defenders handle on average 530 felonies a year, in addition to extraditions, probation revocations, and civil commitment hearings.[58]

The most common form of indigent defense relies not on public defenders, but on private attorneys, many of them solo practitioners, who take on criminal cases for a statutorily prescribed fee. If such systems were adequately funded, they might work, because they would attract good lawyers who could develop experience and make successful careers in the system. But hourly rates commonly range from $20 to $50, far below the hourly rates earned by privately retained counsel, which range from $100 to more than $400.[59] In addition, about one-third of the states also impose a per-case maximum fee. In Kentucky, for example, the statutory maximum fee for defending a capital case is $2,500.[60] Studies have found that attorneys spend between between 100 and 1,500 hours in preparing for and trying a capital case, with the median ranging from 300 to 600 hours.[61] At the Kentucky rate, an attorney who managed to handle a case in only 300 hours would make $8.50 an hour. In Alabama, the statutory maximum is $1,000 for all felonies, and $2,000 for capital cases.[62] Tennessee and Kentucky impose a $1,000 maximum for all noncapital felony cases.[63] South Carolina's statutory maximum is $750.[64] In Virginia, the maximum fee for most felonies is $350.[65] A study prepared for the Virginia General Assembly and State Bar concluded that after taking into account overhead costs, the rate for appointed defense attorneys in capital cases was $13 an hour.[66] Until the mid-1990s, appointed counsel in Detroit's felony trial court were paid a set fee based on the severity of the charges their clients faced: no matter how many hours the attorney devoted to the case, the fee for defending a first-degree murder charge was $1,400, and the fee for any non-murder case with a maximum sentence of life was $750.[67] Although some of these statutory caps may be waived by the judge, waivers are rarely granted.[68]

Prosecutors, by contrast, do not have to deal with per-case ceilings and are funded far more generously than defense attorneys. In Alabama, for example, indigent defense attorneys receive less than one-quarter the funding that Alabama's district attorneys receive. And that figure vastly understates the disparity, because it does not include the funds allocated to the police and other law enforcement services on whom district attorneys rely to investigate their cases, develop and analyze evidence, and find witnesses. Moreover, when Alabama hires outside counsel to represent its own state officials in civil rights and other lawsuits, it pays from $85 to $160 per hour, and imposes no per-case cap.[69] Although precise figures vary from state to state, it is safe to say that every state allocates far more resources to prosecution than defense, and pays more for attorneys representing its own officials than for attorneys representing indigent criminal defendants.

These rates have not gone unchallenged. In one Mississippi capital case, for example, two experienced death penalty attorneys spent 449.5 and 482.5 hours, respectively, on preparation and trial. They filed more than 100 motions, and took two interlocutory appeals. The prosecution sought to use witnesses who had been hypnotized, requiring the defense to retain expert assistance on the effects of hypnosis. There were nine days of pretrial hearings, and the trial itself lasted four weeks. Each attorney logged nearly 200 hours of in-court time alone. Yet the Mississippi statute limited compensation to $1,000 per case, under which the attorneys would have earned just over two dollars an hour.[70] According to Judge Reuben V. Anderson, "the court reporter was paid far more than defense counsel."[71]

The Mississippi Supreme Court nonetheless upheld the cap. Rejecting the claim that such low compensation threatens a defendant's right to effective assistance of counsel, the court stated that "those rare cases where counsel has been ineffective may be handled and determined individually by the appellate courts."[72] Ironically, the court showed more sympathy for the lawyers' claim that appointment at such low wages constituted a taking of their property without just compensation. It addressed that concern by creatively interpreting the statute to permit attorneys to recover their overhead and out-of-pocket expenses, in addition to the $1,000 in the statute, which the court characterized as "pure profit."[73] Thus, although attorneys in Mississippi assigned to indigent defense will now at least break even, they will never receive more than $1,000 above their overhead expenses for any appointed case, no matter how long the trial and no matter how many hours they log.[74]

Many courts have, like the Mississippi Supreme Court, rejected challenges to unrealistically low statutory caps by pointing to the constitutional "ineffective assistance of counsel" standard as a safety net. But because the vast majority of criminal defendants are indigent, the professional standard of criminal representation against which "ineffectiveness" is measured will itself be determined in substantial part by the quality of assistance provided in indigents' cases. Because the ineffectiveness standard accepts as a baseline the quality of defense representation generally provided in indigent cases, and only identifies as "ineffective" radical departures from that baseline, it cannot possibly serve as a check on the quality of representation generated by unrealistically low compensation schemes. In Alabama, for example, the courts found ineffective assistance of counsel in capital cases only three times in fourteen years, at a time when the statutory cap on compensation for handling a capital trial was $1,000.[75]

Low hourly rates and statutory caps not only make it difficult to attract competent attorneys, but also induce the attorneys who do such work to accept more cases than they can reasonably handle.[76] As a result, indigent cases are routinely under-investigated and under-researched. A 1986 study found that in New York, three-quarters of all appointed counsel in homicide cases and 82 percent of appointed counsel in non-homicide cases did not even interview their clients, much less conduct any independent investigation.[77] Appointed counsel filed no discovery motions in 92 percent of homicide cases, and filed no pretrial motions whatsoever in 75 percent of such cases.[78] They consulted with experts in only 17 percent of homicide cases, even though the prosecution uses a medical expert in virtually every homicide case.[79] The study concluded that assigned counsel "were court functionaries, rather than adversarial representatives of the poor. . . . The system sustains only those lawyers who comply with its goals by providing cost-efficient, expeditious dispositions, and alienates those who view the defense function in adversarial terms."[80]

The more serious the charges and the more complicated the case, the more exaggerated the effects of limited resources will be. Precisely where an accused is most in need of competent and diligent representation, statutory caps create the strongest incentives against his receiving such services. From the indigent defendant's point of view, and from the standpoint of fairness, these effects are especially onerous. But from a more perverse perspective, the caps do further society's interests: the more serious the crime, the less likely a competent defense will be presented, and the more likely a conviction will result. Thus, statutory caps not only save money, but also stack the decks against individuals accused of the most serious crimes.

Although inadequate compensation is no doubt the most significant barrier to effective indigent defense, it is not the only barrier. Most jurisdictions have no experiential qualifications for who may be assigned to represent an indigent defendant. As a result, lawyers are routinely appointed with virtually no relevant experience. Charles Bell, facing the death penalty in Mississippi, was represented by a recent law graduate who had never tried a criminal case to final judgment.[81] Donald Paradis's attorney had passed the bar six months before he was appointed to defend a capital murder case, had never taken criminal law, criminal procedure, or trial advocacy in law school, and had never handled a jury trial.[82] Billy Sunday Birt, on trial for murder in Georgia, was represented by court-appointed counsel who, when asked to identify any criminal law decision from any court with which he was familiar, could name only *Miranda v. Arizona* and *Dred Scott v. Sanford*. (*Miranda* is known by virtually anyone who has ever watched a police show on television; *Dred Scott* is not even a criminal case.)[83]

Where standards exist, they are often so minimal as to be meaningless. Until 1986, judges in Philadelphia could appoint anyone with a law license to defend homicide cases. After a conviction was overturned on ineffective-assistance grounds where the appointed attorney had been out of law school for less than a year, the judges adopted rules limiting homicide appointments to experienced attorneys. The "standards," however, turn only on the number of cases tried, and have no quality component. An attorney can be certified based on handling the requisite number of prior cases even if he has mishandled every case. Stanford Shmukler, the first chairman of the certification committee, admitted that the committee certified lawyers for homicide cases whom "committee members wouldn't hire 'to defend them in Traffic Court.'"[84]

Meaningful qualifications are important for at least two reasons. First, the grossly inadequate levels of compensation society has dedicated to indigent defense make it especially likely that lawyers who cannot make a living in the competitive legal market will be driven to indigent defense. Second, because indigent defendants are not allowed to choose their appointed counsel, the usual market forces do not operate within the world of indigent representation, so inefficient and ineffective lawyers who would be driven out of a competitive market will survive (and perhaps even flourish) in the world of indigent defense. Yet for the most part, states do not impose or enforce any meaningful competence standards, and the Supreme Court has also declined to require them.

A final impediment to quality representation is the appointment process itself, which is generally left to the discretion of state judges. Although many state judges no doubt strive to appoint competent counsel, judges may also be tempted to appoint attorneys who they know will not make trouble by being too zealous in their defense. Ron Slick, for example, often gets appointed to defend indigent clients in Long Beach, California. As of 1991, he had had more clients sentenced to death than any other lawyer in California. A local public defender explained that judges liked to appoint Slick because he was always ready to go to trial, even when it seemed he had inadequate time to prepare.[85] According to the *Los Angeles Times*, while it can often "take weeks or months to try complex capital cases . . . Slick sometimes spent just a few days."[86]

Similarly, Joe Frank Cannon, who boasts that he hurries through criminal trials "like greased lightning," has received repeated appointments in capital trials in Houston, Texas. The past president of the Harris County Criminal Lawyers Association stated in an affidavit that it is "generally reputed in the Harris County legal community" that Cannon gets appointments "because he delivers on his promises to move the courts' dockets." He has been accused of falling asleep repeatedly in court. Ten of his clients have received the death penalty.[87]

By contrast, when an attorney demonstrates competence and dedication to his clients, he can find it difficult to get appointed for precisely that reason. George Kendall, an experienced capital punishment defense attorney with the NAACP Legal Defense and Educational Fund, volunteered to represent Victor Roberts in 1984, when Roberts was on death row. He prevailed in federal court in 1992, demonstrating that several constitutional errors in Roberts' trial necessitated a retrial. Yet when Roberts' case was sent back to be retried, the local judge in Fayette County, Georgia, refused to appoint Kendall to the case.[88] Experienced capital defense attorneys Stephen Bright and William Warner faced a similar Georgia welcome after reversing a death sentence in Tony Amadeo's case before the Supreme Court. The trial court refused to appoint them for Amadeo's resentencing, and instead appointed two lawyers with no experience in capital punishment litigation. Bright and Warner had to appeal to the Georgia Supreme Court merely to get appointed to continue to represent the man whose death sentence they'd overturned in the U.S. Supreme Court.[89]

Why might trial judges appoint less than qualified counsel and oppose the appointment of demonstrably effective lawyers? As the O.J. Simpson case demonstrated, capable defense attorneys can make a trial judge's life difficult. Lawyers from Stephen Bright's Southern Center for Human Rights, specialists in death penalty litigation, often file fifty to one hundred pretrial motions, and expend considerable time and resources developing and presenting mitigating evidence at the sentencing phase of the trial, where the life or death decision is made. By contrast, a 1990 National Law Journal study of twenty randomly chosen Alabama death penalty trials found the average length of trial to be 4.2 days, with the penalty phase lasting on average only 3.6 hours.[90] A 1996 study of Alabama capital cases found that the average penalty phase—including jury deliberations—was less than three hours.[91] Competent attorneys are also more likely to ferret out and challenge constitutional error, and judges who rule in favor of a criminal defendant's claims of constitutional error may find re-election difficult.[92] In short, good lawyers make the task of convicting defendants more difficult.

Thus, economic constraints, the absence of meaningful qualifications, and the politics of indigent defense appointments all contribute to a system in which indigent defendants are frequently represented by overworked, underpaid, and unqualified lawyers. Few who could afford to hire an attorney would choose the representation generally available to indigent defendants. This is not to denigrate the talents of those who dedicate their careers to indigent defense. It simply reflects the foreseeable effects of society's choice to pay indigent defense counsel substantially less than attorneys make in virtually any other line of legal work, and to impose no meaningful standards on a group of attorneys whose ability to continue to litigate cases is not affected by the market.

CONSEQUENCES

The difference between a constitutionally "effective" lawyer and a truly effective lawyer can sometimes be the difference between life and death, as Rebecca Machetti will tell you. She and her boyfriend John Eldon Smith both received the death penalty in separate trials in 1975 for the murder of her ex-husband. They were tried within weeks of one another, by juries composed under a system that permitted women to opt out of jury service simply because they were women. Shortly before the trials, the Supreme Court issued a decision declaring such a practice to be unconstitutional gender discrimination. Machetti's lawyer challenged the composition of her jury on these grounds. The state courts rejected Machetti's claim, but on a writ of habeas corpus the federal court of appeals ruled that she was entitled to a new trial with a jury that did not exclude women.[93] On retrial, she received a life sentence.[94]

John Eldon Smith's trial suffered precisely the same constitutional flaw. But because Smith's attorneys were unaware of the Supreme Court decision, announced only six days before Smith's trial began, they failed to object to the jury composition. As a result, the federal courts refused to address the claim on the merits, treating it as a "procedural default."[95] On December 15, 1983, Smith was executed.[96] Had he been represented by Machetti's lawyers, Smith might well have been alive today.

Lloyd Schlup, by contrast, is alive today only because he finally received competent legal assistance in a post-conviction proceeding. Schlup's murder trial lasted two days. He was sentenced to death for allegedly killing a fellow prisoner. His court-appointed trial lawyer, who was paid $2,000 for fees and expenses, talked to Schlup only twice, for a total of seventy-five minutes, before trial. He did not interview any of twenty witnesses who later testified that Schlup wasn't even at the scene when the murder took place. He never investigated Schlup's medical, family, or psychological background, and the only witness he put on at sentencing was Schlup's mother.

Near the end of his post-conviction review process, Schlup was finally able to get help from an experienced capital defense litigator, Sean O'Brien of the Missouri Capital Punishment Resource Center. O'Brien put together a compelling case that Schlup was actually innocent of the crime, because he was in the cafeteria at the time that the fight took place elsewhere. The evidence included sworn statements from the twenty eyewitnesses that Schlup's original lawyer never interviewed, and a videotape showing Schlup in the cafeteria when the incident occurred. The Supreme Court agreed there was sufficient evidence to warrant a hearing on innocence, and on remand the trial court held that Schlup was probably innocent, and reversed his conviction for ineffective assistance of counsel.[97] Had Schlup never received the last-minute assistance of Sean O'Brien, he would have been executed for a crime that the courts now say he probably did not commit.

The difference that effective lawyering can make can also be seen at the systemic level. Indiana is one of the few states to adopt rigorous standards for appointment of defense counsel in death penalty cases. Beginning in 1991, it has required appointment of two experienced attorneys in every capital case. The lead counsel must have at least five years of criminal trial experience, and must have been lead or co-counsel on five completed felony jury trials and one death penalty case. The other lawyer must have three years of trial experience and been lead or co-counsel on at least three complete felony trials. To be eligible for such appointments, lawyers must complete twelve hours of capital litigation training every other year. Lawyers are paid at least $70 per hour, judges must ensure that they are not overloaded with other cases, and public defenders may not be assigned additional cases in the months preceding a capital trial. Experienced prosecutors and defense counsel alike agree that as a result of these requirements, the quality of defense in capital cases has risen dramatically. And in the first three years that the new requirements were in effect, not a single Indiana jury recommended the death penalty. Moreover, knowing that they will face a more capable and prepared defense (and that the county will have to pay for it), Indiana prosecutors have sought the death penalty far more selectively since the new requirements were adopted; from 1991 to 1996, the rate at which prosecutors sought the death penalty fell by more than 50 percent.[98]

The Supreme Court does not deserve all the blame for the miserable state of indigent defense. The ideal it has identified — equality before the law — is admittedly difficult, and perhaps impossible, to achieve in our system. A capitalist economy not only tolerates, but depends on, economic inequality. It is the possibility of earning more than one's neighbor that drives the system. And the notion that one would not be able to spend all one owns to defend oneself in a criminal case is virtually unthinkable. Thus, realization of the Court's ideal is sharply constrained by the realities of our economic system. When the initial right to counsel cases were decided, the Court seemed optimistic that it could deliver on its promise of equality before the law. In hindsight, however, Justice Black's statement that "there can be no equal justice where the kind of trial a man gets depends on the amount of money he has" looks more like a descriptive account of reality than a normative argument for reform.

The Court has taken some steps to alleviate inequality, by requiring the state to provide counsel for those who cannot afford it, and by ruling that counsel must be "effective." Yet as we have seen, the Court's moves in these directions have ultimately proved to be more ceremonial bows than actual reforms. It has stepped in to forestall the starkest inequities, but its interventions have been more successful in legitimizing the gaping inequities that remain than in providing anything approaching substantive equality for the poor.

Although the Court is not the only cause of the problem, it bears a special responsibility. Providing genuinely adequate counsel for poor defendants would require a substantial infusion of money, and indigent defense is the last thing the populace will voluntarily direct its tax dollars to fund. Achieving solutions to this problem through the political process is a pipedream. Unless life-tenured federal judges, and ultimately the Supreme Court, require adequate counsel, politicians and the public will continue to try to get away with allocating as little as possible toward indigent defense. Thus, even if the problem is not entirely attributable to the Court, the Court alone has the power to provide a solution.

More is at stake here than reluctance to spend money on criminal defendants. Consider the fate of death penalty resource centers, a short-lived experiment in federally funded legal aid offices for death row inmates. Congress created the centers in 1987 to save money and reduce delay in the death penalty appeal process. Indigent death row prisoners are entitled by statute to a federally funded attorney in habeas corpus proceedings. Without resource centers, the government has to hire private attorneys to do this work, and pays those private lawyers between $75 and $125 an hour. Resource centers, by contrast, paid lawyers a relatively low salary, even for public interest work. Bryan Stevenson, for example, one of the best capital defense attorneys in the country, headed Alabama's death penalty resource center and drew an annual salary of only $27,000 in 1994. In addition, as "repeat players," resource center lawyers were more efficient. Because death penalty cases are so draining, both emotionally and financially, private attorneys rarely take on more than one such case in their careers. The private appointment system accordingly requires the government to waste resources funding a stream of inexperienced attorneys, each of whom has to start from square one. A 1995 General Accounting Office study reported that hiring private attorneys to represent death row inmates costs the government more than twice as much as using resource centers to do the same work.

Yet in 1995, Congress cut off all funding for the resource centers. Representative Bob Inglis, who introduced the bill, called the centers "think tanks for legal theories that would frustrate the implementation of all death sentences."[99] What bothered the critics was not that the centers were too costly, but that they were too *effective*. Congress was in effect willing to pay more money to ensure that death row inmates got *worse* lawyers, because good lawyers, as Representative Inglis put it, "frustrate the implementation of all death sentences." But a death sentence will be frustrated only if a judge finds constitutional error that cannot be dismissed as "harmless." In those cases, the death penalty should be frustrated.

Congress's decision to pay more money for worse capital defense lawyers only makes economic sense because identifying and vindicating constitutional error is itself extremely costly. It may require resentencing or retrial. In rare cases, it may mean that a guilty man will go free. Better lawyers will raise more issues, investigate and litigate more aggressively, and identify more constitutional errors. All of that makes trying criminal cases more costly. Congress was willing to pay more for worse lawyers in order to avoid those costs—economic and social.

Broadly speaking, the Supreme Court's "right to counsel" jurisprudence has had much the same effect as Congress's decision to defund the resource centers. If the Court required better lawyers for the indigent, it would cost society not only in terms of the resources necessary to pay those lawyers, but also in terms of the costs of fully enforcing criminal defendants' constitutional rights. Better lawyers would mean more hard-fought trials, more evidence thrown out for constitutional error, fewer convictions, more acquittals, and more hung juries. As then-President of Harvard University Derek Bok candidly acknowledged,

> if Congress provided enough funds for legal aid, or if it agreed to offer the same support to legal defenders as it gives the prosecution, it could easily touch off a burst of litigation that would cost huge sums of money and add heavily to the burdens and delays of the legal system.[100]

An adversary system in which both sides are evenly matched costs more than a system in which the prosecution's resources overwhelm the defense's, and despite our surface commitment to equality before the law, apparently neither society nor the Court is willing to require anything like an even playing field.

The present system of assigning indigent defendants poorly funded, overburdened, and often underqualified defense attorneys thus saves money in two ways: first, by reducing the direct costs of providing a decent defense; and second, and more significantly, by systematically underenforcing the constitutional rights of the indigent accused. If one were looking for a mechanism to reduce the costs of constitutional rights without weakening rights protections for the privileged, one could do no better than ensuring that the poor systematically receive less competent legal representation than the rich. By denying the poor adequate lawyers, and then holding their lawyers' mistakes against them, we guarantee that we will never have to pay full cost for the constitutional rights we purport to protect, and we achieve those savings without diluting the protections available to those who can afford competent counsel. The appointed-counsel system creates an across-the-board double standard. As the O.J. Simpson trial illustrated, the inequality created by the ability to hire competent counsel is predicated on class, not race. But because most minority defendants are poor, and because blacks and Hispanics disproportionately find themselves as criminal defendants, this class-based disparity also falls especially heavily on the minority community.

The right to counsel is in theory the linchpin of equality in the criminal justice system, yet in reality differences in the quality of legal assistance available to the rich and poor play probably the most significant systemic role in maintaining a double standard in criminal justice. A constitutional right is only as good as the lawyer one has to assert it. The right to counsel for the indigent should be extended to every stage of the criminal process in which non-indigent defendants hire attorneys, instead of being limited to trial and a first appeal. The standard for effective assistance of counsel should at least require that counsel be *competent to try a criminal case of the complexity involved*; the current standard, by contrast, does little more than ratify a status quo that visits incompetent assistance on indigent defendants with astounding frequency. We must allocate sufficient resources to give defendants a fair shake. And indigent defendants whose court-appointed attorneys negligently fail to object in a timely fashion to constitutional errors should not be punished by "procedural default" rules unless the defendants themselves took part in the decision not to object. We will never achieve perfect equality between the rich and poor in legal assistance, but the current system does little more than place a veneer of legitimacy on a system that is patently inadequate and unjust.

ENDNOTES

1. Anthony Lewis, *Gideon's Trumpet*, 205 (New York: Random House, 1964).
2. See Richard Klein & Robert Spangenberg, *The Indigent Defense Crisis*, 10 (August 1993) (prepared for ABA Section on Criminal Justice Ad Hoc Committee on the Indigent Defense Crisis) (discussing current crisis in indigent defense, and noting that the ABA issued similar reports in 1979, 1982, and 1986); President's Commission on Law Enforcement in Administration of Justice, *The Challenge of Crime in a Free Society*, 128 (1967) (decrying gap between the ideal of a right to counsel for all and the reality of "assembly line justice"); National Legal Aid and Defendar Association, *The Other Face of Justice* (1973) (reporting that indigent defense systems are overburdened and underfunded); S. Krantz, D. Rossmann, P. Froyd & J. Hoffman, *Right to Counsel in Criminal Cases* (1976) (study undertaken for the Law Enforcement Assistance Administration criticizing underfunding of indigent criminal defense); Norman Lefstein, *Criminal Defense Services for the Poor*, 2

(1982) (national study undertaken for the American Bar Association finding that "millions of persons in the United States who have a constitutional right to counsel are denied effective legal representation"); The American Bar Association, The National Legal Aid and Defender Association, *Gideon Undone! The Crisis in Indigent Defense Funding,* 1–3 (1982) (finding that inadequate funding often leads to inadequate indigent representation).

3. Bureau of Justice Statistics, *Sourcebook of Criminal Justice Statistics — 1996,* 2 (Table 1.1) (reporting on figures from fiscal year 1993).

4. Bureau of Justice Statistics, *Sourcebook of Criminal Justice Statistics — 1993,* 2 (Table 1.2) (reporting on total state and federal expenditure figures from fiscal year 1990); Bureau of Justice Statistics, *Sourcebook of Criminal Justice Statistics — 1996,* 14 (Table 1.12) (reporting on federal spending from fiscal year 1993).

5. Bureau of Justice Statistics, *Sourcebook of Criminal Justice Statistics — 1993,* 5 (Table 1.5) (reporting on fiscal year 1990).

6. Edward C. Monahan, "Who Is Trying to Kill the Sixth Amendment?," Crim. Justice 24, 27 (summer 1991).

7. Id.

8. *Powell v. Alabama,* 287 U.S. 45, 64-65 (1932).

9. *Stanley v. Georgia,* 394 U.S. 557 (1969).

10. *Pierce v. Society of Sisters,* 268 U.S. 510 (1925).

11. Bureau of Justice Statistics, *Indigent Defense,* 1 (December 1995).

12. Id.

13. *Powell v. Alabama,* 287 U.S. at 71.

14. 304 U.S. 458 (1938).

15. 304 U.S. at 462–63.

16. 316 U.S. 455 (1942).

17. *Griffin v. Illinois,* 351 U.S. 12 (1956).

18. *Douglas v. California,* 372 U.S. 353 (1963).

19. *In re Oliver North,* 94 F.3d 685 (D.C. Cir. 1996).

20. *United States v. Wade,* 388 U.S. 218, 224 (1967).

21. *Wade,* 388 U.S. 218.

22. *Escobedo v. Illinois,* 378 U.S. 478 (1964); *Massiah v. United States,* 377 U.S. 201 (1964).

23. *Coleman v. Alabama,* 399 U.S. 1 (1970).

24. Stephen A. Saltzburg & Daniel J. Capra, *American Criminal Procedure,* 669–70 (St. Paul, MN: West Pub., 5th ed. 1996).

25. *Kirby v. Illinois,* 406 U,S, 682 (1972).

26. *United States v. Ash,* 413 U.S. 300 (1973).

27. *Ross v. Moffitt,* 417 U.S. 600 (1974).

28. 417 U.S. 600 (1974).

29. *Pennsylvania v. Finley,* 481 U.S. 551 (1987) (defendant has no right to counsel in state post-conviction proceeding); *Murray v. Giarratano,* 492 U.S. 1 (1989) (defendant on death row has no right to counsel in state post-conviction proceeding).

30. *Statistical Abstract — 1997,* 215 (Table 344).

31. Tr. of Habeas Corpus Hearing in *Gibson v. Turpin,* Civ. Action No. 95-V-648 (Sup. Ct. Butts County, GA Sept. 12, 1996), 2–3.

32. Id. at 38, 51, 64.

33. Id. at 67.

34. Randall T. Shepard, "Capital Litigation from State Court Perspective, or, Rushing to Judgment in Fifteen Years," 5 (Presented to Workshop for the Judges of the Seventh Circuit, Kohler, Wis., 2 May 1996).

35. In a study limited to capital cases, the Spangenberg Group reported that Texas and Georgia fail to provide counsel for indigent capital defendants in state post-conviction proceedings. The Spangenberg Group, *A Study of Representation in Capital Cases in Texas,* 129 – 31 (March 1993). Moreover, in several states assistance of counsel in post-conviction proceedings is discretionary, not a matter of right. In 1988, the Spangenberg Group reported that Alabama, Arkansas, Colorado, Mississippi, Montana, Ohio, and Texas all had discretionary provisions for appointment of counsel. See The Spangenberg Group, *Right to Counsel in State Post-Conviction Death Penalty Proceedings* (April 1988). In addition, many of those states that have "mandatory" appointment limit the right to cases that the court finds have merit. These include Delaware, Illinois, Kentucky, Louisiana, Nebraska, New Mexico, Oklahoma, and South Carolina. Id. In some of those states, such as Louisiana, counsel is virtually never appointed.

36. Pub. L. No. 100-690, 102 Stat. 4181 (1988), codified at 21 U.S.C. §848(q)(4)(B).

37. *Powell v. Alabama,* 287 U.S. 45, 71 (1932).

38. 466 U.S. 668 (1984).

39. 466 U.S. 648 (1984).

40. *People v. Tippins,* 173 A.D.2d 512, (N.Y. App. 1991), 570 N.Y.S.2d 581 (1991).

41. *People v. Badia,* 159 A.D.2d 577 (N.Y. App. 1990), 552 N.Y.S.2d 439 (1990).

42. *People v. Murphy,* 96 A.D.2d 625 (N.Y. App. 1983), 464 N.Y.S.2d 882 (1983).

43. *People v. Dalton,* 140 A.D.2d 419 (N.Y. App. 1988), 529 N.Y.S.2d 927 (1988).

44. Stephen B. Bright, "Counsel for the Poor: The Death Sentence Not for the Worst Crime but for the Worst Lawyer," 103 Yale L.J. 1835, 1839 (1994) (describing *Birt v. Montgomery,* 725 F.2d 587, 601 (11th Cir. 1984), *cert. denied,* 469 U.S. 874 (1984)).

45. *People v. Garrison,* 765 P.2d 419 (Cal. 1989), 47 Cal.3d 746 (1989).

46. Klein & Spangenberg, *Indigent Defense Crisis, supra* note 2 at 5 – 6.

47. *Pilchak v. Camper,* 741 F. Supp. 782 (W.D. Mo. 1990), *aff'd,* 935 F.2d 145 (8th Cir. 1991).

48. *Rogers v. Zant,* 13 F.3d 384, 386 (11th Cir. 1994).

49. Bright, *Counsel for the Poor, supra* note 44 at 1864.

50. *State v. Davis,* 561 A.2d 1082, 1116 (N.J. 1989) (Handler, J., dissenting).

51. See, e.g., *Wilkerson v. Collings,* 950 F.2d 1054, 1065 (5th Cir. 1992); *Schlup v. Armontrout,* 941 F.2d 631, 639 (8th Cir. 1991).

52. These figures almost certainly overstate the proportion of successful claims, for many ineffective-assistance claims are rejected in unpublished opinions, while it would be extremely rare for a court to *grant* an ineffectiveness claim without issuing a published decision.

53. *Coleman v. Thompson,* 501 U.S. 722 (1991); *Wainwright v. Sykes,* 433 U.S. 72, 84 – 87 (1977).

54. Ruth Marcus, "Public Defender Systems Tried by Budget Problems," *Wash. Post,* 8 March 1992, A1.

55. *State v. Peart*, 621 So.2d 780, 789 (La. 1993).

56. Id. at 789.

57. Klein & Spangenberg, *Indigent Defense Crisis, supra* note 2 at 8.

58. Bright, *Counsel for the Poor, supra* note 44 at 1850; The Spangenberg Group, *Overview of the Fulton County, Georgia Indigent Defense System* (1990).

59. Alabama, for example, pays $20 an hour for out-of-court work and $40 an hour for in-court work. Ala. Code §15-12-21(d)(1975 & Supp. (1992). For representative billing rates of private attorneys, see "The NLJ 250: 20th Annual Survey," Natl. L.J. (Nov. 10, 1997) (reporting on billing rates at law firms across the country).

60. Governor's Task Force on the Delivery and Funding of Quality Public Defender Service, Interim Recommendations, reprinted in *Advocate*, 3 December 1993, 11.

61. The Spangenberg Group, *A Study of Representation in Capital Cases in Texas*, 61 (March 1993); see also Norman Lefstein, "Reform of Defense Representation in Capital Cases: The Indiana Experience and its Implications for the Nation," 29 Ind. L. Rev. 495, 516–17 (1996) (discussing numerous studies). These studies, moreover, are themselves skewed by the limited compensation paid. Experts estimate that the minimum time required to prepare a capital trial adequately is 1,000 hours — 500 hours for the guilt/innocence phase, and 500 hours for the sentencing phase. "Panel Discussion: The Death of Fairness? Counsel Competence and Due Process in Death Penalty Cases," Hous. L. Rev. 1105, 1108 (1994).

62. Ala. Code §15-12-21(d) (1975 & Supp. 1992). Although the statute limits reimbursement for capital cases to $1,000, the Alabama attorney general has interpreted it to apply separately to the guilt and sentencing phases of a capital trial, so that the effective limit is now $2,000. Op. Ala.A.G. No. 91-00206 (March 21, 1991).

63. Tenn. Code Ann. §40-14-207 (1991); Ky. Rev. Stat. Ann. §31.070 (Michie 1996).

64. S.C. Code Ann. §17-3-50 (Law. Co-op. 1990).

65. Klein & Spangenberg, *Indigent Defense Crisis, supra* note 2 at 6.

66. Id. at 7; The Spangenberg Group, *A Study of Representation in Capital Cases in Virginia* (1993).

67. Andy Court, "Rush to Justice," *American Lawyer*, Jan./Feb. 1993, 56, 57. In 1993, the Michigan Supreme Court ruled that this system did not provide attorneys with the "reasonable compensation" required by Michigan state law. *In the Matter of Recorder's County Bar Assoc. v. Wayne Circuit Court*, 443 Mich. 110, 503 N.W.2d 885 (1993).

68. Albert C. Vreeland, II, "The Breath of the Unfee'd Lawyer: Statutory Fee Limitations and Ineffective Assistance of Counsel in Capital Litigation," 90 Mich. L. Rev. 626, 628 n.23 (1991).

69. All the data in this paragraph come from The Equal Justice Initiative, *A Report on Alabama's Indigent Defense System: Capital Cases*, 3–5 (March 1997).

70. *Pruett v. State*, 574 So.2d 1342 (Miss. 1990).

71. Id. at 1350 (Anderson, J., dissenting).

72. *Wilson v. State*, 574 So.2d 1338, 1341 (quoting *State ex rel. Stephen v. Smith*, 747 P.2d 816, 831 (Kan. 1987) (companion case to *Pruett*).

73. Id.

74. The Louisiana Supreme Court reached a similar result. The court held that while counsel must be reimbursed for out-of-pocket expenses and overhead costs, there

was no need to pay a fee for the lawyer's services, because it was part of the lawyers' "pro bono publico" obligations. The Court rejected the claim that the rights of the indigent defendants had anything to do with the appointed attorney's compensation, and treated the issue as solely a matter of the attorneys' rights. *State v. Wigley*, 624 So.2d 425 (La. 1993).

75. Marcia Coyle, "Counsel's Guiding Hand is Often Handicapped by the System It Serves," *Natl. L.J.*, 11 June 1990, 35.

76. Paul Calvin Drecksel, "The Crisis in Indigent Criminal Defense," 44 Ark. L. Rev. 363, 380 (1991).

77. McConville & Mirsky, "Criminal Defense of the Poor in New York City," 15 N.Y.U. Rev. L. & Soc. Change 581, 758 (1986–87).

78. Id. at 761, 767.

79. Id. at 764.

80. Id. at 901–02.

81. *Bell v. Watkins*, 692 F.2d 999, 1008 (5th Cir. 1982).

82. *Paradis v. Arave*, 954 F.2d 1483, 1490–91 (9th Cir. 1992).

83. *Birt v. Montgomery*, 725 F.2d 587, 598 n.25 (11th Cir.), cert. denied, 469 U.S. 874 (1984); see Bright, *Counsel for the Poor, supra* note 44 at 1839.

84. Fredric N. Tulsky, "Big Time Trials, Small Time Defendants," *Phila. Inquirer*, 14 September 1992, at A1, A8.

85. Ted Rohrlich, "The Case of the Speedy Attorney," *L.A. Times*, 26 September 1991, A1.

86. Id.

87. Paul M. Barrett, "On the Defense: Lawyer's Fast Work on Death Cases Raises Doubts About System," *Wall Street J.*, 7 September 1994, A1.

88. *Roberts v. State*, 438 S.E.2d 905, 906 (Ga. 1994).

89. *Amadeo v. State*, 384 S.E.2d 181, 181 (Ga. 1989).

90. Marcia Coyle, "Counsel's Guiding Hand is Often Handicapped by the System It Serves," *Natl L.J.*, 11 June 1990, 35.

91. Equal Justice Initiative Report, *supra* note 69.

92. See generally, Stephen B. Bright & Patrick J. Keenan, "Judges and the Politics of Death: Deciding Between the Bill of Rights and the Next Election in Capital Cases," 75 B.U.L. Rev. 759 (1995); Thomas M. Ross, "Rights at the Ballot Box: The Effect of Judicial Elections on Judges' Ability to Protect Criminal Defendants' Rights," 7 J. L. & Inequality 107 (1988).

93. *Machetti v. Linahan*, 679 F.2d 236, 241 (11th Cir. 1982), *cert. denied*, 459 U.S. 1127 (1983).

94. *Smith v. Kemp*, 715 F.2d 1459, 1476 (11th Cir.) (Hatchett, J. concurring in part and dissenting in part), *cert. denied*, 464 U.S. 1003 (1983).

95. *Smith v. Kemp*, 715 F.2d at 1472.

96. Bright, *Counsel for the Poor, supra* note 44 at 1859.

97. *Schlup v. Delo*, 115 S. Ct. 851 (1995); *Schlup v. Bowersox*, 1996 U.S. Dist. LEXIS 8887 (E.D. Mo. May 2, 1996); see also Stuart Taylor, "He Didn't Do It," *The American Lawyer*, December 1994, 70.

98. Norman Lefstein, "Reform of Defense Representation in Capital Cases: The Indiana Experience and Its Implications for the Nation," 29 Ind. L. Rev. 495 (1996);

Randall T. Shepard, "Capital Litigation from State Court Perspective, or, Rushing to Judgment in Fifteen Years," 2–4 (Presented to Workship for the Judges of the Seventh Circuit, Kohler, Wis., 2 May 1996). Other states that have adopted experiential standards for appointed capital defense counsel are Ohio, Virginia, and Oklahoma. Louisiana and Tennessese are developing such standards. Lefstein, *supra* at 504.

99. Associated Press, "Judge Uses Keeping Death-Row Lawyers, to Keep Down Costs," The Commercial Appeal, December 12, 1995, A14.

100. Derek Bok, "A Flawed System of Law Practice and Teaching," 33 J. of Legal Education 570, 575 (1983).

3—Judgment and Discrimination

The jury is the heart of the criminal justice system. It renders judgment on the most important question in criminal law—guilt or innocence. Many lawyers believe that cases are won and lost when they pick a jury. The jury has been lauded as a bulwark against government tyranny, a repository of democratic deliberation, and a stirring example of representative government in action. Alexis de Tocqueville described it as placing "the direction of society in the hands of the governed, or of a portion of the governed, and not in that of the government."[1] The Supreme Court has characterized the jury as "an inestimable safeguard against the corrupt or overzealous prosecutor and against the compliant, biased, or eccentric judge."[2] If the state overplays its hand, the jury, reflecting community sentiment, has the freedom to acquit, to convict of lesser charges, or to reach an impasse and require a new trial.

The jury is also, according to the Supreme Court, the "criminal defendant's fundamental 'protection of life and liberty against race or color prejudice.' "[3] Virtually all the attention the Court has paid to race discrimination in criminal justice has been focused on the jury. The first law of any kind that the Supreme Court ever struck down as racially discriminatory was a statute restricting jury service to white men,[4] and the Court has addressed race discrimination in jury selection in more cases than any other form of race discrimination. Justice Lewis Powell described the Court's efforts in this area as "unceasing;"[5] and Justice Anthony Kennedy has proudly characterized the Court's record as "over a century of jurisprudence dedicated to the elimination of race prejudice within the jury selection process."[6]

Yet racial discrimination in jury selection remains a persistent reality to this day. As it did with the right to counsel, the Court has made strong pronouncements about equality, but has not backed them up with meaningful implementation. As with the right to counsel, achieving equality is extremely difficult, in part for reasons beyond the Court's control. But much of the blame for the persistence of discrimination in jury selection must nonetheless be attributed to the Court's historic and continuing tolerance of measures that perpetuate and facilitate discrimination.

The problem of jury discrimination is a microcosm of the problem of discrimination in criminal justice, and indeed of race discrimination generally. The fundamental question is this: How can we ensure that juries treat defendants and victims of different races, genders, and classes equally, when we know that race, gender, and class distinctions play a significant role in how people view the world? Whether we like it or not, race matters in our culture. As Tanya Coke has argued,

> racial identity, though not biological race, informs cultural experience. . . . Racial identity, like gender identity, is an organizing principle of group consciousness: as long as patterns of residential and economic segregation continue to separate the races in different enclaves, blacks, whites, Latinos, and others will exhibit cultural differences in their perceptions of the world.[7]

If we ignore those differences in constructing the rules that govern juries, we risk denying equal justice. But if we construct a system on the premise that race matters, we risk institutionalizing and thereby perpetuating racial stereotypes. This fundamental dilemma is exacerbated by the secret character of jury deliberations. Because juries need not justify their actions with any sort of public account, they exercise virtually unbridled discretion, and that discretion may invite stereotyped judgments, including judgments predicated on race. In addition, nothing breeds skepticism like secrecy. Thus, whether or not the jury is actually a source of discrimination, it is likely to be viewed with distrust by those excluded from participation.

This problem admits of no easy answers, and the Court's approach has been deeply ambivalent. Although selection of jury pools was the first setting in which the Court invalidated racial discrimination, in 1880, selection of trial juries through "peremptory challenges" was also the last setting in which the Court openly tolerated racial discrimination, which it expressly *permitted* until 1986. As it stands today, the Court's jury discrimination doctrine imposes conflicting constitutional mandates on the jury selection process: its Sixth Amendment doctrine is predicated on an acknowledgement that race matters, but its equal protection doctrine requires color-blind jury selection. And while the Court has long condemned jury discrimination in principle, it has consistently adopted weak enforcement mechanisms that have tolerated continuing inequality.

Over the past one hundred years, the Court has reviewed every aspect of jury selection, from the initial processes for identifying a pool, or "venire," of eligible jurors, to the use of "peremptory challenges" by the parties' lawyers to select the trial jury from the jury pool. The Court's focus has shifted over time. It initially paid attention to discrimination in jury pool composition, and only later addressed discrimination in selection of trial juries. This chronology makes sense: As long as blacks were excluded from the jury pool, the issue of discriminatory selection for trial juries was largely moot, because there were no blacks in the pool to discriminate against in selecting the trial jury. "Peremptory challenges," used in selecting trial juries, grew in importance as a mechanism for discrimination as blacks began to appear in the jury pools. This chapter therefore first reviews the Court's approach to discrimination in the selection of jury pools, and then turns to its treatment of the discriminatory use of "peremptory strikes" to obtain a trial jury.

"A VIOLENT PRESUMPTION"

Three facts about jury discrimination are largely undisputed. First, the all-white jury has been a staple of the American criminal justice system for most of our history.[8] Second, the Supreme Court has long condemned discrimination in jury selection.[9] And third, race discrimination in jury selection remains a pervasive feature of our justice system to this day.[10] The interesting question is how all these facts can be true at the same time. A historical review of jury discrimination suggests the answer: while the Supreme Court has long condemned overt racism in jury selection, it has been reluctant to adopt measures that would make selection processes fair in practice. The Court's record has improved over the century, but its doctrine remains conflicted and compromised to this day, thereby permitting disproportionately white juries to endure.

Although procedures vary from state to state, several basic features are common to all jury selection processes. Jury commissioners start by creating a jury list or roll, which identifies all persons eligible for jury service. Voter registration lists are most commonly used as a source, in some instances supplemented by other sources, such as driver's license lists. Some southern states still rely on the "key man" system to compile their jury rolls. In Alabama, for example, jury commissioners are directed to place on the rolls persons in the community who are "generally reputed to be honest and intelligent and . . . esteemed in the community for integrity, good character and sound judgment."[11]

From the jury roll, jury commissioners then select a jury pool, or venire, which consists of those persons actually summoned to appear in court on a given day for jury service. Trial juries, or "petit juries," which judge guilt or innocence in individual cases, are then selected by a process of elimination from the jury pool. First, the court excuses those citizens who are exempt by virtue of occupation or other obligations. Then prospective jurors are asked about potential biases: are they related to any of the participants, have they been victimized by crime, do they have relatives who are in prison or in law enforcement, etc. Parties may challenge "for cause" any juror who cannot judge the facts objectively and fairly by virtue of such biases. Finally, each side ordinarily uses a number of "peremptory challenges," which permit them to strike jurors without explanation, to obtain the requisite number for the petit jury.

Each of these stages may result in the exclusion of minorities from jury service. Voter registration and even driver's license lists underrepresent poor people and racial minorities.[12] Key man lists tend to be filled with persons who belong to the same social circles as the jury commissioners, and therefore also underrepresent minorities and the poor. Because minorities and the poor move more frequently than whites and the rich, these groups are less likely to receive jury summonses. For a number of reasons, from skepticism and alienation to the inability to take time off from their jobs, minorities and the poor are also less likely to respond to those summonses they receive.[13] Finally, and most significantly today, because peremptory challenges need not be explained, they are especially fertile soil for racial discrimination.

The history of racial discrimination in jury selection is long and sordid. No black person sat on a jury in the United States until 1860.[14] During the post-Civil War Reconstruction, blacks began to serve on juries in the South for the first time.[15] Not coincidentally, integrated juries at that time began to convict whites for racially motivated violence against blacks.[16] But Democratic conservatives soon regained power in the South, Klan violence intimidated Republicans and blacks alike, and the all-white jury returned.[17] In 1875, Congress responded by making it a federal crime to exclude a juror on the basis of race, but violations of the law have rarely been prosecuted.[18]

A lawyer reading the 1880 decision in *Strauder v. West Virginia*,[19] the Supreme Court's first word on jury discrimination, might well have predicted that the all-white jury would soon go the way of slavery. At issue was a West Virginia statute that expressly reserved jury service to white males. The Court squarely held that barring blacks from serving on juries violated the recently enacted Fourteenth Amendment, which it construed as "securing to a race recently emancipated, a race that through many generations had been held in slavery, all the civil rights that the superior race enjoys."[20] It portrayed the exclusion of blacks from jury service as "practically a brand upon them, affixed by the law, an assertion of their inferiority, and a stimulant to that race prejudice which is an impediment to securing . . . equal justice."[21] The Court asked:

> how can it be maintained that compelling a colored man to submit to a trial for his life by a jury drawn from a panel from which the State has expressly excluded every man of his race, because of color alone, however well qualified in other respects, is not a denial to him of equal protection?[22]

In reaching its result, the Court in *Strauder* acknowledged what could hardly be denied in post-Civil War America: Race matters. In particular, by finding that the black *defendant's* right to equal protection was infringed by the exclusion of black *jurors*, the Court necessarily presumed that white and black jurors would react differently to prosecutions against black defendants, that is, that jurors are not color-blind. The Court expressly noted that "prejudices often exist against particular classes in the community, which sway the judgment of jurors," and asserted that "[t]he framers of the [Fourteenth A]mendment must have known full well the existence of such prejudice and its likelihood to continue against the manumitted slaves and their race, and that knowledge was doubtless a motive that led to the amendment."[23]

Notwithstanding its strong rhetoric, however, *Strauder* had virtually no impact on the practice of jury discrimination. From the end of Reconstruction through the New Deal, "the systematic exclusion of black men from Southern juries was about as plain as any legal discrimination could be short of proclamation in state statutes or confession by state officials."[24] The Supreme Court repeatedly upheld convictions of black defendants by all-white juries in situations where intentional exclusion of black jurors was self-evident. In *Smith v. Mississippi*, to cite one of many examples, the Court in 1896 upheld the conviction of a black man for murder where the defendant alleged that although there were 1,300 black and 300 white voters in Bolivar County, no black person had been summoned for jury service since the end of the Civil War.[25]

Until 1935, the only Supreme Court decision other than *Strauder* itself that invalidated a conviction on jury discrimination grounds was *Neal v. Delaware*.[26] William Neal, a black man, was indicted for the rape of a white woman, an offense punishable by death. Delaware law explicitly restricted jury service to white males, but a state court had ruled that ban inoperative in light of the Fourteenth Amendment. The state conceded, however, "that no colored citizen had ever been summoned as a juror in the courts of the State," in a county where blacks numbered more than 26,000 among a total population of less than 150,000.[27] The Delaware Supreme Court had denied Neal's equal protection challenge with the following reasoning:

> That none but white men were selected is in nowise remarkable in view of the fact—too notorious to be ignored—that the great body of black

men residing in this State are utterly unqualified by want of intelligence, experience, or moral integrity to sit on juries. Exceptions there are, unquestionably, but they are rare . . .[28]

The U. S. Supreme Court reversed, noting that the state had conceded that it excluded all black jurors, and that the only explanation offered—that "the great body of black men residing in this State are utterly unqualified by want of intelligence, experience, or moral integrity"—was "a violent presumption" that the Court could not sanction.[29]

The most remarkable thing about *Neal*, however, is how little distinguishes it from the legion of cases that followed in which the Supreme Court *upheld* convictions of black men by all-white juries. In case after case, the Supreme Court, much like the Delaware Supreme Court in *Neal*, discounted showings of stark disparities as insufficient, deferred to lower court findings of no discrimination, and indulged a presumption that public officials would not exclude jurors on the basis of race unless the law explicitly directed them to do so. What made *Neal* different was that the Delaware Supreme Court had made *explicit* the violent presumption that black citizens were unqualified for jury service. Apparently, so long as the presumption was left unstated, the Supreme Court in the pre-New Deal era was willing to condone discriminatory results.

Professor Benno Schmidt has sought to explain the Supreme Court's dismal record of tolerating all-white juries for so long after declaring race discrimination in jury selection unconstitutional by noting that defendants were required to develop the facts underlying their claims in often hostile state courts. In *Strauder* and a companion case, *Virginia v. Rives*,[30] the Supreme Court ruled that state defendants could not bring such claims in federal court, where judges would be more sympathetic. Instead, defendants had to litigate their race discrimination claims before state judges, who were often extremely reluctant to find their own jury commissioners guilty of the federal criminal offense of racial exclusion. Although U.S. Supreme Court review was theoretically available on appeal from state court convictions, the Supreme Court could not possibly review every claim of jury discrimination that arose in a state criminal proceeding. When it did review such claims, it adopted a highly deferential attitude toward the trial court's factfinding regarding discrimination. Thus, at the very moment that it declared jury discrimination unconstitutional, the Court relegated enforcement of such claims to unsympathetic state courts, where most would fail.

Schmidt attributes this result to the Court's ambivalence about the shift in federal-state relations brought about by the Civil War amendments to the Constitution.[31] Prior to the Civil War, states were seen as the prime protectors of individual rights, and the federal government's authority was sharply limited. In retrospect, historians now view the Civil War, and the Civil War amendments, as fundamentally shifting the power and responsibility for assuring equal rights from the states to the federal government. This shift, Schmidt argues, was not an easy one, and the Court was reluctant to assert its newly dominant federal role.

Schmidt also posits another motive. Had the Court actually put an end to the all-white jury, it might have encouraged widespread private vigilantism of the type practiced by the Ku Klux Klan.[32] The unstated concern — speculative at best — was that if discrimination could not be effected through judicial channels, it would be effected through extrajudicial methods, such as lynchings. In any event, the Court announced a broad principle of nondiscrimination in *Strauder*, but left its enforcement to state courts. In Schmidt's view:

> The advantages of [such an approach] are clear: shift the everyday burden of enforcement to the state courts and officialdom. At least make them say the right things about nondiscrimination. If profession of principle is to force actual effects in life, make the state courts the forcing institutions. If there is to be hypocrisy between judicial profession and judical process, let the state courts dirty their hands. Keep the federal trial judges out of the picture. Hold the Supreme Court at appellate remove, a distant keeper of the Ark of the (paper) Covenant, unembarrassed by hands-on confrontations with the frustration of federal guarantees.[33]

Of course, prudence can also be a cover for a lack of courage. And the costs of the Court's cautious approach were substantial. By tolerating official discrimination at the core of the criminal justice system as long as it was not explicit, the Court may well have done more damage to the cause of racial equality than the feared Klan violence. Such violence would have been seen for what it was—extralegal and illegitimate—and might have prompted more substantial federal intervention. By instead channeling racial subordination through a facially race-neutral judicial system that imposed official violence on blacks through imprisonment and capital punishment, the Court arguably contributed to the "normalization" and institutionalization of subordination, rendering it even more insidious and difficult to confront.

The Court's performance in these early jury discrimination cases unfortunately is consistent with its approach to discrimination in criminal justice to this day. The Court announced a constitutional right, but then implemented it in a manner that spared mainstream society the cost of realizing that right across the board. In the jury setting, the cost to mainstream society would likely have come in increased tensions and hostilities between Democrats and Republicans, between the South and the North, and between state and federal institutions, at a time when the mainstream was seeking to suppress such hostilities and achieve a renewed union. The Court's approach spared mainstream society by shifting the cost to black defendants and permitting white domination of the jury to continue under the cover of formal race neutrality, long after it could not openly be justified.

"PLAIN AS PUNCH"

In 1935, the Supreme Court abruptly shifted course, invalidating a second round of convictions in the high-profile Scottsboro case on the ground that the state had discriminatorily applied a race-neutral selection scheme to exclude black citizens from the jury rolls.[34] After the Supreme Court reversed the initial convictions in the Scottsboro case for lack of effective counsel, the Communist Party hired Samuel Leibowitz, an experienced New York trial attorney, to represent the defendants on retrial. Leibowitz aggressively challenged the racial composition of the jury rolls. He put on witnesses who testified that they could not remember a black man serving on any jury in the county in their lifetimes. He interrogated jury commissioners, who admitted that they designated black citizens as "col."—for "colored"—on the lists from which they drew the jury venire. And he subpoenaed the books containing the jury roll.

Those books became a central exhibit in the case. Alabama officials pointed to the names of six black citizens on the jury roll as evidence that they had not systematically excluded black citizens. But Leibowitz called a handwriting expert, who testified that the six black names had been entered *after* the jury rolls were completed. Red lines had been drawn at the bottom of each page when the lists were initially recorded, and the black men's names appeared to have been written in later, over the red lines.

The Alabama courts nonetheless found no discrimination. Like so many courts before, they credited the jury commissioners' general denials of discriminatory intent, presumed that the commissioners had faithfully followed their obligations, and found that they had not tampered with the jury rolls. This case's conclusion was to be different, however. In part the difference may have been due to the nationwide attention that the case had achieved. But in part the difference lay in Leibowitz's marshalling of the evidence. At the Supreme Court oral argument, Leibowitz made the brute fact of discrimination dramatically visible in a way that no argument had before. Supreme Court arguments are usually exercises in technical legal discourse far removed from the facts of a case. But Leibowitz brought the jury books with him to the argument, and invited the Justices to witness the tampering for themselves. Although the Court rarely reviews evidence during argument, each Justice in turn examined the books with a magnifying glass as Leibowitz explained how the black men's names were added after the fact. When Justice Willis Van Devanter, saw the books, he whispered to his colleague Chief Justice Charles Evans, in a voice loud enough to be heard by spectators, "Why it's plain as punch!"[35]

The Court reversed the convictions, finding that the Alabama jury commissioners had intentionally excluded black jurors because of their race.[36] Where the Court had in previous cases presumed good faith on the part of government officials absent a direct showing of racist motive, it now stated that a case of discrimination could be made by a sufficiently strong statistical showing that blacks were qualified for jury service but absent from juries.[37] A direct showing of intentional discrimination was no longer necessary. And the Court abandoned its previous stance of deference to lower court factfinding on the issue of whether intentional discrimination occurred, insisting now that its duty was to "analyze the facts in order that the appropriate enforcement of the federal right may be assured."[38]

After the Scottsboro case, the Court reviewed jury discrimination claims with much more care, at the rate of about one a year, and frequently reversed convictions based on statistical showings.[39] The Court's record was by no means consistent, however. In 1945, the Court rejected a race discrimination challenge to a grand jury where Dallas County had adopted a practice of placing one, and only one, black juror on each grand jury.[40] The Court upheld this practice, even though jury commissioners admitted that once they found one black juror, they "felt like that was satisfactory representation," and "had no intention of placing more than one negro on the panel."[41] In dissent, Justice Murphy argued that "clearer proof of intentional and deliberate limitation on the basis of color would be difficult to produce."[42]

In the early 1970s, the Court began to look beyond tokenism, and invalidated selection schemes where defendants showed a "substantial disparity" between the racial makeup of the community and that of the jury list, absent a specific explanation for the disparity from state officials. In 1970, for example, the Court upheld a constitutional challenge to a Georgia jury selection scheme where blacks comprised 37 percent of a jury venire, but 60 percent of the population, and the state had not adequately explained the difference.[43]

While the Court's decisions from 1935 to 1975 exhibit a relatively consistent effort to ferret out the most blatant racially exclusionary selection measures, the very persistence of the cases illustrated the limits of the Court's approach. It could review only a small number of jury selection cases each year, and many cases with strong showings of discrimination went unreviewed. In 1943, for example, the Supreme Court declined to review a lower court decision finding no discrimination where the jury roll contained only 3 percent black jurors in a county whose population was 19 percent black.[44] In 1965, the Court refused to review a case in which the lower court had upheld a death penalty for a black man accused of raping a white woman, notwithstanding evidence that the jury list had been marked with a handwritten "c" next to each potential black juror's name.[45] And in 1971 it declined to review a case finding no discrimination in New York City's grand jury list even though, in a city that was 24 percent black and 12 percent Puerto Rican, only 1.65 percent of those summoned for jury service were black and only 0.3 percent were Puerto Rican.[46] The Court's method of case-by-case review was time consuming, factually intensive, and inefficient—in short, an administrative nightmare. The Court may well have been looking for a way out. If so, it found it in an unlikely case, that of Billy Taylor, a white male defendant complaining of discrimination against women jurors.

"A FAIR CROSS SECTION"

Like many defendants before him, Billy Taylor, convicted of aggravated kidnapping in 1972, objected to the composition of the jury list from which his jury was chosen. But unlike most defendants, Taylor did not complain that persons of his own race or sex—white men—were excluded, but that women were. Under Louisiana law at the time, women were not placed on the jury roll unless they affirmatively requested in writing that they be listed. As a result, no more than 10 percent of the names on the jury roll were female. Taylor, a man, could not advance a traditional equal protection claim, because such claims were predicated on the harm that a defendant suffered when members of his own race or gender were excluded from the jury that judged him. In any event, in 1961 the Court had unanimously rejected an equal protection challenge to a similar law excusing women from jury service, reasoning that women could be presumptively excused because a "woman is still regarded as the center of home and family life."[47]

Taylor therefore relied on the Sixth Amendment, arguing that its guarantee that he be tried by an "impartial jury" included the right to have a jury selected from a representative cross section of the community. The exclusion of women, he argued, rendered the cross section unrepresentative. The Court agreed, holding that "the selection of a petit jury from a representative cross section of the community is an essential component of the Sixth Amendment right to a jury trial."[48] It found that Louisiana's rule disproportionately excluded women, and therefore violated the Sixth Amendment. The doctrine has since been extended to other "distinctive" groups, including racial and ethnic groups.

There are two significant features to the Sixth Amendment doctrine articulated in *Taylor v. Louisiana*. First, the Court expressly acknowledged, as it had in *Strauder*, that group identity matters. It insisted that although men and women do not necessarily vote as a class, a jury that includes only men is presumptively different from a jury that includes both men and women. Quoting Justice Thurgood Marshall (who was writing about racial exclusion), the Court explained, "It is not necessary to assume that the excluded group will consistently vote as a class in order to conclude, as we do, that its exclusion deprives the jury of a perspective on human events that may have unsuspected importance in any case that may be presented."[49] Thus, the Court's Sixth Amendment doctrine is predicated on race and gender consciousness.

Second, the Court ruled that a Sixth Amendment violation does not require any showing that the state *intentionally* excluded jurors because of their race or gender.[50] A selection process that underrepresents women or blacks violates the Sixth Amendment regardless of whether it was intended to have that effect. Because the doctrine focuses on easily measured effects rather than on the ever-elusive question of intent, the "fair cross section" requirement can be meaningfully enforced. As a result, the Court's Sixth Amendment doctrine has in large measure solved the problem of discrimination in jury roll and venire composition.

The solution, however, is not necessarily stable. Its premise — that race (and sex) matter — is in direct conflict with the the principal lesson of the Court's Equal Protection Clause jurisprudence, which insists on color-blindness and says the state *cannot* take race or sex into account in selecting a jury. Since *Strauder*, intentional exclusion of jurors from jury service because of their race or sex violates the Equal Protection Clause. Yet because it requires a representative result rather than a color-blind process, the Sixth Amendment creates an incentive for jury commissioners to consider race and gender in selecting jurors for the venire.[51] Thus, the Sixth Amendment is predicated on, and practically mandates, race consciousness, while the Fourteenth Amendment prohibits race consciousness and mandates color-blindness. Today's Supreme Court is more committed to color-blindness than ever before, so much so that it views race-conscious efforts to assist African Americans with practically the same skepticism with which it views race-conscious efforts to harm them. That approach threatens to dismantle affirmative action efforts in employment, education, and voting rights.[52] An equal protection challenge to race-conscious jury selection measures cannot be far off.[53]

The tension between race consciousness and color-blindness can also be found in the Court's refusal to extend the Sixth Amendment fair cross-section principle to the trial jury. In *Taylor*, the Court stressed that the Sixth Amendment imposes "no requirement that petit juries actually chosen [from jury venires] must mirror the community and reflect the various distinctive groups in the population. Defendants are not entitled to a jury of any particular composition."[54] It is not obvious why this is so. The Sixth Amendment on its face guarantees an impartial *jury*, not an impartial *venire*. A defendant plainly cares more about the actual jury that judges her case than about the venire from which that jury is chosen. If representative perspectives of race and gender are important to include in the jury venire, it would seem even more important to include them on the actual jury that decides guilt or innocence.

The Court has justified its refusal to extend Sixth Amendment requirements to the trial jury on the ground that "it would be impossible to apply a concept of proportional representation to the petit jury in view of the heterogeneous nature of our society."[55] But this cannot be a complete explanation, for in many communities and for particular groups (e.g., women), it would probably not be so difficult to apply the fair cross-section requirement to the trial jury. With respect to sex, for example, trial juries would simply have to be roughly half women and half men. What makes extension of the fair cross-section requirement to the petit jury unacceptable is not that it is unworkable, but that it would require the application of race and gender presumptions to *individuals* rather than *groups*. It is one thing to say that women as a class generally will offer different perspectives than men; it is another thing to say that a particular individual juror, because she is female, will do so. Generalizations may be accurate at a general level, but they begin to look like invidious stereotypes when translated to the specific level of identifiable individuals. The larger numbers of the jury venire permit generalizations; the smaller numbers on the petit jury and the individualized selection process make race and gender consciousness much more problematic.

The Court's ambivalent jury discrimination doctrine reflects the genuine difficulty of constructing fair rules in a world in which, descriptively, race and sex matter, but normatively, they should not. As Andrew Kull laments, "We stand caught between what we can't realistically deny and what we can't afford to admit."[56] It is only because race and sex matter that jury discrimination happens. In a truly race- and gender-blind world, jurors' race and gender would be of no more significance than their eye color, and jury discrimination would not even be a coherent concept. The Sixth Amendment fair cross-section requirement, with its focus on results and its rough requirement of proportionality, has come close to solving the problem of discrimination in jury rolls and venires, but only by effectively requiring that race and sex be consciously taken into account. What remains to be seen is whether a Court committed to the ideology of color-blindness will continue to tolerate such race consciousness.

THE PEREMPTORY CHALLENGE

The Sixth Amendment fair cross-section requirement has largely made discrimination in the composition of jury rolls and venires a thing of the past. But that has not eliminated the all-white jury, for one reason: the peremptory challenge. The peremptory challenge allows a party to "strike" a potential juror from the trial jury without offering any explanation. It is used in virtually all jurisdictions as a way to select a trial jury from the larger pool of eligible jurors. Because this challenge requires no explanation, and because it is exercised on the basis of very limited information — often the parties know little more about a prospective juror than the juror's race, sex, age, and perhaps employment — it will almost necessarily be based on stereotyped judgments. Yet the Court expressly condoned race-based peremptory strikes as late as 1965, did not declare them unconstitutional until 1986, and to this day has failed to adopt an effective mechanism for prohibiting them. Thus, for more than a century after the Court held that it was unconstitutional to exclude jurors from a jury venire because of their race, it *permitted* parties to use peremptory challenges to exclude jurors from trial juries on the basis of race. And because it still has not solved the problem of race-based peremptories, the all-white jury endures.

The peremptory challenge serves several legitimate purposes. It gives the parties a direct role in shaping the jury, which theoretically increases their acceptance of verdicts. It allows the parties to strike jurors they believe are biased, but who won't admit their biases sufficiently to support a challenge for cause. And it offers parties a check on judges who may be reluctant to declare potential jurors biased absent extremely strong evidence. But peremptory strikes are notoriously based on stereotypes. Jury selection manuals have been quite candid about this fact. Consider, for example, the following advice from a 1973 Texas prosecutors' manual:

> You are not looking for any member of a minority group which may subject him to oppression — they almost always sympathize with the accused . . .

> I don't like women jurors because I can't trust them. They do, however, make the best jurors in crimes against children . . .

> Extremely overweight people, especially women and young men, indicates a lack of self-discipline and often times instability. I like the lean and hungry look . . .

> People from small towns and rural areas generally make good State's jurors. People from the east or west coasts often make bad jurors . . .

> Intellectuals such as teachers, etc., generally are too liberal and contemplative to make good State's jurors . . .

Ask if the venireman has any hobbies or interests that occupy their spare time. Active, outdoors type hobbies indicate the best State's jurors. Hunters always make good State's jurors . . .

Jewish veniremen generally make poor State's jurors. Jews have a history of oppression and generally empathize with the accused. Lutherans and Church of Christ veniremen usually make good State's jurors.[57]

In a similar vein, the great Clarence Darrow advised defense attorneys to "[n]ever take a wealthy man on a jury. He will convict, unless the defendant is accused of violating the anti-trust law, selling worthless stocks or bonds, or something of that kind."[58] Darrow favored Irishmen, because "I never met [one] who didn't think that someday he might be in trouble himself."[59] Melvin Belli, a renowned trial attorney, advised that "generally a male juror is more sound than a woman juror," especially when the client "is a woman and has those qualities which other women envy—good looks, a handsome husband, wealth, social position," because women "are the severest judges of their own sex."[60]

The effects of the race-based peremptory challenge have long been noted. A *New York Times* reporter wrote in 1935 that "a Negro on a trial jury is as rare as ever in the deep South . . . Negroes can be—and are—easily eliminated by one or both sides through the [peremptory strike]."[61] Professor Douglas Colbert has found that all-white juries remained a staple of American justice in both the North and South from 1935 to 1965, largely because of the peremptory strike.[62] And the Alabama Supreme Court candidly admitted in 1963 that "Negroes are commonly on trial venires but are always struck by attorneys in selecting the trial jury."[63]

In Dallas County, Texas, prosecutors in 100 criminal trials in 1983 and 1984 used the peremptory challenge to strike 405 of 467 eligible black jurors, and struck five times as many black as white jurors.[64] From 1974 to 1981 in several counties in Georgia, one prosecutor used almost 90 percent of his peremptory strikes against black jurors in capital cases with black defendants, and used 94 percent of his strikes against black jurors where the defendant was black and the victim white.[65] Even after the Supreme Court declared race-based peremptory challenges unconstitutional in 1986, prosecutors have continued to strike many prospective black jurors to obtain disproportionately white juries.[66]

The persistence of this practice was confirmed in 1997 with the release of a videotape from a Philadelphia district attorney's training session for prosecutors, in which Jack McMahon, then an assistant district attorney, explicitly advocated that prosecutors strike black jurors because of their race. McMahon advised that

> . . . young black women are very bad. There's an antagonism. I guess maybe they're downtrodden in two respects. They are women and they're black. . . . So they somehow want to take it out on somebody, and you don't want it to be you.

> Let's face it, the blacks from the low-income areas are less likely to convict. I understand it. There's a resentment for law enforcement. There's a resentment for authority. And as a result, you don't want those people on your jury.

> It may appear as if you're being racist, but you're just being realistic. You're just trying to win the case.[67]

This training film was made in 1987, a year after the Supreme Court declared the use of race-based peremptory challenges unconstitutional. More significantly, when McMahon was questioned about it on national television after the videotape was disclosed in 1997, he unapologetically defended the practice as a simple recognition of reality:

> My point is, you have to recognize that people in those communities . . . have different human experiences. And they're less — they've had bad experiences with police. And if you're a prosecutor trying to have them believe police officers, they're going to be less likely to believe a police officer because of their human experience. And you have to recognize that if you're going to be a strong advocate.[68]

Three Philadelphia judges confirmed to local reporters after the McMahon story broke in 1997 that these techniques are still routinely used by both prosecutors and defense counsel.[69] Similarly, Harvard Law Professor Arthur Miller complained that "Jack McMahon is being scapegoated for something that every lawyer in the United States, including those defense lawyers . . . do[es]."[70]

Given such practices, the peremptory challenge means that a

racially mixed jury venire can easily produce an all-white trial jury. A minority group will by definition constitute a minority of a representative venire, and often a few peremptory challenges will suffice to eliminate all prospective minority jurors. Yet the Supreme Court did not even take up the issue of race-based peremptory challenges until 1965, at the height of the civil rights movement, and when it did so, it expressly *approved* of them.

Robert Swain, the defendent in *Swain v. Alabama*,[71] was a nineteen-year-old black man accused of raping a seventeen-year-old white woman. He was convicted and sentenced to death by an all-white jury after the prosecutor struck all six prospective black jurors. Represented by the NAACP Legal Defense and Educational Fund's Constance Baker Motley (now a federal judge), Swain showed that no black had ever served on a trial jury in Talladega County, Alabama, where he was tried and convicted, even though blacks comprised more than one-quarter of the county's population. Blacks had been consistently underrepresented on jury venires, but more significantly, black jurors on the venire had been eliminated by peremptory challenges *in every case*.

The Supreme Court was not troubled. It reasoned that the "essential nature of the peremptory challenge is that it is one exercised without a reason stated, without inquiry, and without being subject to the court's control," and therefore the challenge "would no longer be peremptory" if it had to be explained.[72] The Court admitted that peremptory challenges are often based on "'sudden impressions and unaccountable prejudices,'" and on "grounds normally thought irrelevant to legal proceedings or official action, namely . . . race, religion, nationality, occupation or affiliations."[73] But in reasoning that echoed *Plessy v. Ferguson*[74]—which found segregation on trains to be nondiscriminatory because whites were barred from riding with blacks just as blacks were barred from riding with whites—the Court in *Swain* explained that "[i]n the quest for an impartial and qualified jury, Negro and white, Protestant and Catholic, are alike subject to being challenged without cause."[75] Thus, at the height of the civil rights movement, in a case involving the most racially charged of crimes, in a county where peremptory challenges against blacks had been used so successfully that no one could remember a black person ever sitting on a trial jury, the Court expressly approved the practice of race-based exclusion of black jurors.

That remained the law until 1986, when the Supreme Court decided *Batson v. Kentucky*.[76] In a burglary case against a black defendant, the prosecutor struck all four black jurors to obtain an all-white jury. Although the defendant invoked the Sixth Amendment, presumably to avoid the dictates of *Swain*, the Supreme Court resolved his case on equal protection grounds, overruled *Swain*, and held that race-based peremptory challenges violate the Equal Protection Clause. In *Batson*, however, the Court continued its practice, begun in *Strauder*, of pronouncing strong equal protection principles but failing to ensure their realization in practice.

Batson has by all accounts done relatively little to eliminate the use of race-based peremptory strikes for two reasons.[77] First, the Court in *Batson* made it extremely easy for attorneys to recharacterize their race-based peremptory strikes as race neutral after the fact. The essence of the peremptory strike is that it requires no explanation at all, and may be wholly arbitrary. The Court in *Batson* sought to retain as much of the peremptory challenge as possible, while surgically excising those peremptories predicated on race. But under that approach, courts must accept *any* explanation for a challenge that is not race-based, no matter how ridiculous, unless they are willing to brand the prosecutor a liar. Because peremptories need not even be rational, the most irrational reason, if deemed credible, suffices to defeat a *Batson* challenge.

Michael J. Raphael and Edward J. Ungvarsky reviewed all published decisions involving *Batson* challenges from 1986 to January 1992, and concluded that "in almost any situation a prosecutor can readily craft an acceptable neutral explanation to justify striking black jurors because of their race."[78] Courts have accepted explanations that the juror was too old, too young, was employed as a teacher or unemployed, or practiced a certain religion. They have accepted unverifiable explanations based on demeanor: the juror did not make eye contact or made too much eye contact, appeared inattentive or headstrong, nervous or too casual, grimaced or smiled. And they have accepted explanations that might often be correlated to race: the juror lacked education, was single or poor, lived or worked in the same neighborhood as the defendant or a witness, or had previously been involved with the criminal justice system.[79]

As a result of *Batson*'s underenforcement, prosecutors are not shy about continuing to use peremptory strikes against black jurors. Consider the following examples, from Alabama trials in the late 1980s and 1990s:

> the prosecutor in Jesse Morrison's case . . . remove[d] twenty of the twenty-one blacks who had qualified for jury service; twelve of thirteen black venire members were eliminated from Darrell Watkins' capital trial; Earl McGahee had to face an all-white jury after the state removed all sixteen black venire members; David Freeman was convicted and sentenced to death by an all-white panel after the state removed nine of ten prospective black jurors.[80]

The Supreme Court has, if anything, encouraged this trend of accepting any race-neutral rationale after the fact. In *Purkett v. Elem*,[81] the prosecutor offered the following rambling explanation to justify his strikes of two black jurors:

> I struck [juror] number twenty-two because of his long hair. He had long curly hair. He had the longest hair of anybody on the panel by far. He appeared to not be a good juror for that fact, the fact that he had long hair hanging down shoulder length, curly, unkempt hair. Also, he had a mustache and a goatee type beard. And juror number twenty-four also has a mustache and goatee type beard. Those are the only two people on the jury . . . with facial hair. . . . And I don't like the way they looked, with the way the hair is cut, both of them. And the mustaches and the beards look suspicious to me. And number twenty-four had been in a robbery in a supermarket with a sawed-off shotgun pointed at his face, and I didn't want him on the jury as this case does not involve a shotgun, and maybe he would feel to have a robbery you have to have a gun, and there is no gun in this case.[82]

The Court of Appeals for the Eighth Circuit held that the prosecutor's reliance on long hair and facial hair was insufficient because those factors were not plausibly related to "the person's ability to perform his or her duties as a juror." The Supreme Court reversed, holding that *any* racially neutral reason, no matter how fantastic, silly, or superstitious, is sufficient to satisfy the prosecutor's burden, provided that the trial court finds the reason genuine. Although "a trial judge *may choose to disbelieve* a silly or superstitious reason,"[83] if believed, even silly and superstitious reasons suffice to defeat a *Batson* claim.

This standard practically invites after-the-fact rationalizations. As Professor Sheri Johnson has suggested, "[i]f prosecutors exist who . . . cannot create a 'racially neutral' reason for discriminating on the basis of race, bar exams are too easy."[84] Even assuming good faith, attorneys will often exercise race-based judgments without realizing it. As Justice Thurgood Marshall explained,

> A prosecutor's own conscious or unconscious racism may lead him easily to the conclusion that a prospective black juror is 'sullen' or 'distant,' a characterization that would not have come to his mind if a white juror had acted identically. A judge's own conscious or unconscious racism may lead him to accept such an explanation as well supported.[85]

Batson does nothing to address this problem, and is generally ineffective at stopping even blatant racists, as long as they can manufacture a "neutral explanation" after the fact.

The second weakness in the *Batson* inquiry is its deference to trial judges. Because prosecutors should always be able to proffer some race-neutral reason for their strikes, the *Batson* test reduces to a question of credibility: should the prosecutor's asserted neutral reason be accepted as genuine, or is the prosecutor lying to cover up a race-based strike? It is notoriously difficult for an appellate court to second-guess a trial judge's determination on such credibility issues, as the appellate court lacks the benefit of first-hand observation of the prosecutor's demeanor. Reviewing courts therefore defer to the trial court's finding regarding the prosecutor's motive unless the finding is clearly erroneous.[86]

Trial judges are likely to be reluctant to find discrimination. It is no minor matter to find that a fellow officer of the court and representative of the state has *both* lied and acted for discriminatory reasons. In many localities, the prosecutor will have appeared quite often before the same judge, will travel in the same social circles, may well have contributed to the judge's election campaign, and may be personal friends with the judge. Not surprisingly, the vast majority of state trial courts accept prosecutors' "neutral explanations" as genuine, and such findings are only rarely overturned on appeal.[87] As with *Strauder*, the Supreme Court has left enforcement of the equal protection principle it pronounced to those least likely to enforce it effectively.

The peremptory challenge doctrine has allowed the Supreme Court to articulate and enforce a principle of nondiscrimination without incurring the social costs of actually requiring integrated juries in criminal trials. What are those costs today? One might be more hung juries and acquittals. A National Law Journal study of 800 jurors found that where a police officer's and a defendant's stories conflict, 42 percent of whites but only 25 percent of blacks believe that the police officer's version should be credited.[88] Jury studies tend to support attorneys' intuitions that jurors are in general more sympathetic to victims of their own race, and more forgiving of defendants of their own race.[89] In any event, the consistency with which prosecutors strike black jurors in cases against black defendants suggests that they believe race matters to their conviction rates. Race-based peremptory challenges, expressly tolerated until 1986 and tolerated in practice to this day, allow society to maintain the appearance of race neutrality while avoiding the costs of including blacks and other members of minority groups on juries in proportion to their representation in the general population.

ACKNOWLEDGING THAT RACE MATTERS

The Supreme Court has never come to terms with the fact that race matters in our culture. Nor has it been willing to confront the full costs of guaranteeing equality in this critical area of the criminal justice system. A better approach would be to acknowledge the contradiction candidly: race matters *and* racial stereotypes are pernicious. Such an approach would not require major revisions of the Court's doctrine, but would require the Court to confront the difficulties and tensions more honestly. The tension can be mediated structurally, by permitting (and even encouraging) race consciousness at the more general level of jury venire selection, and demanding true color-blindness at the petit jury selection stage. The current

Sixth Amendment regime, in which significant departures from rough proportionality trigger constitutional review, effectively ensures that jury venires are representative. It often leads to race-conscious decisionmaking on the part of jury commissioners, but taking race into account at this very general level, and for a legitimate purpose, should be permissible. It does minimal damage to the principle of individual treatment, since venires are constructed not through individualized selection but through the use of aggregate data, with respect to which generalizations are both more accurate and less offensive than when applied to individuals. Thus, the Sixth Amendment approach should be maintained, and when the Court faces the inevitable equal protection challenge to a race-conscious venire selection process, it should uphold race-conscious processes so long as they are designed to ensure a representative venire.

At the level of selecting the individuals who will serve on the trial jury, however, racial stereotypes should play no role. Unlike the construction of venires, trial jury selection is by definition an individualized process. The application of race or gender generalizations to individuals in the petit jury selection process offends basic principles of individual treatment. To say so merely restates the principle announced in *Batson*. But if that principle is to be made a reality, the Court must either impose a heightened justification requirement where a pattern of racial strikes has been shown, or eliminate peremptory challenges altogether. Until then, the peremptory strikes will be color-blind in theory only.

Once a pattern of racial strikes has been shown, the Court should require the prosecutor to defend her strikes with reasonable grounds for suspecting that the prospective juror was biased, something akin to the showing required for "for cause" strikes. This approach would retain the benefits of the peremptory challenge, so long as race and other impermissible criteria are avoided. But where a party engages in a pattern of apparently race-based strikes, she would effectively forfeit the benefits of the peremptory strike, and be required to justify her strikes on something approaching a for-cause standard.

If this system does not succeed in halting race-based strikes, the

Court should eliminate peremptory strikes altogether. In that event, some adjustment of the current regime of for-cause strikes would be necessary. Under today's strict for-cause standard, judges will strike a prospective juror only if the facts strongly suggest that the juror cannot be fair; because few jurors admit their prejudices, for-cause challenges for bias are rare.[90] If peremptories were eliminated, courts would have to liberalize the for-cause standard; instead of asking whether the juror can be impartial, the judge might ask if the party objecting has reasonable grounds for suspecting that the juror might be biased—a lower standard that would exclude more marginal jurors. It is precisely because it is backed up with the peremptory challenge that the for-cause standard can afford to be so strict. A relaxed for-cause standard could be relatively deferential to the suspicions of counsel, but would nonetheless require counsel to articulate a reason for each strike. Race or sex should of course be an impermissable ground, and courts should engage in heightened scrutiny where rationales appear to be correlated with race or gender. The result would be a process in which, as now, the parties would participate in the shaping of the jury that decides their case, but all suspicious strikes would have to be justified by articulated, noninvidious reasons.

The regime proposed here openly acknowledges that race matters, but at the same time avoids the most pernicious instances of race-based decision making. It admits the tension that the Supreme Court has sought to suppress, and adopts a structural solution as a mediating mechanism. By permitting the consideration of race at the general level of venire creation, we can ensure that jury venires will generally be representative of the ethnic groups in the community. And by rigorously cleansing the trial jury selection process of racial considerations, trial juries should also, on the whole, be representative of the community. Once a representative venire has been constructed, insisting on a color-blind process of selection should not have negative consequences. Without first ensuring such a representative venire, however, insisting on color-blindness will only foster discriminatory results, and lead to still more disproportionately white juries.

One of the traditional explanations for the jury system is that it promotes the acceptability of criminal sanctions by involving the community in the process. If the criminal justice system is to be accepted by the black community, the black community must be represented on juries. The long history of excluding blacks from juries is one important reason why blacks as a class are more skeptical than whites about the fairness of the criminal justice system.[91] But the problem feeds on itself. Because African Americans are more skeptical of the criminal justice system, they are less likely to participate in jury service. And for the same reason, prosecutors are inclined to disfavor those who do volunteer to serve, as Philadelphia prosecutor Jack McMahon's comments illustrate. As long as the criminal justice system disproportionately stops, arrests, tries, and convicts blacks, that skepticism is likely to remain. Thus, even though black participation in the jury system might legitimate the results of the criminal justice system, prosecutors remain suspicious of black jurors as pro-defense, and therefore are inclined to do what they can to keep them off their juries. And so the cycle continues, with exclusion feeding skepticism, and skepticism feeding exclusion.

ENDNOTES

1. Alexis de Tocqueville, *Democracy in America*, 282–83 (Phillips Bradley, ed. 1991) (original ed. 1835).
2. *Duncan v. Louisiana*, 391 U.S. 145, 156 (1968).
3. *McCleskey v. Kemp*, 481 U.S. 279, 310 (1987) (quoting *Strauder v. West Virginia*, 100 U.S. 303, 309 (1880)).
4. *Strauder v. West Virginia*, 100 U.S. 303 (1880).
5. *Edmonson v. Leesville Concrete Co., Inc.*, 111 S. Ct. 2077, 2081–82 (1991).
6. *Batson v. Kentucky*, 476 U.S. 79, 85 (1986).
7. Tanya E. Coke, "Lady Justice May Be Blind, But Is She a Soul Sister? Race-Neutrality and the Ideology of Representative Juries," 69 N.Y.U. L. Rev. 327, 359 (1994).
8. Randall Kennedy, *Race, Crime and the Law*, 168–230 (New York: Pantheon, 1997); Benno C. Schmidt, Jr., "Juries, Jurisdiction, and Race Discrimination: The Lost Promise of *Strauder v. West Virginia*," 61 Tex. L. Rev. 1401 (1983); Douglas L. Colbert, "Challenging the Challenge: The Thirteenth Amendment as a Prohibition Against the Racial Use of Peremptory Challenges," 76 Cornell L. Rev. 1, 13–32 (1990).
9. See, e.g., *Strauder v. West Virginia*, 100 U.S. 303 (1880); *Batson v. Kentucky*, 476 U.S. 79 (1986).

10. Bryan A. Stevenson & Ruth E. Friedman, "Deliberate Indifference: Judicial Tolerance of Racial Bias in Criminal Justice," 51 Wash. & Lee. L.Rev. 509, 519–24 (1994) ("The reality of the administration of criminal justice in the South is that a black defendant can still find himself facing a jury from which the overwhelming majority, if not all, of the prospective jurors of his race have been excluded."); Albert Alschuler & Andrew G. Deiss, "A Brief History of the Criminal Jury in the United States," 61 U. Chi.L.Rev. 867, 894–96 (1994); Stephanie Domitrovich, "Jury Source Lists and the Community's Need to Achieve Racial Balance on the Jury," 33 Duq. L. Rev. 39, 42 (1994); Tanya E. Coke, *Lady Justice, supra* note 7 at 345–46.

11. Ala. Code § 12-16-60(a) (1986). Georgia law similarly requires that trial jurors be "intelligent and upright," and requires that grand jurors be "among the most experienced, intelligent and upright persons of the county." O.C.G.A. § 15-12-60.

12. Hayward R. Alker, Jr., et al., "Jury Selection as a Biased Social Process," 11 L. & Soc'y Rev. 9, 31–33 (1976); Nancy J. King, "Racial Jurymandering: Cancer or Cure? A Contemporary Review of Affirmative Action in Jury Selection," 68 N.Y. U.L. Rev. 707, 712–19 (1993).

13. Hiroshi Fukurai, et al., *Race and the Jury*, 21–24, 64 (New York: Plenum Press, 1993); Kennedy, *supra* note 8 at 233; Morris B. Hoffman, "Peremptory Challenges Should Be Abolished: A Trial Judge's Perspective," 64 U.Chi. L. Rev. 809, 851 n.192 (1997) (federal judge noting that blacks, Hispanics, and the young have a "shockingly high" failure to appear rate after receiving jury summonses).

14. Leon F. Litwack, *North of Slavery: The Negro in the Free States 1790–1860*, 102 (Chicago: Univ. of Chicago Press, 1961).

15. Colbert, *Challenging the Challenge, supra* note 8 at 49–50.

16. Id. at 54–55 (noting that successful federal prosecutions for white-on-black violence increased from forty-three cases in 1870 to over 500 in 1872).

17. Id. at 62.

18. Act of March 1, 1875, ch. 114, § 4, 18 Stat. 335. See, e.g., *Cassell v. Texas*, 339 U.S. 282, 303 (1950) (Jackson, J., dissenting) (characterizing *Ex parte Virginia* as "solitary and neglected authority" for criminal prosecutions based on racially motivated jury exclusion).

19. *Strauder v. West Virginia*, 100 U.S. 303 (1880). The same day that the Court decided *Strauder*, it also upheld a conviction of a state judge for violating the 1875 jury selection statute. *Ex Parte Virginia*, 100 U.S. 339 (1880).

20. 100 U.S. at 306.

21. Id. at 308.

22. Id. at 309.

23. 100 U.S. at 309.

24. See Schmidt, *Juries, Jurisdiction, supra* note 8 at 1406. Indeed, Schmidt adds, during this time period, "virtually every embodiment of the legal process in the South, from the sheriff and police to the prosecutor, to the courtoom functionaries, to defense counsel, to the judges, was white." Id. at 1407.

25. 162 U.S. 592 (1896); see also *Gibson v. Mississippi*, 162 U.S. 565 (1896); *Brownfield v. South Carolina*, 189 U.S. 426 (1903); Schmidt, *Juries, Jurisdiction, supra* note 8 at 1463.

26. 103 U.S. 370 (1880).

27. 103 U.S. at 397.

28. 103 US. at 402–03 (quoting Delaware Supreme Court opinion).

29. 103 U.S. at 397.

30. 100 U.S. 313 (1880).

31. Schmidt, *Juries, Jurisdiction, supra* note 8 at 1488–99.

32. Id. at 1485–86.

33. Id. at 1486.

34. The Scottsboro case is discussed in Chapter 2, at pp. 67–68.

35. Schmidt, *Juries, Jurisdiction, supra* note 8 at 1478–79 (reporting the observation of Columbia Law School Professor Herbert Wechsler, who attended the argument).

36. *Norris v. Alabama*, 294 U.S. 587 (1935).

37. 294 U.S. at 598.

38. 294 U.S. at 590.

39. Jeffrey Abramson, *We, the Jury: The Jury System and the Ideal of Democracy*, 109 (New York: Basic Books, 1994); see, e.g., *Hale v. Kentucky*, 303 U.S. 613 (1938); *Pierre v. Louisiana*, 306 U.S. 354 (1939).

40. *Akins v. Texas*, 325 U.S. 398 (1945).

41. 325 U.S. at 406.

42. 325 U.S. at 410 (Murphy, J., dissenting).

43. *Turner v. Fouche*, 396 U.S. 346, 359 (1970).

44. *United State ex rel. Jackson v. Brady*, 133 F.2d 476, 478 (4th Cir.), *cert. denied*, 319 U.S. 746 (1943).

45. *Maxwell v. Stephens*, 348 F.2d 325, 333–34 (8th Cir.), *cert. denied*, 382 U.S. 944 (1965).

46. *United States ex rel. Chestnut v. Criminal Court of City of New York*, 442 F.2d 611, 614–16 (2d Cir.), *cert. denied*, 404 U.S. 856 (1971).

47. *Hoyt v. Florida*, 368 U.S. 57, 61–62 (1961).

48. *Taylor v. Louisiana*, 419 U.S. 522, 528 (1975). The Court's constitutional interpretation followed Congress's statutory lead. In 1968, Congress had enacted the Federal Jury Selection and Service Act, which declared that "all litigants in Federal courts entitled to trial by jury shall have the right to grand and petit juries selected at random from a fair cross section of the community in the district or division wherein the court convenes." 28 U.S.C. §1861.

49. 419 US. at 532 n.12 (quoting *Peters v. Kiff*, 407 U.S. 493, 502–04 (1972) (opinion of Marshall, J., joined by Douglas and Stewart, JJ.)).

50. *Castaneda v. Partida*, 430 U.S. 482, 510 (1977) (Powell, J., dissenting).

51. The Judicial Council of Georgia's *Jury Commissioner's Handbook*, for example, directs jury commissioners to take race and gender into account because "the percentage of each distinct group in the jury box must parallel the percentage of each group in the county's population of the eligible age." Judicial Council of Georgia, Administrative Office of the Courts, *Jury Commissioner's Handbook*, 18 (1993); see generally id. at 18–27 (on "balancing the box"). In DeKalb County, Georgia, jury commissioners have programmed a computer to ensure that each jury venire reflects the race and gender proportions of the county at large, because the voter registration list from which they generate the jury roll underrepresents particular groups, and therefore venires selected at random would not be representative. Andrew Kull, "Ra-

cial Justice," *The New Republic*, 30 November 1992, 18; see generally Nancy J. King, "Racial Jurymandering: Cancer or Cure? A Contemporary Review of Affirmative Action in Jury Selection," 68 N.Y.U.L. Rev. 707, 724 (1993) (listing different techniques used to create racially proportional jury venires). The pattern is repeated across the country, as jury commissioners seek to avoid Sixth Amendment challenges by ensuring that their jury venires reflect the race and sex composition of their districts.

52. *Adarand Constructors, Inc. v. Pena*, 515 U.S. 200 (1995); *Shaw v. Reno*, 509 U.S. 630 (1993).

53. This tension exists not merely between the Sixth Amendment and the Equal Protection Clause, but is also found within the Court's interpretation of each provision. Under the Equal Protection Clause, for example, while the Court expressly bans only *intentionally* race-based selection mechanisms, the test it has developed for identifying when jury discrimination has occurred, much like the Sixth Amendment test, looks in part to *effects*. In *Castaneda v. Partida*, 430 U.S. 482 (1977), the Court ruled that a criminal defendant makes out a prima facie claim of jury discrimination under the Equal Protection Clause by demonstrating that his or her ethnic group was "a recognizable, distinct class," and that over a significant period of time that group was substantially underrepresented in the jury venire relative to its proportion of the total population. The fact that statistical underrepresentation will make out a prima facie equal protection claim adds to the incentives to construct jury venires that roughly match the ethnic and gender percentages in the population at large.

   In addition, the Court's recognition — first noted in *Strauder* — that discriminatory exclusion of black jurors denies the black *defendant* equal protection of the laws is premised on the conclusion that race matters. Exclusion of jurors of the defendants' race can deny the black *defendant* equal protection only if having a black juror may make a difference in deliberations. Thus, while *Strauder*'s rule appears to require color-blindness in jury selection, the application of the rule is predicated on the recognition that race matters in jury deliberations, i.e., that jurors are not color-blind in their decisionmaking.

   Sixth Amendment doctrine reflects a similar tension, although here the dominant note is race consciousness, and the minor key is color-blindness. The Court insists, for example, that the Sixth Amendment does not require proportional representation, but merely bars the exclusion of distinctive groups. In theory, this mandate is reconcilable with color-blindness; all other things being equal, a race-neutral random-selection mechanism should achieve proportional representation or something close to it. But in practice, virtually every source of jury lists seems to disproportionately underrepresent some groups, and therefore, to provide a "fair cross section," that underrepresentation needs to be offset by affirmative consideration of factors such as race and gender.

54. 419 U.S. at 538; see also *Holland v. Illinois*, 110 S. Ct. 803 (1990) (Sixth Amendment does not apply to peremptory strikes used to construct petit jury).

55. *Batson v. Kentucky*, 476 U.S. 79, 85 n.6 (1986); see also *Akins v. Texas*, 325 U.S. 398, 403 (1945) ("The number of our races and nationalities stands in the way of evolution of such a conception" under the Equal Protection Clause).

56. Andrew Kull, *Racial Justice, supra* note 51 at 21.

57. Albert W. Alschuler, "The Supreme Court and the Jury: Voir Dire, Peremptory Challenges, and the Review of Jury Verdicts," 56 U.Chi. L. Rev. 153, 210–11 (1989).

58. Pluckik & Schwarts, "Jury Selection: Folklore or Science," 1 Crim. L. Bull. 4 (May 1965) (quoting Darrow, "Attorney for the Defense," Esquire, May 1936, 211).

59. Ted Gest & Constance Johnson, "The Justice System: Getting a Fair Trial," *U.S. News and World Rep.*, 25 May 1992, 36 (quoting Darrow). William H. Arpaia, a trial attorney of less renown, went further, opining that certain nationalities — namely the Italians, French, Jews (sic), Spanish, Greeks, Slavs, and the Irish — "are emotional and react to sympathy," while others — the Germans, Swedes, Norwegians, Finns, English, and the other Nordics — "are generally less apt to be swayed emotionally and less apt to return an excessive verdict." William H. Arpaia, "Hints to a Young Lawyer on Picking a Jury," 6 J. Mar. L.Q. 344, 345 (1941).

60. Melvin M. Belli, Sr., 3 *Modern Trials*, §§ 51.6-51.68 at 446–47 (St. Paul, MN: West Pub. Co., 2d ed. 1982); see also Joseph Kelner, "Jury Selection: The Prejudice Syndrome," 56 N.Y. St. B.J. 34, 36 (1984) ("hell may have no fury like a woman juror who is to decide the case of a young and attractive woman").

61. *N.Y. Times*, 17 November 1935, §4, at 7, col. 1 (quoted in Colbert, *Challenging the Challenge, supra* note 8 at 85 n.424).

62. Colbert, *Challenging the Challenge, supra* note 8 at 75–93.

63. *Swain v. State*, 375 Ala. 505, 515, 156 So.2d 368, 375 (1963), *aff'd*, 380 U.S. 202 (1965).

64. Steve McGonigle & Ted Timms, "Prosecutors Routinely Bar Blacks, Study Finds," *Dallas Morning News*, 9 March 1986, A1.

65. *Horton v. Zant*, 941 F.2d 1449, 1458 (11th Cir. 1991).

66. Ted Gest & Constance Johnson, "The Justice System: Getting a Fair Trial," *U.S. News & World Rep.*, 25 May 1992, 36, 38 (quoting NAACP Legal Defense Fund attorney George Kendall); see also *Georgia v. McCollum*, 112 S. Ct. 2348, 2360 n.1 (1992) (Thomas, J., concurring) (noting that the phrase "all-white jury" appeared over 200 times in the preceding five years in coverage of trials by the *New York Times*, *Los Angeles Times*, and *Chicago Tribune*).

67. Barry Siegel, "Storm Still Lingers Over Defense Attorney's Training Video," *L.A. Times*, 29 April 1997, A5 (quoting from Philadelphia district attorney training videotape).

68. Transcript from ABC "Good Morning America," 4 April 1997, "Do Prosecutors Try to Keep Blacks Off Juries?" (quoting Jack McMahon).

69. Barry Siegel, *L.A. Times*, 29 April 1997, *supra* note 67.

70. Tr. from ABC "Good Morning America," 4 April 1997, *supra* note 68.

71. 380 U.S. 202 (1965).

72. Id. at 220, 222.

73. Id. at 220.

74. 163 U.S. 537 (1896).

75. 380 U.S. at 221. Justice Rehnquist expressed the same view twenty years later, dissenting from the Court's ruling in *Batson v. Kentucky*, 476 U.S. 79, 137–38 (1986) (Rehnquist, J., dissenting): "In my view, there is simply nothing 'unequal' about the State's using its peremptory challenges to strike blacks from the jury in cases involving black defendants, so long as such challenges are also used to exclude whites in

cases involving white defendants, Hispanics in cases involving Hispanic defendants, Asians in cases involving Asian defendants, and so on."

76. 476 U.S. 79 (1986).

77. Kenneth J. Melilli, "Batson in Practice: What We Have Learned About Batson and Peremptory Challenges," 71 Notre Dame L. Rev. 447, 503 (1996); Jere W. Morehead, "When a Peremptory Challenge Is No Longer Peremptory: Batson's Unfortunate Failure to Eradicate Invidious Discrimination from Jury Selection," 43 DePaul L. Rev. 625 (1994); Jeffrey S. Brand, "The Supreme Court, Equal Protection, and Jury Selection: Denying that Race Still Matters," 1994 Wis. L. Rev. 511, 596–613 (1994).

78. Michael J. Raphael and Edward J. Ungvarsky, "Excuses, Excuses: Neutral Explanations Under *Batson v. Kentucky*," 27 U. Mich. J.L. Reform 229, 236 (1993).

79. Id. at 236–67; see also Brian J. Serr & Mark Maney, "Racism, Peremptory Challenges, and the Democratic Jury: The Jurisprudence of a Delicate Balance," 79 J. Crim. L. & Criminology 1, 44–47 (1988).

80. Bryan Stevenson & Ruth Friedman, *supra* note 8 at 520.

81. 115 S. Ct. 1769 (1995).

82. Id. at 1773 n. 4 (Stevens, J., dissenting) (quoting prosecutor)

83. Id. at 1771 (original emphasis).

84. Sheri Lynn Johnson, "The Language and Culture (Not to Say Race) of Peremptory Challenges," 35 Wm. & Mary L. Rev. 21, 59 (1993).

85. *Batson*, 476 U.S. at 106 (Marshall, J., concurring).

86. *Batson*, 476 U.S. at 98 n.21; *Hernandez*, 500 U.S. at 364.

87. Raphael & Ungvarsky, *supra* note 78 at 234–35.

88. "Racial Divide Affects Black, White Panelists," *Nat'l. L.J.*, 22 February 1993, 58–59.

89. See Nancy J. King, "Postconviction Review of Jury Discrimination: Measuring the Effects of Juror Race on Jury Decisions," 92 Mich. L. Rev. 63, 75–100 (1993) (reviewing jury discrimination studies and finding that race of jurors generally affects outcomes); Sheri Lynn Johnson, "Black Innocence and the White Jury," 83 Mich. L. Rev. 1611 (1983) (same); but cf. Jeffrey E. Pfeifer, "Reviewing the Empirical Evidence on Jury Racism: Findings of Discrimination or Discriminatory Findings?," 69 Neb. L. Rev. 230 (1990) (critiquing jury discrimination studies).

90. For-cause standards are set by state law, but they generally require a finding that the jurors "had such fixed opinions that they could not judge impartially the guilt of the defendant." *Mu'Min v. Virginia*, 500 U.S. 415, 430 (1991). If a juror shows some bias but says that he can render an impartial verdict nonetheless, he will not be struck for cause unless the judge finds him to lack credibility. Wayne R. LaFave & Jerold H. Israel, *Criminal Procedure*, 973 (St. Paul, MN: West Pub. Co., 2d ed. 1992); V. Hale Starr and Mark McCormick, *Jury Selection: An Attorney's Guide to Jury Law and Methods*, 303–4 (Boston: Little, Brown, 1985).

91. Randall Kennedy, "The Angry Juror," *Wall St. J.*, 30 September 1994, A12.

4—The Color of Punishment

On Friday, September 6, 1991, Donald "Peewee" Gaskins was executed in Columbia, South Carolina. He had confessed to stabbing, shooting, or drowning thirteen people, and had been convicted of ten murders. The last one, the murder of fellow inmate Rudolph Tyner, occurred while Gaskins was already serving multiple consecutive life sentences. The son of Tyner's victims paid Gaskins to commit the murder. Gaskins did it by giving Tyner a bomb disguised as a homemade radio.

The electric chair has seen people with better and worse records than Gaskins. What made Gaskins' execution unusual was not the number of prior murders, but the fact that Gaskins was white and Tyner, the man for whose death he was executed, was black. The last time South Carolina had executed a white person for killing a black person was more than a century earlier, in 1880. Gaskins was the first white person in the nation to be put to death for murdering a black person since 1976, when the death penalty was revived. (The Supreme Court declared the death penalty unconstitutional in 1972, but in 1976 it held that as long as jurors' discretion was guided by certain factors, the death penalty could be imposed constitutionally.) As of June 1998, only six other white men had been executed in the United States for killing black victims.[1] In the same 1976–1998 period, 115 black men were executed for killing white victims.

RACE AND THE DEATH PENALTY

Virtually every study of race and the death penalty has concluded that, all other things being equal, defendants who kill white victims are much more likely to receive the death penalty than those who kill black victims. The evidence regarding disparities based on the defendant's own race is more equivocal; some studies have found such discrimination, while others have not.[2] That disparities in death sentencing tend to be based on the race of the victim rather than the defendant should probably not be surprising. Whether a jury votes for death or life turns in large part on the jurors' sympathies for the victim; jurors at sentencing will rarely be sympathetic to the defendant, whatever his race, for they will have just found him guilty of murder. Juries remain predominantly white in most of the country, and apparently their sympathies lie more strongly with white than black victims.

The most exhaustive study of the racial breakdown of the death penalty was conducted by Professors David Baldus, George Woodworth, and Charles Pulaski. They studied more than 2,000 murder cases in Georgia in the 1970s. They divided the cases into three categories. At one extreme, such as multiple murders of strangers, nearly everyone convicted was sentenced to death. At the other extreme, such as murders of abusive husbands by battered women, the death penalty was almost never imposed. In the middle range, however, where the death penalty was sometimes but not always imposed, they found significant racial disparities.[3]

Baldus and his colleagues found that defendants charged with killing white victims received the death penalty eleven times more often than defendants charged with killing black victims. Black defendants charged with killing white victims received a death sentence 22 percent of the time, while white defendants charged with killing black victims received the death penalty in only 3 percent of the cases. Much of the disparity seemed attributable to Georgia prosecutors, who sought the death penalty in 70 percent of cases involving black defendants and white victims, but only 19 percent of cases involving white defendants and black victims.[4]

Raw numbers, however, can be misleading. If certain features, such as multiple murders, long criminal records, or strong eyewitness testimony, happen to be correlated with race in the sample, what appears to be a racial disparity may have a race-neutral explanation. Baldus and his colleagues therefore subjected the raw data to sophisticated statistical analysis to see if nonracial factors might explain the differences. But even after they accounted for thirty-nine nonracial variables, they found that defendants charged with killing white victims were 4.3 times more likely to receive a death sentence than defendants charged with killing blacks. Racial disparities based on the defendant's race, however, were minimal; black defendants were 1.1 times more likely to get the death penalty than white defendants. Still, when these figures were put together, black defendants who killed white victims had the highest chance of being sentenced to death.[5]

These are very troubling statistics. What's more, they have been replicated in virtually every other study of race and the death penalty. In 1990, the General Accounting Office reviewed twenty-eight empirical studies of race and the death penalty, and concluded that 82 percent of the studies demonstrated that the race of the victim influenced the likelihood of the defendant being charged with or receiving the death penalty.[6]

In 1987, the Supreme Court considered the constitutional significance of the Baldus statistics. Warren McCleskey, a black man facing the death penalty for killing a white police officer during an armed robbery, challenged the constitutionality of his sentence by relying on the Baldus study. McCleskey argued that by administering the death penalty in such a way that defendants who killed white victims were substantially more likely to receive a death sentence than defendants who killed black victims, Georgia had violated the Equal Protection Clause. In addition, he argued that the *risk* that race played a role in whether a defendant received life or death rendered the death penalty arbitrary, and therefore "cruel and unusual punishment" in violation of the Eighth Amendment.[7]

McCleskey v. Kemp, handled by Jack Boger and a team of lawyers from the NAACP Legal Defense and Educational Fund, was closely watched. On one hand, the statistical evidence of discrimination that Baldus had developed was the strongest ever presented to a court regarding race and criminal sentencing. On the other hand, a ruling in McCleskey's favor would for all practical purposes end (or at least greatly impede the imposition of) the death penalty in Georgia, and, to the extent such studies could be replicated in other states as well, perhaps across the country. The case was therefore widely viewed as the last systemic challenge to capital punishment in America. Because most members of the Supreme Court were not opposed to the death penalty, it seemed unlikely that the Court would rule for McCleskey. However, when the Court in 1972 had briefly declared the death penalty unconstitutional, it did so at least in part out of concern—at that time based only on anecdotal evidence—that the sanction was being implemented in a racially discriminatory fashion.[8]

By a one-vote margin, the Court rejected McCleskey's challenge. Turning first to his equal protection challenge, the Court stated that McCleskey had failed to prove that there was any racial discrimination in *his* case. The statistical showing was not particularly revealing on that issue, the Court reasoned, because each jury is unique. Thus, the fact that *other juries* imposed the death penalty more often on blacks who killed whites did not shed light on whether *McCleskey's jury* had been motivated by race. McCleskey could prevail only if he could prove that the prosecutor in his case had sought the death penalty, or that the jury in his case had imposed it, for racial reasons.

It is nearly impossible to make such a showing. For one thing, long-standing rules generally bar criminal defendants from obtaining discovery from the prosecution. Thus, unless the prosecutor admits to acting for racially biased reasons, it will be difficult to pin discrimination on the prosecutor. A similar rule bars inquiry into jury deliberations, and generally forbids introduction of evidence about jury deliberations even where a juror has chosen to make it public. So defendants are precluded from discovering evidence of intent from the two actors whose discriminatory intent the *McCleskey* Court required them to establish.

The difficulty of making a showing in the face of such hurdles is illustrated by a subsequent case from Georgia, *Dobbs v. Zant*.[9] Like McCleskey, Wilburn Dobbs had no access to the jury deliberations or to the prosecutor's motives, so he sought to prove discrimination with what other evidence was available. He used questions asked during jury selection to show that all the jurors on his case had expressed reservations about interracial dating and marriage, that several of the jurors referred to blacks as "colored," and that two admitted to using the word "nigger." He established that the judge who presided over his trial had opposed integration, and referred to Dobbs as "colored" at trial. Dobbs's own court-appointed attorney admitted to using the word "nigger," opined that blacks make good basketball players but not good teachers, and referred to the black community as a "black boy jungle." Both the district court and the court of appeals found this evidence insufficient to demonstrate that Dobbs had received the death penalty because he was black and his victim was white. Absent an explicit admission that a prosecutor, judge, or jury acted because of racial bias, the *McCleskey* standard cannot be met. Indeed, it never has been.

In view of the virtual impossibility of demonstrating bias in a particular case, McCleskey argued that his showing of a significant racial disparity across a wide range of cases ought to create at least an inference of discrimination, requiring the state to show that McCleskey's case was *not* affected by race. In other areas of the criminal law, such as the selection of jury venires or the use of peremptory strikes, the Court has permitted such inferences to be drawn from statistical patterns. But the Court declined to adopt such a rule in *McCleskey*. It reasoned that because each death penalty decision is unique and every jury is different, one cannot know what the racial breakdown of death sentences would look like absent discrimination. And seemingly without irony, the Court noted that the rules against inquiring into jurors' and prosecutors' motives would make it difficult for *prosecutors* to rebut the inference.

McCleskey also sought to assign responsibility to the Georgia legislature, arguing that it engaged in intentional discrimination by maintaining the death penalty with the knowledge that it was being administered in a racially disproportionate way. In other areas of the law, such as the rules governing civil and criminal liability for harming others, engaging in conduct with knowledge of its foreseeable consequences is sufficient to establish "intent."[10] The Court, however, defined intentional discrimination for equal protection purposes much more narrowly, as action taken to harm blacks "because of, not in spite of" their race. At most, the Baldus study showed that Georgia had continued to apply the death penalty in spite of its race-based effects; there was no showing that it did so for the purpose of harming blacks. Foreseeable consequences, the Court said, are not enough.

Unlike his equal protection claim, McCleskey's Eighth Amendment claim did not require a finding of invidious intent. Arbitrary punishment is "cruel and unusual" regardless of its intent. McCleskey argued that the *risk* of discrimination demonstrated by the Baldus study rendered capital punishment in Georgia arbitrary. The Court characterized the question as whether the Baldus study demonstrated a "constitutionally unacceptable risk" of discriminatory results. There is, of course, no objective yardstick for what risks are "constitutionally unacceptable." Justice William Brennan, dissenting, noted that it was more likely than not that had McCleskey killed a black man he would not have received the death penalty. Brennan argued that that level of risk was constitutionally unacceptable in capital sentencing, particularly given that we require certainty beyond a reasonable doubt before allowing a jury to impose a death sentence.

The majority, however, found the risk "constitutionally acceptable." Its rationale: discrimination is inevitable. It is a by-product of discretion, and discretion plays a necessary role in the implementation of the death penalty. The Court had previously ruled, for example, that mandatory death penalties were unconstitutional: a jury must have the option of not sentencing a defendant to death, because the decision to impose death must be tailored to the individual. Discretion is constitutionally required in order to provide individualized justice. In *McCleskey*, however, the Court confronted evidence that discretion was being used not to make individualized judgments, but to discriminate on group-based grounds. Race discrimination is the very antithesis of individualized judgment; it judges an individual not on the basis of his personal traits, but on the basis of his group identity. Yet the majority determined that this was an inevitable cost of discretion, and therefore not constitutionally unacceptable.

McCleskey may be the single most important decision the Court has ever issued on the subject of race and crime. The case's significance extends beyond Warren McCleskey, beyond the death penalty, and beyond the criminal justice system itself. Ultimately, it provides an important lesson in the limits of obtaining judicial relief for racial inequality. On both claims presented in McCleskey, reasonable people could disagree. There was nothing in the text of the Constitution, the history of its framing, or the Court's prior doctrine which required the Court to resolve either question for or against McCleskey. The Court split on both questions by the narrowest of margins. The question of what amounts to a "constitutionally unacceptable risk" has no determinate answer. And while the Court had previously rejected the argument that racial disparities in and of themselves constituted discrimination, it had been willing in related areas to adopt inferences of discrimination from strong statistical showings of racial disparity, and it had long recognized that "death is different," requiring heightened safeguards in the capital punishment setting.

What drove the majority to reach its result was not formal legal doctrine but pragmatic concerns about the judiciary's role in addressing racial disparity in America. The Court's most revealing passage comes at the very end of its opinion. Presented almost as an afterthought, it is in fact the key to the Court's approach to racial disparities in criminal justice. The passage begins with an understatement: "Two additional concerns inform our decision in this case." The first concern was that McCleskey's claim, "taken to its logical conclusion, throws into serious question the principles that underlie our entire criminal justice system."[11] If the Court were to accept the notion that racial disparities invalidated the death penalty, how would it treat other statistical disparities in criminal justice? The Court noted that racial disparities had been found in other criminal settings, and that disparities along other lines, such as gender, were also known to exist. Concerned about embarking on the slippery slope of policing the demographic distribution of criminal justice, the Court refused to take the first step.

This concern led to an "additional concern": "McCleskey's arguments are best presented to the legislative bodies."[12] Legislatures are better at assessing statistical studies and assigning moral significance to their findings. McCleskey's arguments were nothing less than a fundamental challenge to "the validity of capital punishment in our multi-racial society," and the sheer magnitude of that question, the Court believed, made it more appropriately addressed by the legislature. This was not a Court eager to go down the path that the Court had taken some fourteen years earlier in *Furman v. Georgia*, when the Court struck down the death penalty nationwide because its administration was arbitrary and capricious. The *McCleskey* Court seemed to be saying that the significance of racial disparity in criminal justice poses a political, not a legal question, better decided by a politically elected branch.

These institutional concerns explain not only the Court's decision in *McCleskey*, but its approach to racial disparity in the criminal justice system generally. Put most charitably, the Court's concern is that there is a vast discrepancy between the limits of what it can do and the depth and breadth of the racial problem. Racial disparities appear at virtually every point in the criminal justice system. Disparities within the criminal justice system in turn reflect disparities in social and economic conditions beyond that system. The problem of racial disparity is so widespread and deeply rooted that attempts to solve it at any particular point appear to be either hopelessly partial or steps on a slippery slope toward massive social restructuring. As an unelected institution, the Court cannot engage in the latter exercise, which would require the commitment of society at large. And the Court is equally reluctant to engage in the former, as such exercises may only underscore its impotence. In the face of a problem much bigger than it felt it could handle, the Court in *McCleskey* defined the problem away by declaring it not constitutional in nature, and deferred to the legislature.

Although this approach may be understandable, it is deeply problematic. First, it abandons perhaps the judiciary's most important role in a constitutional democracy—protecting interests otherwise unprotected in the political process. As Professor John Hart Ely has argued, the Court, an undemocratic institution in the heart of a democracy, is at its most legitimate where it counteracts defects in the majoritarian process.[13] One such defect—and the reason for the Bill of Rights and the Fourteenth Amendment—is that majorities tend to trample on the rights of disfavored minorities. And in the United States, African Americans are the paradigmatic disfavored minority group.

Perhaps the only people more disfavored than African Americans are accused criminals. Other than a promise to reduce taxes, few positions are easier for an American politician to espouse today than being tough on crime. Legislators have little interest in protecting the rights of accused criminals. So if the judiciary doesn't protect them, nobody will. To tell a member of a doubly disfavored minority such as Warren McCleskey to seek his remedy through the majoritarian process is to relegate him to no remedy at all.

This lesson has been borne out by recent history. Citing *McCleskey*'s final paragraph, civil rights advocates repeatedly proposed federal legislation to redress racial disparity in capital punishment. The proposed bills would direct courts to adopt a presumption of discrimination where defendants make a statistically significant demonstration of racial disparity. The government would then be required to come forward with a race-neutral explanation. These measures have always failed.[14] Opponents of the legislation inconsistently claim that there is no discrimination, and that enactment of the bills would effectively end the death penalty. If there really were no discrimination, the bills would have no impact; they would invalidate death sentences only where a defendant demonstrates statistically significant racial disparities and the state cannot rebut that showing. But reason is not what drives this issue; politicians simply have too little to gain from protecting the rights of death row inmates or African Americans, and too much to lose by being portrayed as soft on crime.

The second problem with the *McCleskey* Court's institutionally based reticence about providing relief is that the judiciary is already inextricably involved in the problem it seeks to avoid. Criminal justice is, after all, meted out through the courts. The Court's refusal to do anything to redress racial imbalances in criminal justice, therefore, is far less defensible than a refusal to redress imbalances in other institutions, such as private or public employment, where the court confronts a threshold question about whether it is appropriate to intrude on another institution. In criminal justice, the threshold of judicial involvement has already been passed, and declining to "intervene" is indistinguishable from abdicating responsibility.

Third, by declaring that the Baldus study presented no constitutional problem, the Court deflated much of the pressure for a legislative response. The reader of *McCleskey* comes away with conflicting messages. On the one hand, the Court states that discretion is fundamental to criminal justice, that discrimination is an inevitable by-product of discretion, and that therefore Baldus's statistics establish no constitutional violation. On the other hand, the Court suggests that legislative reform may be appropriate. But if discretion and the accompanying discrimination are inevitable, and not constitutionally problematic, there would seem to be no workable alternative and, in any event, little reason to change things.

The problems reflected by the Baldus study and the Court's and Congress's responses to it are not limited to the death penalty. As noted in the introduction, African Americans bear the brunt of the criminal law punishment that our society metes out. Blacks make up 12 percent of the population, but fill half the nation's jail and prison cells.[15] The per capita incarceration rate among blacks is seven times higher than among whites;[16] among men aged 25 to 29 the black incarceration rate is ten times the rate for whites.[17] In the District of Columbia in 1997, nearly 50 percent of young black men between the ages of eighteen and thirty-five were under criminal justice supervision.[18] There are more young black men under correctional supervision than in college.[19] And we increasingly rely on incarceration as our primary response to the problem of crime. As of December 1996, we incarcerated 1.6 million adults, giving us the second highest per capita incarceration rate in the world, behind only Russia.[20]

These figures are astonishing. But they are quietly accepted as "inevitable" by politicians and policy makers who seek above all to look tough on crime. The Supreme Court not only failed to step into the breach, but legitimated that attidude of inevitability in its *McCleskey* decision, by holding that such racial disparities need not even be explained, much less justified. The ultimate effect is to allow the white majority to assume "tough on crime" attitudes while imposing most of the cost of tough criminal sanctions on minorities.

THE WAR ON DRUGS

Tonya Drake, a twenty-five-year-old mother of four on welfare, needed the money. So when a man she hardly knew gave her a $100 bill and told her she could keep the change if she mailed a package for him, she agreed, even though she suspected it might contain drugs. The change amounted to $47.40. The package contained crack cocaine. And for that, Tonya Drake, whose only prior offenses were traffic violations, received a ten-year mandatory minimum prison sentence. When federal judge Richard A. Gadbois, Jr., sentenced her, he said, "This woman doesn't belong in prison for 10 years for what I understand she did. That's just crazy, but there's nothing I can do about it." Had the cocaine in the package been in powder rather than crack form, she would have faced a prison sentence of less than three years, with no mandatory minimum.[21]

Tonya Drake is joined by thousands of prisoners serving lengthy mandatory prison terms for federal crack cocaine violations.[22] What unites them is skin color. About 90 percent of federal crack cocaine defendants are black. Indeed, a 1992 U.S. Sentencing Commission study found that in seventeen states, not a single white had been prosecuted on federal crack cocaine charges.[23]

Crack cocaine is nothing more than powder cocaine cooked up with baking soda. Wholesalers deal in powder; retailers deal in crack. But under the federal sentencing guidelines, a small-time crack "retailer" caught selling 5 grams of crack receives the same prison sentence as a large-scale powder cocaine dealer convicted of distributing 500 grams of powder cocaine. The U.S. Sentencing Commission has estimated that 65 percent of crack users are white.[24] In 1992, however, 92.6 percent of those convicted for crimes involving crack cocaine were black, while only 4.7 percent were white; at the same time, 45.2 percent of defendants convicted for powder cocaine crimes were white, and only 20.7 percent were black.[25] In Minnesota, where state sentencing guidelines drew a similar distinction between crack and powder cocaine, African Americans made up 96.6 percent of those charged with possession of crack cocaine in 1988, while almost 80 percent of those charged with possession of powder cocaine were white.[26] Sentencing guidelines were ostensibly adopted to eliminate disparity in sentencing, yet the crack/powder distinction has ensured that significant racial inequities remain.

Black defendants have challenged the crack/powder disparity on constitutional grounds, but every federal challenge has failed.[27] The courts, echoing the Supreme Court in *McCleskey*, have held that "mere" statistical disparities do not prove that Congress or the Sentencing Commission adopted the disparities for the purpose of harming African Americans. And it is not wholly irrational to treat crack as more harmful than powder cocaine, because crack is more often associated with violence, is more potent as typically ingested, and is more accessible to low-income people. Accordingly, even though black cocaine offenders in the federal system serve sentences on average five years longer than white cocaine offenders, the courts see no constitutional problem.

In 1995, however, the U.S. Sentencing Commission, which administers the federal sentencing guidelines, concluded that the disparities could not be justified by qualitative differences between the two drugs, particularly as powder cocaine distributors provide the raw material for crack. It proposed to reduce the differential, noting the racial disparities and their corrosive effect on criminal justice generally.[28] Congress and President Clinton responded like politicians; they reframed the issue as whether we should be "tough on crime," and opposed any change. For the first time since the sentencing guidelines were created in 1984, Congress passed a law overriding a Sentencing Commission recommendation to alter the guidelines.[29]

In 1995, the Georgia Supreme Court very briefly took a different approach. Georgia has a "two strikes and you're out" sentencing scheme that imposes life imprisonment for a second drug offense. As of 1995, Georgia's district attorneys, who have unfettered discretion to decide whether to seek this penalty, had invoked it against only 1 percent of white defendants facing a second drug conviction, but against more than 16 percent of eligible black defendants. The result: 98.4 percent of those serving life sentences under the provision were black. On March 17, 1995, the Georgia Supreme Court ruled, by a 4-3 vote, that these figures presented a threshold case of discrimination, and required prosecutors to explain the disparity.[30]

Instead of offering an explanation, however, Georgia Attorney General Michael Bowers took the unusual step of filing a petition for rehearing signed by every one of the state's forty-six district attorneys, all of whom were white. The petition warned that the Court's approach was a "substantial step toward invalidating" the death penalty, and would "paralyze the criminal justice system," presumably because racial disparities in other areas might also have to be explained. Thirteen days later, the Georgia Supreme Court took the highly unusual step of reversing itself, and held that the figures established no discrimination and required no justification. The court's new decision relied almost exclusively on the U. S. Supreme Court's decision in *McCleskey*.[31]

The crack/powder differential and the Georgia experience with "two strikes and you're out" life sentences are but two examples of the widespread racial disparities caused by the war on drugs. Between 1986 and 1991, arrests of members of racial and ethnic minorities for all crimes increased by twice as much as nonminority arrests.[32] Yet when that figure is broken down by type of crime, drug offenses were the *only* area in which minority arrests actually increased more than nonminority arrests. The five-year increase in arrests of minorities for drug offenses was *almost ten times* the increase in arrests of white drug offenders.[33]

In 1992, the United States Public Health Service estimated, based on self-report surveys, that 76 percent of illicit drug users were white, 14 percent black, and 8 percent Hispanic—figures which roughly match each group's share of the general population.[34] Yet African Americans make up 35 percent of all drug arrests, 55 percent of all drug convictions, and 74 percent of all sentences for drug offenses.[35] In Baltimore, blacks are five times more likely than whites to be arrested for drug offenses.[36] In Columbus, Ohio, black males are less than 11 percent of the population, but account for 90 percent of drug arrests; they are arrested at a rate eighteen times greater than white males.[37] In Jacksonville, Florida, black males are 12 percent of the population, but 87 percent of drug arrests.[38] And in Minneapolis, black males are arrested for drugs at a rate twenty times that for white males.[39]

Similar racial disparities are found in incarceration rates for drug offenses. From 1986 to 1991, the number of white drug offenders incarcerated in state prisons increased by 110 percent, but the number of black drug offenders increased by 465 percent.[40] In New York, which has some of the most draconian drug laws in the country—selling two ounces of cocaine receives the same sentence as murder—90 percent of those incarcerated for drugs each year are black or Hispanic.[41] The "war on drugs" is also responsible for much of the growth in incarceration since 1980. Federal prisoners incarcerated for drug offenses increased nearly tenfold from 1980 to 1993, and that increase accounted for nearly three-quarters of the total increase in federal prisoners.[42] The number of state prisoners incarcerated for drug offenses during the same period increased at a similar rate.[43]

The same pattern emerges in the treatment of juveniles. Between 1986 and 1991, arrests of minority juveniles (under age eighteen) for drug offenses increased by 78 percent, while arrests of nonminority juveniles for drugs actually *decreased* by 34 percent.[44] As with adults, black youth are also treated progressively more severely than whites at each successive stage of the juvenile justice process. In 1991, white youth were involved in 50 percent of all drug-related cases, while black youth accounted for 48 percent.[45] Yet blacks were detained for drug violations at nearly twice the rate of whites.[46] Four times as many black juvenile drug cases were transferred to criminal courts for adult prosecution as white cases.[46] And black youth involved in drug-related cases were placed outside the home almost twice as often as white youth. These disparities are only getting worse: from 1987 to 1991, such placement for black juveniles in drug cases increased 28.5 percent, while placement for whites *decreased* 30 percent.[48] The situation in Baltimore is illustrative. In 1980, eighteen white juveniles and eighty-six black juveniles were arrested for selling drugs—already a fairly stark five-to-one disparity. In 1990, the number of white juveniles arrested on drug charges fell to thirteen, while the number of black juveniles arrested grew to 1,304—a disparity of more than one hundred to one.[49]

Thus, the victims of the war on drugs have been disproportionately black. Some argue that this is neither surprising nor problematic, but simply reflects the unfortunate fact that the drug problem itself disproportionately burdens the black community.[50] If more blacks are using and selling drugs, equal enforcement of the drug laws will lead to disproportionate arrests and incarceration of African Americans. Even if that were the case, the fact that the disparities increase at each successive stage of both the criminal and juvenile justice processes suggests that greater drug use by blacks is not the whole story. In addition, as noted earlier, official estimates of drug use by race do not reflect the disparities evident in the criminal justice system, and in fact suggest very little racial disparity in drug use.

The effects of the drug war are difficult to measure. Critics contend that drugs are just as prevalent and cheap today as they were before the crackdown began in the mid-1980s. Proponents point to signs that crack use has declined, and that teen use of drugs generally has also fallen. But it is extremely difficult to say whether these trends are a result of the war on drugs. Scholars find that drug use goes in cycles, but they have never been able to find a correlation between fluctuations in drug use and criminal-law enforcement. One thing is certain, however: the stigmatization and incarceration of such a high proportion of young African-American males for drug crimes will have significant adverse long-term effects on the black community. A criminal record makes it much more difficult to find a legitimate job. We are disabling tens of thousands of young black men at the outset of their careers. The short-term "benefits" of removing offenders from the community may well come back to haunt us in the long term.

THREE STRIKES

Not so long ago, "three strikes and you're out" was just a baseball slogan. Today, it passes for a correctional philosophy. And here again, African Americans are disproportionately the losers. Between 1993 and 1995, twenty-four states and the federal government adopted some form of "three strikes and you're out" legislation, under which repeat offenders face life sentences for a third felony conviction.[51] (Georgia and South Carolina went even further, adopting "two strikes and you're out" laws). California's three-strikes law, one of the first, was sparked by a repeat offender's abduction and murder of twelve-year-old Polly Klaas in Petaluma in 1993.[52] Under California's version, a second felony conviction doubles the sentence otherwise authorized, and a third felony conviction receives a mandatory twenty-five-year-to-life term, no matter how insubstantial the third conviction, so long as the prior convictions were for "violent" or "serious" crimes. The "three strikes" idea has been wildly popular; 72 percent of California's voters approved it in a popular referendum, and President Clinton himself jumped on the three-strikes bandwagon during the 1994 mid-term election campaign.[53] But the implementation of the laws has led to many problems.

First, the laws lead to draconian results. Jerry Dewayne Williams, for example, received a twenty-five-year sentence for stealing a slice of pizza from four young men at a Los Angeles beach.[54] Another defendant's third strike consisted of stealing five bottles of liquor from a supermarket.[55] In its first two years, California's law led to life sentences for twice as many marijuana users as murderers, rapists, and kidnappers combined.[56] A California Department of Corrections study reported that 85 percent of those sentenced under the law were convicted most recently of a nonviolent crime.[57] Some have argued that focusing on the third strike is an unfair basis for criticism, because most offenders sentenced under the law have long criminal histories.[58] But the law is triggered even where a defendant's prior offenses are in the distant past, the third conviction is for a minor offense, and there is little likelihood that public safety requires anything like a life sentence. Robert Wayne Washington, for example, received twenty-five years to life for a minor cocaine possession charge; his prior offenses were two eight-year-old burglaries and an intervening conviction for possession of contraband.[59]

Second, if the purpose of the law is to incapacitate those who would otherwise repeatedly prey on society, it is overinclusive. Most violent criminals have a relatively limited "criminal career," tailing off after ten years or so.[60] An individual's third strike often will not occur until his criminal career is on the wane. Thus, the three-strikes laws will impose life sentences on many offenders who pose little future danger to the community.

Third, such laws increase the costs of administering the criminal justice system. They make police work more dangerous, because a repeat offender facing a life sentence, in the words of Los Angeles Police Department spokesman Anthony Alba, is like "a cornered animal. If he knows he is going to get life in jail, he is definitely going to up the ante in eluding his captors."[61] Once apprehended, many defendants facing a third strike are unwilling to plead guilty, leading to a marked increase in criminal trials. Michael Judge, the chief public defender for Los Angeles County, said, "The law has created the single greatest increase in workload in the thirty years since I've been associated with the criminal justice system."[62] Two years into the California law's existence, an auditor estimated that it had cost Los Angeles County alone an extra $169 million.[63] The increase in criminal trials causes backlogs in the civil justice system, as the courts must increasingly devote themselves to criminal trials; as of 1996, 47 of California's 125 civil courts had to be diverted to hearing criminal cases.[64]

Three-strikes and other mandatory minimum laws have contributed to startling growth in our prison population. From 1980 to 1994, the national prison and jail population increased 195.6 percent.[65] By comparison, the general population increased from 1980 to 1990 by only 9.8 percent.[66] If the prison population continues to grow at the rate of increase from 1995–96, it would top 3.2 million in 2009. California alone has built seventeen new jails in the last fifteen years. Its prison spending has increased over that period from 2 percent to almost 10 percent of its state budget, and it now spends more on corrections than on higher education.[67]

Despite these problems, the three-strikes approach remains extraordinarily popular. Why? One possibility is that, as with many other "get tough" policies, its direct burdens fall disproportionately on minorities. The Georgia case discussed above involving racially disparate application of a two-strikes law is not unique. In California, for example, blacks make up only 7 percent of the general population, yet as of 1996 they accounted for 43 percent of the third-strike defendants sent to state prison. Whites, by contrast, make up 53 percent of the general population in California, but only 24.6 percent of third-strike prisoners. This means that blacks are being imprisoned under California's three-strikes law at a rate 13.3 times that of the rate for whites. And because three-strikes convicts serve such long sentences, their proportion of the prison population will steadily increase; third-strikers comprised 8 percent of the total prison population in 1996, but the California Department of Corrections estimates that by 2024 they will amount to 49 percent.[68] Without a change in direction, the already stark racial disparities in our nation's prisons will only get worse. Yet it is precisely for that reason that there is unlikely to be a change in direction. As long as the effects of this get-tough measure are felt principally in minority communities, there is not likely to be sufficient political pressure for change.

WHEN IS DISPARITY DISCRIMINATION?

As the figures above illustrate, it is beyond dispute that criminal sentencing is marked by stark racial *disparities*. But does this amount to *discrimination*? Everyone agrees that black defendants should not receive harsher penalties simply because they are black, and that criminals who attack white victims should not be punished more severely because the victims were white. But the disparities identified above may be attributable to factors other than race discrimination. Perhaps blacks commit more serious crimes per capita than whites. Social scientists and criminologists have long sought to determine through statistical analysis whether criminal sentencing is impermissibly affected by race, and have reached contradictory conclusions.

In the death penalty setting, as we have seen, most studies conclude that there is discrimination based on the race of the victim, even after controlling for other possible factors. In non-death penalty cases, however, the results are more mixed. In a 1993 study of the racial impact of the federal sentencing guidelines, for example, the U.S. Justice Department's Bureau of Justice Statistics found that although blacks on average received sentences that were almost two years longer than whites, the bulk of this disparity was due to the crack/cocaine sentencing disparity.[69] The study concluded that other racial differences in sentencing for drug trafficking, fraud, and embezzlement could be explained by nonracial factors such as prior prison records, guilty pleas, and severity of offense.[70] But the study also found that even after controlling for such factors, black offenders were 50 to 60 percent more likely to be sentenced for larceny than white offenders, and twice as likely as whites to be sentenced for weapons offenses.[71] Several other studies have concluded that racial disparities in sentencing are largely attributable to race-neutral factors, such as offense severity or prior criminal record.[72] Most criminologists agree that a substantial part—but not all—of sentencing disparity is attributable to blacks committing more serious crimes than whites.[73] However, all of these findings—both those that find discrimination and those that do not—are plagued by several inescapable problems.

First, in order to determine whether a racial *disparity* is the result of racial *discrimination*, one must compare similar cases. Where defendants similar in all respects but race are treated differently, one may reasonably conclude that discrimination has occurred. The rub lies in defining "similar." As Barbara Meierhoefer has argued,

> There is no disagreement that similar offenders should be sentenced similarly. The problem . . . is that there is no consensus as to what defines "similar offenders." Even outwardly empirical assessments of whether unwarranted disparity has been reduced will be strongly influenced by which offense and offender characteristics are selected to define "similarly situated" offenders.[74]

Thus, for example, critics of the Baldus study used in *McCleskey* have argued that it did not sufficiently identify "similar" cases, and that therefore its conclusion that the remaining disparities were racial in nature was flawed.[75]

Second, even if we could identify and agree on all relevant race-neutral factors that might conceivably explain a disparity, no study can possibly measure all such factors.[76] Some of the most important factors, such as strength of evidence, credibility of witnesses, or the effectiveness of a lawyer's representation, are simply not susceptible to quantification. Quantifiable factors may be missing from available data. No study can absolutely eliminate the possibility that some unaccounted-for race-neutral variable that correlates with race has caused the apparent racial disparity.

Third, statistical studies may also err in the opposite direction, by concealing racial discrimination. A study of sentencing decisions that found that all racial disparities could be explained by offense severity and prior criminal records, for example, might conceal racial discrimination in police or prosecutorial practices. If police officers observe, stop, and arrest blacks at a higher rate than whites because of their race, blacks are more likely to develop criminal records, all other things being equal. Similarly, if prosecutors offer more generous plea bargains to white than black defendants because of their race, black defendants' sentencing reports will reflect higher "offense severity" and more serious criminal records. By focusing only on one stage of the criminal justice system, a statistician may miss discrimination occurring at another stage. At the same time, statistical studies may miss discrimination if, in the aggregate, two forms of discrimination cancel each other out. For example, some biased sentencers might assign a longer sentence for a black-on-black crime because the *defendant* is black; others might impose a shorter sentence because the *victim* is black. If these biases cancel each other out in the aggregate, statistics may conceal actual discrimination.

For these reasons, statistical studies can rarely prove intentional discrimination. But even if none of the sentencing disparities outlined above is attributable to discrimination as the Supreme Court has defined it, they nonetheless raise serious questions about the racial fairness of our criminal justice policy. To see that this is so, one need only imagine the public response if the current racial disparities in criminal justice were reversed. Imagine what kind of pressure legislatures would feel, for example, if one in three young *white* men were in prison or on probation or parole. Imagine what the politics of the death penalty would look like if prosecutors sought the death penalty 70 percent of the time when whites killed blacks, but only 19 percent of the time when blacks killed whites. Or imagine what our juvenile justice policies would be like if white youth charged with drug offenses were four times as likely as black youth to be tried as adults, and twice as likely to be placed outside the home. One thing is certain: the nation would not accept such a situation as "inevitable."

Indeed, turning the tables on some of these statistics is almost beyond comprehension. If the per capita incarceration rate for whites were equal to that for blacks, more than 3.5 million white people would be incarcerated today, instead of 570,000, and we would need more than three times the prison capacity (and prosecution and court capacity) that we currently have. And because white people comprise about 80 percent of the general population, it would be literally impossible for whites to be overrepresented in the prison population to the same degree that black people currently are—four times their representation in the general population.

To see what happens when the criminal law begins to affect large numbers of white middle- and upper-class people, one need only look at the history of marijuana laws. The country's first marijuana users were largely nonwhite, mostly Mexicans.[77] By 1937, every state had criminalized marijuana. In the 1950s, federal penalties for the sale of marijuana ranged from two to five years imprisonment; a second offense brought a sentence of five to ten years; and a third brought ten to twenty years. State penalties followed suit. In 1956, Congress imposed mandatory minimum sentences for marijuana possession and sale.

In the 1960s, however, marijuana spread to the white middle and upper classes. By 1970, some college campuses reported that at least 70 percent of their student population had tried marijuana. As one author wrote in 1970, "Vast numbers of people have recently adopted the drug as their principal euphoriant; however, by all estimates, the new users are the sons and daughters of the middle class, not the ethnic minorities and ghetto residents formerly associated with marijuana."[78] The harsh penalties imposed when their effect was primarily felt by minorities were no longer acceptable, and marijuana laws were liberalized. As Dr. Stanley Yolles explained in 1970,

> Nobody cared when it was a ghetto problem. Marijuana—well, it was used by jazz musicians or the lower class, so you didn't care if they got 20 years. But when a nice, middle-class girl or boy in college gets busted for the same thing, then the whole community sits up and takes notice. And that's the name of the game today. The problem has begun to come home to roost—in all strata of society, in suburbia, in middle-class homes, in the colleges. Suddenly, the punitive, the vindictive approach was touching all classes of society. And now the most exciting thing that's really happening is the change in attitude by the people. Now we have a will-

ingness to examine the problem, as to whether it's an experimentation, or an illness rather than an "evil."[79]

Police and prosecutors began to leave users alone, and instead targeted dealers and sellers. The courts limited enforcement, using their discretion to invalidate convictions on a variety of grounds. And the legislatures amended the laws, eliminating strict penalties for possession. As one commentator described the development, "In response to the extraordinary explosion in marijuana consumption and the penetration of its use into the mainstream of American life, every state amended its penalties in some fashion between 1969 and 1972, the overall result being a massive downward shift in penalties for consumption-related offenses. Simple possession of less than one ounce was classified as a misdemeanor in all but eight states by the end of 1972."[80] In 1973, Oregon went further and actually decriminalized possession of small amounts of marijuana, and by 1981 ten other states had followed suit.[81]

When the effects of a criminal law reach the sons and daughters of the white majority, our response is not to get tough, but rather to get lenient. Americans have been able to sustain an unremittingly harsh tough-on-crime attitude precisely because the burden of punishment falls disproportionately on minority populations. The white majority could not possibly maintain its current attitude toward crime and punishment were the burden of punishment felt by the same white majority that prescribes it.

ENDNOTES

1. Death Penalty Information Center, "Facts About the Death Penalty," June 29, 1998.
2. See, e.g., U.S. Gen. Accounting Office, *Death Penalty Sentencing: Research Indicates Pattern of Racial Disparities*, 6 (1990) (overview of studies, finding evidence of race-of-defendant disparity equivocal); David C. Baldus, George Woodworth, & Charles A. Pulaski, Jr., "Reflections on the 'Inevitability' of Racial Discrimination in Capital Sentencing and the 'Impossibility' of its Prevention, Detection, and Correction," 51 Wash. & Lee L.Rev. 359, 386 n.115 (1994) (citing studies finding racial disparities in death penalty by race of defendant).
3. Mark Tushnet, *The Death Penalty*, 82 (New York: Facts on File, 1994).
4. *McCleskey v. Kemp*, 481 U.S. 279, 327 (1987) (Brennan, J., dissenting).
5. Id. at 321.
6. U.S. Gen. Accounting Office, *Death Penalty Sentencing*, *supra* note 2 at 5.
7. *McCleskey*, 481 U.S. at 367 (Stevens, J., dissenting).

8. *Furman v. Georgia*, 408 U.S. 238, 245 (1972) (Douglas, J., concurring).

9. 720 F. Supp. 1566 (N.D. Ga. 1989), *aff'd*, 963 F.2d 1403 (11th Cir. 1991), *rev'd and remanded on other grounds*, 506 U.S. 357 (1993).

10. In criminal law, for example, a person is "presumed to intend the natural and probable consequences of his acts." Wayne R. LaFave & Auston W. Scott, Jr., *Criminal Law* §3.5 at 225 (St. Paul, MN.: West Pub. Co., 2d ed. 1986). Similarly, in tort law intent "extends to those [actions] which the actor believes are substantially certain to follow from what the actor does." W. Page Keeton, et al., *Prosser and Keeton on Torts* §8 at 35 (St. Paul, MN: West Pub. Co., 5th ed. 1984).

11. 481 U.S. at 314–15.

12. Id. at 319.

13. John Hart Ely, *Democracy and Distrust: A Theory of Judicial Review* (Cambridge, MA: Harvard Univ. Press, 1980).

14. See generally Baldus et. al., *Reflections, supra* note 2 at 404 nn. 172–73.

15. Darrell K. Gilliard & Allen J. Beck, U.S. Dep't of Justice, *Prisoners in 1993*, 9 (1994).

16. Michael H. Tonry, *Malign Neglect: Race, Crime, and Punishment in America*, 29 (New York: Oxford Univ. Press, 1995).

17. Fox Butterfield, "Prison Population Growing Although Crime Rate Drops," *N.Y. Times*, 9 August 1998, 18; see also Marc Mauer, *Intended and Unintended Consequences of State Racial Disparities in Imprisonment*, 1 (Washington, D.C.: The Sentencing Project, January 1997); Darrell K. Gilliard & Allen J. Beck, *Prisoners in 1997*, 11 (Washington, D.C.: Bureau of Justice Statistics, 1998).

18. National Center on Institutions and Alternatives, *Hobbling a Generation: Young African Males in Washington, D.C.'s Criminal Justice System* (1997); Cheryl W. Thompson, "Young Blacks Entangled in Legal System; Report Puts D.C. Rate at 50% of Men 18 to 35," *Wash. Post*, 26 August 1997, B1.

19. In 1995, there were 711,600 black men in jail or prison. Bureau of Justice Statistics, *Sourcebook of Criminal Justice Statistics — 1996*, Table 6-12 (1997). The same year, there were 710,000 black men enrolled in college. *Statistical Abstract of the United States, 1997*, Table 286 (Lathan, MD: Bernam Press, 117th ed. 1997).

20. Christopher J. Mumola and Allen J. Beck, "Prisoners in 1996" (Bureau of Justice Statistics Bulletin, June 1997); Michael J. Sniffen, "Prison Population Increase is Slowing; Down from 8.1% Annual Rate," *Arizona Republic*, 23 June 1997, A1 (U.S. incarceration rate is 615 inmates per 100,000 U.S. residents, second only to Russia, which had a rate of 690 inmates per 100,000).

21. Jim Newton, "Judges Voice Anger Over Mandatory U.S. Sentences," *L.A. Times*, 21 August 1993, A1.

22. As of 1995, there were 14,000 people in prison for federal crack convictions, 80 percent of whom were black. Ronald Smothers, "Wave of Prison Uprisings Provokes Debate on Crack," *N.Y. Times*, 24 October 1995, A18.

23. H. R. Rep. No. 104-272 at 20 (1995), reprinted in 1995 U.S.C.C.A.N. 335, 353 (citing U.S. Sentencing Commission study).

24. *United States v. Armstrong*, 517 U.S. 456 (1996) (Stevens, J., dissenting) (citing United States Sentencing Commission, Special Report to Congress: *Cocaine and Federal Sentencing Policy*, 39, 161 (1995).

25. *United States v. Clary*, 846 F. Supp. 768, 787 (E.D. Mo. 1994); see also *United States v. Walls*, 841 F. Supp. 24, 28 (D.D.C. 1994).

26. *State v. Russell*, 477 N.W.2d 886, 887 n.1 (Minn. 1991). In the Eastern District of Missouri, 98.2 percent of defendants convicted of crack cocaine charges from 1988 to 1992 were black. *United States v. Clary*, 846 F. Supp. at 786.

27. See, e.g., *United States v. Richardson*, 130 F.3d 765 (7th Cir. 1997); *United States v. Andrade*, 94 F.3d 9 (1st Cir. 1996); *United States v. Teague*, 93 F.3d 81 (2d Cir. 1996), *cert. denied*, 117 S. Ct. 708 (1997); *United States v. Lloyd*, 10 F.3d 1197 (6th Cir. 1993), *cert. denied*, 513 U.S. 883 (1994); *United States v. Jackson*, 67 F.3d 1359 (8th Cir. 1995), *cert. denied*, 517 U.S. 1192 (1996).

28. United States Sentencing Comm., Special Report to the Congress, *supra* note 24.

29. In 1997, the Sentencing Commission recommended reducing rather than eliminating the disparity, and the Clinton Administration supported the proposal. As of this writing, Congress has not acted on the recommendation.

30. *Stephens v. State*, 1995 WL 116292 (Ga. S. Ct. Mar. 17, 1995).

31. *Stephens v. State*, 456 S.E.2d 560 (Ga. 1995).

32. American Bar Association, *The State of Criminal Justice*, 9 (February 1993) (23 percent minority increase, 10 percent nonminority).

33. Id.

34. Jerome G. Miller, *Search and Destroy: African American Males in the Criminal Justice System*, 81 (New York: Cambridge Univ. Press, 1996).

35. Marc Mauer & Tracy Huling, The Sentencing Project, *Young Black Americans and the Criminal Justice System: Five Years Later*, 12 (1995).

36. David J. Rothman, "The Crime of Punishment," *New York Rev. of Books*, 17 February 1994, 34, 37.

37. Jerome G. Miller, *Search and Destroy*, *supra* note 34 at 82.

38. Id.

39. Id.

40. Marc Mauer, *Intended and Unintended Consequences: State Racial Disparities in Imprisonment*, 10 (Sentencing Project, Jan. 1997).

41. Human Rights Watch, *Cruel and Unusual: Disproportionate Sentences for New York Drug Offenders*, 2 (March 1997).

42. Dep't of Justice, Bureau of Justice Statistics Bulletin, *Prisoners in 1994*, 10, Table 13 (1995).

43. Id. at 11, Table 14 (state prisoners incarcerated on drug offenses increased from 19,000 in 1980 to 186,000 in 1993).

44. American Bar Association, *State of Criminal Justice*, *supra* note 32 at 11.

45. Office of Juvenile Justice and Delinquency Programs, *Juvenile Court Statistics 1991*, 25, Table 35, 71, Table 114 (May 1994). In this source, Hispanic youth were included in the "white" racial category.

46. 13,800 black juveniles were detained for drug violations, as compared to 7,400 white juveniles. Id. at 74, Table 118, 28, Table 39.

47. Id. at 29, Table 40.

48. Id. at 25, Table 37.

49. National Center on Institutions and Alternatives, *Hobbling a Generation: Young African American Males in the Criminal Justice System of America's Cities: Baltimore, Maryland* (September 1992).

50. See, e.g., Randall Kennedy, "The State, Criminal Law, and Racial Discrimination: A

Comment," 107 Harv. L. Rev. 1255 (1994). For a detailed response, see David Cole, "The Paradox of Race and Crime: A Comment on Randall Kennedy's 'Politics of Distinction,'" 83 Geo. L.J. 2547 (1995); see also Randall Kennedy, "A Response to Professor Cole's 'Paradox of Race and Crime,'" 83 Geo. L.J. 2573 (1995).

51. National Institute of Justice, Department of Justice, *Three Strikes and You're Out: A Review of State Legislation*, 1 (September 1997); Tom Rhodes, "Third Strike and Pizza Thief Is Out for 25 Years," *The Times*, 4 April 1996 (available on NEXIS).

52. Maura Dolan & Tony Perry, "Justices Deal Blow to '3 Strikes,'" *L.A. Times*, 21 June 1996, A1.

53. Id.; see also The President's Radio Address, Weekly Comp. Pres. Doc. 1493 (July 16, 1994) (supporting "three strikes and you're out" provision in federal crime bill).

54. Rhodes, *supra* note 51.

55. Daniel B. Wood, "Softer Three-Strikes Law Brings Wave of Appeals," *Christian Science Monitor*, 24 June 1996, 3.

56. Christopher Davis, Richard Estes, and Vincent Schiraldi, *"Three Strikes:" The New Apartheid* (Report of the Center on Juvenile and Criminal Justice, San Francisco, March 1996).

57. Fox Butterfield, "Tough Law on Sentences is Criticized," *N.Y. Times*, 8 March 1996, A14.

58. See, e.g., Andy Furillo, "Most Offenders Have Long Criminal Histories," *Sacramento Bee*, 31 March 1996, A1.

59. Id.

60. William Spelman, *Criminal Incapacitation*, 15 (New York: Plenum Press, 1994) ("the typical criminal career lasts only 5 to 10 years"); 1 *Criminal Careers and Career Criminals*, 94 (Alfred Blumstein et al., eds.) (Washington, D.C.: National Academy Press, 1986) (same).

61. Daniel B. Wood, "LA Police Lash Out Against Three Strikes," *Christian Science Monitor*, 29 March 1996, 3.

62. Fox Butterfield, *supra* note 57.

63. Id.

64. Ian Katz, "Bull Market in Prisons and Knee-Jerk Politics," *The Guardian*, 25 May 1996 (available on NEXIS).

65. Bureau of Justice Statistics, *Sourcebook of Criminal Justice Statistics — 1995*, Table 6.11 (1996).

66. Ann Golenpaul, ed., *Information Please Almanac*, 829 (Boston: Houghton Mifflin, 1997).

67. Ian Katz, *supra* note 64.

68. Christopher Davis, et al., *supra* note 56 at 2.

69. Douglas C. McDonald & Kenneth E. Carlson, *Sentencing in the Federal Courts: Does Race Matter? The Transition to Sentencing Guidelines, 1986–90: Summary*, 1–2 (Washington, D.C.: Bureau of Justice Statistics, 1993).

70. Id. at 13–17.

71. Id. at 16–17.

72. See, e.g. Stephen Klein, Joan Petersilia, and Susan Turner, "Race and Imprisonment Decisions in California," 247 *Science* 812–16 (Feb. 16, 1990) (studying California sentences and concluding that race did not improve the accuracy of predicting what

THE COLOR OF PUNISHMENT — 157

type of punishment offenders would receive); Alfred Blumstein, "On the Racial Disproportionality of United States Prison Populations," 73 J. of Crim. L. & Crim. 1259 (1983) (finding little evidence of racial bias in incarceration for serious crimes); M. Tonry, *Malign Neglect, supra* note 16 (concluding that most racial disparity in incarceration is due to racial disparity in offending); but see Jerome Miller, *Search and Destroy, supra* note 34 at 61–71 (reviewing studies finding evidence of racial discrimination); Crutchfield, et. al, "Analytical and Aggregation Biases in Analysis of Imprisonment: Reconciling Discrepancies in Studies of Racial Disparity," 31 J. of Res. in Crime & Delinquency 178 (1994) (critiquing prior studies for aggregating information in a way that might conceal discrimination; finding evidence of discrimination).

73. M. Tonry, *Malign Neglect, supra* note 16 at 34.

74. Barbara S. Meierhoefer, "Individualized and Systemic Justice in the Federal Sentencing Process," 29 Am. Crim. L.Rev. 889, 891 (1992).

75. William Wilbanks, *The Myth of a Racist Criminal Justice System* (Monterey, CA: Brooks/Cole, 1986).

76. Stephen P. Klein, *Racial Disparities in Sentencing Decisions*, 5 (Santa Monica, CA: Rand, 1991).

77. Unless otherwise indicated, the information in the next two paragraphs is drawn from Bonnie Whitebread, "Marijuana Prohibition," 56 U.Va. L. Rev. 983 (1970).

78. Whitebread, 56 Va. L. Rev. at 1096.

79. Gertrude Samuels, "Pot, Hard Drugs, and the Law," *N.Y. Times Magazine*, 15 February 1970, 14.

80. Richard J. Bonnie, "The Meaning of 'Decriminalization': A Review of the Law," Contemporary Drug Problems 277, 278 (Fall 1981).

81. Id. at 279; see also Bureau of Justice Statistics, U.S. Dept of Justice, *Drugs, Crime and the Justice System*, 84–85 (1992) (reporting that when large numbers of white middle-class youth were arrested for marijuana possession in the late 1960s and early 1970s, public complaints led Congress and eleven states to decriminalize or reduce substantially the penalties for that crime).

5—See No Evil, Hear No Evil

In April 1992, federal and state agents on a joint drug crime task force raided Room 203 of La Mirage, a seedy motel in Los Angeles, and arrested Christopher Lee Armstrong and four of his companions. That month, a federal grand jury in Los Angeles indicted the men for conspiracy to distribute more than fifty grams of crack cocaine. All five were black. To the public defenders who were assigned to represent the men, the pattern was all too familiar. Of the twenty-four crack cocaine cases the public defender office closed in the prior year, all the defendants were black. And of the fifty-three crack cases the office completed over the prior three years, forty-eight defendants were black, five Hispanic, and none white. At the same time, they knew that many whites used crack, and that white defendants had been tried for crack cocaine charges in California's state court system, where the penalties are much less harsh. Armstrong's lawyers suspected that the authorities might be routing black defendants through the federal system, while directing white defendants into the more lenient state court system. If prosecutors were treating defendants differently based on their race, they reasoned, that conduct would violate equal protection and should require dismissal of the cases. However, the best evidence of what the prosecutors were doing and why they were doing it was in the prosecutors' control. So the defense lawyers submitted to the court the evidence of racial disparity that they had, and asked for the right to conduct "discovery" of the prosecution's files to determine whether their suspicions were in fact well-founded.

SELECTIVE PROSECUTION

In making their charge of "selective prosecution," Armstrong's lawyers were not advancing a new theory. The Supreme Court had recognized long before that selective enforcement of the laws based on race violates equal protection. In *Yick Wo v. Hopkins*,[1] the Court in 1886 unanimously overturned convictions of two Chinese men for operating laundries without a license. San Francisco authorities had arrested about 150 persons for operating laundries without a license—every one of them Chinese. They had denied licenses to all Chinese applicants. And they had granted licenses to all but one of the eighty or so non-Chinese laundry operators who applied. In a unanimous decision invalidating Yick Wo's conviction, the Supreme Court stated, "Though the law itself be fair on its face, and impartial in appearance, yet, if it is applied and administered by public authority with an evil eye and an unequal hand, so as practically to make unjust and illegal discriminations, between persons in similar circumstances, material to their rights, the denial of equal justice is still within the prohibition of the constitution."[2]

The principle the Court established in *Yick Wo* is straightforward: where the government discriminates based on race in its enforcement of the criminal law, it denies equal protection of the laws. Yet at the time Christopher Armstrong's lawyers made their selective prosecution claim, there had been no reported federal or state cases since 1886 that had dismissed a criminal prosecution on the ground that the prosecutor acted for racial reasons. It seems unlikely that this is because no federal or state prosecutor in over 100 years had engaged in racial discrimination. The more likely explanation is that it is virtually impossible to prove such a claim in court.

Criminal defendants making selective prosecution claims face a classic catch-22. To establish selective prosecution, a defendant must prove that the prosecutor singled him out for prosecution because of his race, and did not prosecute others engaged in the same conduct. The best—and usually the only—evidence on these issues is in the prosecutor's control. But the courts have ruled that defendants have no right to see the prosecutor's files until they first make a "colorable showing" of selective prosecution. Thus, a defendant must provide evidence of selective prosecution *before* he gets any access to the documents and other evidence necessary to establish the claim. In the vast majority of cases, this is an insurmountable hurdle. Absent a public admission from the prosecutor of racial animus, or a remarkable racial pattern of prosecutions, defendants are not likely even to obtain discovery, much less dismissal of their claims.

The pattern Armstrong's lawyers presented to the court was

quite remarkable: no white crack defendants prosecuted in federal court over a three-year period. In addition, defendants submitted two sworn statements. The first related a halfway house intake co-ordinator's observation that in his experience treating crack cocaine addicts, whites and blacks dealt and used the drug in equal propor-tions. (The United States Sentencing Commission subsequently re-ported in 1995 that 65 percent of those who have used crack are white.) Another, from a defense attorney experienced in state pros-ecutions, stated that many nonblack defendants were prosecuted for crack cocaine offenses in state court. The government's own evi-dence seemed to support the defendants' suspicions: it submitted a list of some 2,400 persons charged with federal crack cocaine vio-lations over a three-year period, of which all but eleven were black, and none were white.

The trial court deemed this evidence enough to justify discov-ery, to determine whether the allegations of racial selectivity were in fact well-founded. But the prosecutors refused to submit to the dis-covery, and appealed. In May 1996, the Supreme Court reversed.[3] It stated that Armstrong's evidence was insufficient because he had failed to identify any similarly situated white defendants who had been prosecuted in state court. The Court seemed to go out of its way to ensure that Armstrong's claims of race discrimination would not see the light of day. It dismissed the criminal defense attorney's affidavit, which presented precisely the information the Court said was missing, as "hearsay" that "reported personal conclusions based on anecdotal evidence." Yet the prosecutors had never ob-jected to the evidence in the trial court, and the general rule — which the Supreme Court enforces rigorously against criminal defen-dants — is that if one fails to object when evidence is introduced, the objection is waived. Only a single Justice, John Paul Stevens, dis-sented.

As the *Armstrong* decision suggests, and as the absence of any successful claims over more than a century confirms, the selective-prosecution defense is available in theory, but unattainable in prac-tice. Much like the guarantee of effective assistance of counsel, the nominal availability of the selective-prosecution defense does more to legitimate the status quo as nondiscriminatory than it does to protect defendants from discrimination. The Court's tactic for dealing with the issue—effectively blocking at the threshold the very investigation necessary to establish the claim—ensures that the courts will rarely if ever be forced to confront evidence of race discrimination in criminal prosecutions.

STANDING TO CHALLENGE RACIAL DISCRIMINATION IN CRIMINAL LAW ENFORCEMENT

The tactic of burying race discrimination claims before they can be made is not limited to selective prosecution; it is a consistent theme throughout virtually all of the Supreme Court's doctrine governing legal challenges to discrimination in the administration of criminal justice. The Court has imposed nearly insurmountable barriers to persons challenging race discrimination at all stages of the criminal justice system, from policing to judging to sentencing. With the exception of jury discrimination, the barriers are so high that few claims are even filed, notwithstanding shocking racial disparities and widespread belief among minority groups that criminal justice is enforced in a discriminatory manner. The few suits involving claims of criminal justice abuses along racial lines that have reached the Supreme Court have almost all been dismissed on technical grounds before the issue of discrimination could even be aired. This frees the Court from having to address the messy and troubling reality of racial inequality in criminal justice, but it is also likely to breed distrust and cynicism among those who feel that the system is unfairly administered.

Adolph Lyons, a twenty-four-year-old black man, filed such a suit, and his experience is illustrative. While driving his car in Los Angeles early in the morning of October 6, 1976, Lyons was pulled over by four police officers for a burnt-out taillight. Drawing their guns, the police ordered Lyons out of his car. He complied. They told him to face the car and spread his legs. He did so. They told him to put his hands on his head. Again, he followed their orders. After they subjected him to a patdown search, Lyons dropped his hands, at which point an officer slammed Lyons's hands back on his head. When Lyons complained of pain from the car keys he was holding, the officer applied a chokehold. Lyons lost consciousness and fell to the ground. When he came to, he was spitting up blood and dirt, had urinated and defecated, and had suffered permanent damage to his larynx. The officers issued a traffic ticket for the burnt-out taillight and sent him on his way.

Lyons sued to challenge the use of the chokehold in such circumstances. Between 1975 and 1980, the LAPD had applied the chokehold on 975 occasions. By the time Lyons's case reached the Supreme Court, sixteen persons had been killed by police use of the chokehold; twelve of the victims were black men. The Supreme Court, however, dismissed the case, ruling that Lyons lacked "standing" to seek an injunction against the practice.

The "standing" doctrine holds that courts may provide relief only where they are presented with a specific and concrete dispute. At a minimum, an individual must identify some injury caused by the defendant that will be remedied through the lawsuit. Lyons sought a court order limiting the LAPD's use of chokeholds in the future. The Supreme Court said he had no right to bring such a suit, because he could not show that he would encounter another chokehold again. That Lyons had been victimized by a chokehold in the past did not mean that he faced a threat of being subjected to one in the future. In the absence of a threat of future harm, the Court concluded, there was no concrete dispute between the parties justifying judicial intervention. In essence, the Court deemed the case too abstract to decide.

The matter was hardly abstract to Lyons. He argued that, as a black man, he could not drive his car in Los Angeles without fearing that he would be pulled over again and subjected to another chokehold. Because the police had applied the chokehold even though Lyons had cooperated fully, there was nothing short of a lawsuit he could do to protect himself. Yet the Court held that in order to have standing,

> Lyons would have had not only to allege that he would have another encounter with the police but also to make the incredible assertion either (1) that *all* police officers in Los Angeles *always* choke any citizen with whom they happen to have an encounter, whether for the purpose of

arrest, issuing a citation or for questioning, or (2) that the City ordered or authorized police officers to act in such manner.[4]

Lyons did not explicitly allege race discrimination, although the statistics on chokehold deaths suggest that black men had particular reason to fear its application. But the Court's holding makes it difficult to challenge any discriminatory applications of criminal law authority. Because criminal law is by its nature enforced selectively and intermittently, individuals will rarely be able to satisfy the Court's requirement that they show that an encounter with the police, a prosecutor, or judge, is sufficiently likely to recur to them in the future.

Two racially charged precursors to *Lyons* illustrate the point. *O'Shea v. Littleton*[5] arose out of the civil rights struggle in Cairo, Illinois, in the early 1970s. The plaintiffs were seventeen blacks and two whites who had been engaged in peaceful demonstrations and boycotts against racially discriminatory stores. They alleged that Cairo's criminal justice authorities were conducting a race war in retaliation for their political activities. They specifically charged that the state prosecutor, investigator, and police commissioner sought harsher penalties against black criminal defendants, and impeded black citizens' ability to have the law enforced against whites who harmed them. They also charged the local judges with setting bail rates higher for black than for white defendants. Several plaintiffs had been subject to the practices they complained of, which they claimed were motivated both by their race and by their continuing involvement in civil rights activities.

As in *Lyons*, the Supreme Court ruled that the case should be dismissed for lack of a "case or controversy." Although some of the plaintiffs had been victimized in the past, the Court stated, "past exposure to illegal conduct does not in itself show a present case or controversy regarding injunctive relief . . . if unaccompanied by any continuing, present adverse effects."[6]

Two years later, the Court reaffirmed its resistance to judicial oversight of criminal law enforcement. *Rizzo v. Goode*[7] involved the notorious Philadelphia police department, and the equally notorious Frank Rizzo, who was police chief when the case began and mayor when it ended. Rizzo prided himself on being tough on crime. During his mayoral campaign he vowed, "I'm gonna make Attila the Hun look like a faggot after this election's over," and stated that "the way to treat criminals is *spacco il capa*" — to bust their heads.[8] During his eight years as mayor, fatal shootings by Philadelphia police officers increased by about 20 percent *per year*.[9] The *Rizzo* case involved two consolidated class action lawsuits, both of which charged that the Philadelphia police force had engaged in a pattern and practice of police misconduct, and had adopted a civilian complaint procedure that was more effective at deterring civilians from filing complaints than at controlling or punishing police abuse. The district court heard 250 witnesses over the course of twenty-one days, and made detailed factual findings on approximately forty incidents of alleged police abuse. The district court found that "it is impossible to avoid the conclusion that, in the absence of probable cause for arrest, at least two classes of individuals are particularly likely to be subjected to [abuse]: poor blacks, and individuals who question or protest the initial police action."[10] It also concluded that the constitutional violations it found "cannot be dismissed as rare isolated instances."[11] Finding that the civilian complaint procedure was grossly inadequate, the court ordered the police department to implement an improved complaint procedure.

The Supreme Court reversed. Citing *O'Shea*, it expressed serious doubts as to whether the case presented a case or controversy, again because there was insufficient likelihood that the plaintiffs would be subjected to police misconduct in the future. After the Supreme Court issued its decision in *Rizzo*, the Civil Rights Division of the Justice Department launched an eight-month federal investigation into allegations of police brutality in Philadelphia. At the close of that investigation, the Justice Department itself sued the City of Philadelphia, claiming that it had discovered an extensive pattern of constitutional violations, that the police department exercised inadequate supervision, and that the misconduct was disproportionately directed at black and Hispanic citizens.[12] Backed by resources not available to private plaintiffs, the Justice Department was armed with evidence of hundreds of incidents of misconduct and abuse. It found that blacks and Hispanics comprised about a third of Philadelphia's population, but accounted for about 60 to 70 percent of the complaints of physical abuse, illegal searches and seizures, and unlawful detentions.[13] Nonetheless, the district court, reading the signs from *Rizzo* and *O'Shea*, dismissed the complaint on its own initiative.[14] The court of appeals affirmed. If the Justice Department itself could not prevail in such a suit, there is little hope for anyone else to do so.

In *Lyons*, *O'Shea*, and *Rizzo*, the Supreme Court repeatedly turned back legal challenges to constitutional violations in the administration of criminal justice, each of which involved claims of racial discrimination or racially disparate impact. It did so, moreover, not on the merits, but by barring such suits at the threshold. It defined standing to sue in such narrow terms that few will ever be able to satisfy its requirements in connection with a challenge to criminal law enforcement. Much like the selective prosecution cases, these rulings have the effect of foreclosing claims of discrimination before they are even aired. Because the bars operate at the threshold of the lawsuit, cases are frequently dismissed before the allegations of discrimination can even be developed. They never see the light of day. In this way, the illusion is maintained that the system forbids discrimination; the reality is that the system for all practical purposes forbids discrimination *cases*.

LIMITS ON SUITS FOR DAMAGES

The restrictions erected in *O'Shea*, *Rizzo*, and *Lyons* apply only to suits for injunctive relief. Thus, the Supreme Court stated that Adolph Lyons could have sued the LAPD for money damages for the injuries he suffered. But suits for monetary compensation face their own set of hurdles, in many instances more formidable even than those that apply to requests for injunctions. Consider a situation faced by many black parents: your son is stopped without cause by a state police officer, ordered out of his car, and searched illegally. You want to challenge the conduct, which appeared to be predicated on nothing more than your son's race. You can't sue for injunctive relief, because you can't show that he will be stopped again, so you want to sue for damages. Who can you sue?

Not the state and not the state police. The Supreme Court has held that the state and its offices are immune from federal suits for damages under the Eleventh Amendment to the Constitution.[15] The Eleventh Amendment literally protects states only from being sued in federal court "by citizens of another state," but the Supreme Court has interpreted it broadly to bar *any* federal suits for damages against states absent their consent. The Court has also held that states cannot be sued for damages for constitutional rights violations in state court.[16] Thus, the state, the defendant with the deepest pocket, is immune.

If the police officer were employed by a city rather than by the state, you could sue the city, but only if you could point to a city policy or custom authorizing such illegal stops and searches.[17] Because most cities do not have such policies, and "custom" is notoriously hard to prove, suing the city is often not a realistic option either.

That leaves the individual officer. But the Supreme Court has also granted government officials substantial protection from suit. Some officials are absolutely immune: judges, for example, can't be sued for damages for discrimination in the courtroom, nor can prosecutors be sued for damages for discriminatory prosecutions, no matter how strong the evidence of wrongdoing. Police officers and other government officials may be sued, but they, too, have a form of immunity: under the judicially created doctrine of "qualified immunity," they may be held liable for constitutional violations only if it was clearly established at the time the conduct occurred that their actions were illegal.[18] The idea behind this doctrine makes some sense standing alone: individual officers should not be held personally liable for their wrongdoing if they could not reasonably have known that their conduct was illegal. But the Supreme Court has interpreted this immunity so broadly that, in its own words, "all but the plainly incompetent or those who knowingly violate the law" are immune.[19] As a result, shockingly few damages actions for government misconduct succeed. For example, of some 12,000 actions filed against federal officials for constitutional violations from 1971 to 1985, only four led to a successful judgment or settlement for the plaintiff.[20] When the qualified immunity rule is combined with the bars on suits against states and cities, the result often means that *no one* can be sued for a constitutional violation. The victim is made to bear the costs of the violation himself.

In addition to these legal barriers to relief, there are numerous practical hurdles to bringing a suit for damages. In many instances the violation of constitutional rights does not lead to any tangible harm. An illegal search motivated by race, for example, may be extremely intrusive and humiliating, but as long as the police do no physical damage, it will be difficult to point to harm for which one should be compensated. In addition, many such suits reduce to a swearing match between a police officer and the individual stopped. Because those who are stopped are disproportionately poor and members of minority groups, they may find it difficult to convince a judge or jury to accept their word over a police officer's.

Finally, as the *McCleskey* case demonstrated, to establish an equal protection violation, one must prove *intentional* discrimination, and it is extremely difficult to do so. Government officials do not commonly admit that their actions were motivated by prejudice. Indeed, because there is such a strong social sanction against racial prejudice, few people are even willing to admit to themselves that they have acted for racial reasons. Yet racial stereotypes affect all of us in subtle and not-so-subtle ways. The Court's prohibition of intentional discrimination weeds out the bigots who admit they are racist, but ignores (and thereby effectively legitimates) all other discrimination.

Thus, despite the Supreme Court's assurances to Lyons that he could seek damages, the likelihood of obtaining any relief in any case challenging discriminatory law enforcement is slim. This is true whether one seeks to raise selective prosecution as a defense to a particular criminal prosecution, whether one seeks injunctive relief to forestall future violations, or whether one seeks only monetary compensation for an individual case. In each setting, the Court has constructed a set of all-but-impassable barriers. And in each area, the hurdles operate at the threshold, stopping the complaint from even being aired. In this way, the illusion of a constitutional prohibition against discrimination in criminal justice is maintained, but the avenue left open for enforcing it is so narrow and difficult that few will succeed in navigating its course. At one level, that may have the effect of legitimating the system; the courts can say that they abhor and forbid race discrimination, but that they simply do not see it. But as I suggest in the next chapter, at a deeper level this strategy eats away at the system's legitimacy. The charade cannot be maintained forever. Ultimately members of minority groups are likely to conclude that the courts and the law cannot be counted on to guarantee equal protection.

ENDNOTES

1. 118 U.S. 356 (1886).
2. Id. at 373–74.
3. *United States v. Armstrong*, 517 U.S. 456 (1996).
4. *City of Los Angeles v. Lyons*, 461 U.S. 95, 105 (1983).
5. 414 U.S. 488 (1974).
6. 414 U.S. at 495–96.
7. *Rizzo v. Goode*, 423 U.S. 362 (1976).
8. Ralph Cipriano & Tom Infield, "You Either Loved Him or Hated Him," *Phila. Inquirer*, 17 July 1991, 1A.
9. Jerome H. Skolnick & James J. Fyfe, *Above the Law: Police and the Excessive Use of Force*, 140 (1993).
10. *COPPAR v. Rizzo*, 357 F. Supp. 1289, 1317 (E.D. Pa. 1973).
11. Id. at 1319.
12. *United States v. City of Philadelphia*, 644 F.2d 187 (3d Cir. 1980).
13. 644 F.2d at 210 (Gibbons, J., dissenting from denial of petition for rehearing).
14. Id. at 209.
15. *Quern v. Jordan*, 440 U.S. 332 (1979).
16. *Will v. Mich. Dept. of State Police*, 491 U.S. 58 (1989).
17. *Monell v. Dept. of Social Services*, 436 U.S. 658 (1978).
18. *Harlow v. Fitzgerald*, 457 U.S. 800 (1982).
19. *Malley v. Briggs*, 475 U.S. 335, 341 (1986).
20. Written Statement of John J. Farley, III, Director, Torts Branch, Civil Division, U.S. Dept. of Justice, to the Litigation Section of the Bar of the District of Columbia (May 1985); cited in Cornelia Pillard, *Taking Fiction Seriously*, manuscript on file with author.

6—The Costs of Inequality

T
he inequalities and disparities discussed in the preceding chapters are for the most part not the result of intentional discrimination, at least in the narrow sense that the Supreme Court has defined that term. Rather, I think it more likely that they reflect human nature; it is human nature to avoid difficult choices, and the rules set out above are "useful" in avoiding the difficult choices inevitably posed by the administration of criminal justice. But while the inequalities are "useful" in this sense, they also have substantial costs. The costs begin with the obstruction of law enforcement but ultimately extend much further, contributing to crime and deepening race and class divisions.

OBSTRUCTING LAW ENFORCEMENT

Consider the following stories:

- Richmond, Virginia's Police Chief Marty Tapscott called it a "conspiracy of silence." Twenty-four-year-old Isham Draughn, Richmond's first murder victim of 1993, was shot in the back of the head early one morning in the parking lot of a McDonald's, where he worked as a security guard. He had been trying to make an arrest in an unruly crowd of 300 to 500 persons. Although hundreds of witnesses saw the slaying, no one would cooperate with the police in the investigation.[1]
- The Des Moines, Iowa police thought they knew who killed Mark Atkins in March 1996—two cousins, Howard and Antonio Nelson. But they had to drop charges against them because witnesses were unwilling to cooperate. As Rev. Keith A. Ratliff, president of the local NAACP chapter, explained to a *Des Moines Register* reporter, cooperation can be elusive because police officers are not viewed as "friends and co-workers in the inner city because of the historic treatment of minorities and poor whites."[2]
- In Baltimore, a jury of eleven blacks and an Asian American acquitted Davon Neverson of murder, despite hearing four witnesses testify that they saw Neverson commit the crime and two others testify that Neverson told them he did it. The Asian-American juror reported to the judge that race may have played a role in the decision.[3]
- Eric Holder, currently the Deputy Attorney General for the United States, served for five years as a trial judge in the District of Columbia.

Holder, an African American, estimates that he presided over at least ten trials involving nonviolent drug possession charges in which hung juries were caused by a "holdout" who said, in Holder's words, "I just was not going to vote to send another young black man to prison." Holder elaborates, "There are some folks who have been so seared by racism, who are so affected by what has happened to them because they are black, that, even if you're the most credible, upfront black man or woman in law enforcement, you're never going to be able to reach them."[4]

- In the Bronx, where juries are more than 80 percent black and Hispanic, juries acquit black defendants in felony cases 47.6 percent of the time, and Hispanics 37.6 percent of the time, as compared to a national acquittal rate of 17 percent for all races.[5]
- In Chicago, 60 percent of residents in African-American neighborhoods do not even respond to calls for jury service. By contrast, only 8 percent fail to respond in white neighborhoods. Standish Wills, Chair of the Chicago Conference on Black Lawyers, says that part of the problem is that "black people, to a great extent, don't have a lot of faith in the criminal justice system."[6]

These stories are increasingly common, and they illustrate one of the costs of exploiting inequality to avoid the hard choices presented by a system of criminal justice. While "using inequality" may seem less costly than extending constitutional protections equally to all, crime control turns largely on people's faith and trust in the criminal justice system, and on the cohesive strength of communities. Double standards directly undermine the faith of poor and minority communities in the criminal law, and indirectly contribute to the weakening of community ties. When the law loses its legitimacy within a particular community, law enforcement is left to rely on a far less effective tool: brute force. As the U.S. Court of Appeals for the Second Circuit stated twenty-five years ago, "[n]othing can corrode respect for the law more than the knowledge that the government looks beyond the law itself to arbitrary considerations such as race . . . as the basis for determining its applicability."[7]

Polls routinely demonstrate that blacks distrust the criminal justice system in greater numbers than whites. A 1995 Gallup poll found that 77 percent of blacks and 45 percent of whites think the criminal justice system treats blacks more harshly than whites.[8] A 1995 U.S. Justice Department survey found that only 31 percent of blacks nationwide "expressed a great deal or quite a lot" of confidence in the police, as compared with 65 percent of whites.[9] A 1994 New York Times poll found that 58 percent of blacks viewed the police as corrupt, as compared to 32 percent of whites.[10] The dramatically different responses of most black and white citizens to the acquittal in *California v. O.J. Simpson* brought home to all Americans the depth of the division in black and white perceptions of crime and criminal justice.[11]

The rich and poor also have divergent views on criminal justice, although the differences here are less stark (and less studied) than the differences between whites and blacks. When a 1992 Louis Harris poll asked respondents to rate police officers in their area, those with incomes above $50,000 had a much better view of the police than those with incomes under $7,500. Asked to rank police officers on treating people fairly, 27 percent of those in the upper-income bracket rated them "excellent," while only 11 percent of those in the lower-income bracket did so. At the other end of the scale, 28 percent of the wealthy rated officers' performance as "only fair" or "poor," while 46 percent of the poor gave those assessments. When asked to rank police officers' use of force, 31 percent of the wealthy but only 17 percent of the poor ranked the police as "excellent."[12]

As the anecdotes that opened this chapter illustrate, popular faith in the criminal justice system is critical because without public cooperation, criminal law enforcement is deeply compromised. Police officers rely on citizens' information to prevent and detect crime. Prosecutors rely on citizens to testify as witnesses. And prosecutors and courts rely on citizens to serve as jurors and to apply the law to their peers. Where a community views the criminal law as just, such cooperation can be assumed. But where a community views the law as unjust, enforcement is subverted. Police find it more difficult to get leads, prosecutors find witnesses more reluctant to testify, and jurors may engage in nullification.

ENCOURAGING CRIME

The community's faith in the criminal justice system is also important at a deeper level. The vast majority of people obey the criminal law. They do so not because they fear imprisonment, but because they think it is the right thing to do — in other words, because their personal and peer group values are consonant with the criminal law, and because they believe in the legitimacy of legal authority. Fear of incarceration plays little role because the chances of being apprehended and punished for most crimes are very small. For example, the odds of going to prison for assault, burglary, larceny, or motor-vehicle theft are one hundred to one.[13] Victimless crimes such as drug possession and distribution are even more unlikely to lead to incarceration. As a result, the deterrent effects of incarceration are not likely to play a significant role in a citizen's decision to obey or to violate the law.[14]

Two factors appear to play a much more significant role than does the threat of incarceration: (1) the extent to which the individual views the legal system as legitimate, and therefore internalizes the mores reflected in the criminal law; and (2) the extent to which the individual fears shame within his or her community or family. These factors are closely interrelated. One's views about the legitimacy of the legal system and internalization of its mores will be shaped by the views of the community in which one lives.

Social psychologist Tom Tyler has found that those who view legal authority as legitimate are generally more likely to comply with the law, and that those who have a favorable view of the performance of the police and the courts are especially likely to comply. Those who view the performance of police and courts negatively, by contrast, are less likely to play by the rules.[15] Most significantly, people's "[v]iews about authority are strongly connected to judgments of the fairness of the procedures through which authorities make decisions."[16] Indeed, people's beliefs about *procedures* are often *more* important to their evaluations of the legitimacy of a justice system than their beliefs about the fairness of substantive outcomes. Studies have found this to be true in many settings, including judicial proceedings and police encounters.[17] These findings suggest that where people view criminal justice procedures as unfairly biased, they will be especially likely to consider the law illegitimate, and therefore less likely to comply with the law. As Austin Sarat has argued, "the perception of unequal treatment is the single most important source of popular dissatisfaction with the American legal system."[18]

A second important factor in why people obey the law is fear of disapproval within their communities. In one study, for example, children reported that they were much more afraid of what their parents or friends might think if they were apprehended for delinquent behavior than of what punishment the system would mete out.[19] Sociologists Robert Meier and Weldon Johnson similarly found that fear of peers' disapproval is more important than formal legal sanctions in explaining why people obey the law.[20] And Charles Tittle found that social control is predicated not on formal sanctions, but is instead "rooted almost entirely in how people perceive the potential for negative reactions from interpersonal acquaintances."[21]

The importance of social ties is reinforced by noting which demographic groups are most likely to commit crime in our society: men more than women; youth more than adults; single people more than married persons; the unemployed more than those with steady jobs; children who do poorly in school or feel alienated from their parents more than children who are successful students and attached to their parents; people living in large cities or areas characterized by high residential mobility more than people in small towns with stable populations; and racial minorities and the poor more than the white majority or the privileged.

Australian criminologist John Braithwaite has argued that these widely accepted demographic facts are best explained by reference to community ties.[22] The groups more likely to commit crime tend to lead more isolated lives, while the groups less likely to commit crime are typically more connected to their communities. Women, for example, are historically raised with an emphasis on their interrelationships with others in the community, while men are historically raised to be independent.[23] Teenage boys and young men, the highest offenders, are at a point in their lives when they are asserting their independence, breaking out of the families that raised them, and not yet settled into new families. Unmarried persons, the unemployed, children alienated from family and/or school, and people living in large cities often lack supportive social networks.

Racial minorities and the poor are more likely to be found in urban settings of concentrated poverty, in broken families, and in communities characterized by high mobility and joblessness. In addition, because of segregation and discrimination, racial minorities are less likely to feel closely tied to mainstream social structures. These facts suggest that as interconnectedness to community goes up, crime goes down, and as individuals are increasingly alienated from social ties, crime rises.

Studies of the interrelationships between crime and neighborhood conditions further support the importance of community ties to preventing crime. Sociologists Robert Sampson and William Julius Wilson argue that conditions in the urban ghetto create substantial barriers to controlling crime, and that crime in turn aggravates the disastrous conditions of the ghetto by driving out those who might provide stability in the community.[24] Areas featuring residential instability, high-rise housing, and a concentration of single-parent families are almost always plagued by high crime as well.[25] Sampson and Wilson report that these neighborhoods are frequently characterized by relative anonymity and minimal participation in community organizations (other than gangs and churches). The "community" has largely broken down, and crime fills the vacuum: such settings foster "a system of values . . . in which crime, disorder, and drug use are less than fervently condemned and hence expected as part of everyday life."[26]

Most urban ghettos in the United States have been ceded to the minority underclass. In 1980, fewer than 7 percent of poor whites lived in extreme poverty areas, but 38 percent of poor blacks did. The proportion of poor blacks living in ghetto areas doubled between 1970 and 1980.[27] Thus, the oft-noted correlation between race and crime may be in large part a correlation between the urban ghetto and crime. In any event, these studies support what anyone looking to buy or rent a home or apartment well knows: community matters when it comes to crime.

Where community ties are strong, the shame associated with contravening social norms will also be strong; where those ties have already been broken, the would-be offender has correspondingly less to lose. The French sociologist Emile Durkheim has argued that "[t]o act morally is to act in terms of the collective interest."[28] Thus, "[f]or morality to have a sound basis, the citizen must have an inclination toward collective life."[29] Those who feel less tied to their communities are more likely to violate society's mores. As criminologist Elliott Currie argues, "the best deterrent to crime is the creation and maintenance of stable communities in which people may reasonably expect that good behavior will lead to esteemed and rewarding social roles."[30]

The criminal justice system's exploitation of inequality directly undermines both of these important conditions for encouraging compliance with the law: the law's legitimacy, and the community's cohesion. Double standards rob the criminal law of legitimacy among minority and poor communities. As a result, lawbreaking in those communities is likely to be viewed with less disapproval. Increased criminal conduct in turn undermines the very community ties that might deter crime. Absent legitimacy or community ties to deter crime, authorities will rely increasingly on incarceration, which further decimates the community by severing the community ties of its youth. The negative ripple effects extend far beyond urban ghettos, because the criminal justice system's double standards reinforce racial divisions that render the very notion of "community" in the United States a problematic one. Rather than being viewed as the voice of the community's mores, the criminal law is likely to be perceived as the forcible imposition of one community's values on another.

Richard Cloward and Lloyd Ohlin have argued that where people blame their inadequate opportunities on an unjust social order, they are less likely to view the legal system as legitimate, more likely to take advantage of illegitimate opportunities, and more likely to develop delinquent and criminal subcultures. Cloward and Ohlin suggest that the two factors most likely to lead people to blame the system and to enter delinquent subcultures are: (1) a discrepancy between official criteria for success (hard work, talent, etc.) and actual criteria for success (connections, family ties, wealth); and (2) a perception of systemic prejudice against particular groups.[31] The criminal justice system's exploitation of inequality fuels both sentiments. It creates a discrepancy between the formal rules, under which criminal responsibility is a function of individual culpability and all are equal before the law, and actual practice, in which who you know, how much money you have, and the color of your skin all play an important role in criminal justice outcomes. And as the polls reviewed earlier suggest, minorities and the poor often attribute the criminal justice system's disparate outcomes to systemic race and class prejudice in its procedures.[32]

Thus, it should not be surprising that scholars of the criminal justice system have concluded that the black community's distrust and suspicion "is one of the most corrosive and consequential features of crime in this society."[33] This is not to suggest that perceptions of the criminal justice system are the only determinants of criminal behavior, but simply to insist that they play a significant role. The likelihood and severity of criminal sanctions no doubt also play some role, although in general the public seems vastly to overestimate the correlation between the severity of sanctions and their deterrent effect. The availability of legitimate opportunities for achieving one's desires and needs quite evidently has a significant part to play in the decision whether to commit crime, so employment conditions and educational options are also important. But social scientists generally agree that perceptions of legal legitimacy and fear of community disapproval are substantial factors in why people obey the law. We know this as an intuitive matter; anyone who wields authority — from a parent to a soccer coach to the President of the United States — knows that the perceived legitimacy of his or her power makes a big difference in whether that authority will be obeyed. It is therefore not only morally wrong, but self-defeating, to maintain a criminal justice system that is widely perceived as imposing double standards. Although inequality in criminal justice may at first blush appear to be useful in minimizing the costs of crime associated with protecting constitutional rights, that very inequity is in all likelihood responsible for *encouraging* crime, by directly undermining faith in the criminal law among those groups and communities already most plagued by crime.

DEEPENING SOCIETAL DIVISIONS

In addition to impeding law enforcement and encouraging crime, the criminal justice system's double standards do even more damage by exacerbating our society's race and class divisions. As I have shown, the double standards develop because our society is not willing to pay the full cost of constitutional rights, and is only willing to bear the cost of mass incarceration because the incarcerated mass is predominantly nonwhite and poor. This strategy depends on the exploitation of race and class divisions. Without those divisions, the white majority could not afford to write off the costs of incarceration, nor could it "save" on the full cost of constitutional rights. But the strategy also contributes to such divisions. The polls discussed at the opening of this chapter illustrate that as a society, we fundamentally disagree — along race and class lines — about the fairness of the criminal justice system. Incidents such as the O.J. Simpson trial underscore that we are living in different worlds. A democratic society cannot thrive where such deep divisions persist.

Moreover, there is a circular quality to the relationship between criminal justice policy and race and class divisions. That crime has a young black man's face in our culture has, tragically, made it easier to justify our collective failure to respond adequately to past and ongoing inequality within and beyond the criminal justice system. Stigmatizing African Americans and the poor as "criminals" eases the guilt that the privileged might otherwise feel for the gulf between their opportunities and those available to African Americans and the poor. At the same time, our reliance on stigmatization and incarceration is made easier because the majority is not locking up its own, but those who are already defined as "other." There is a mutually reinforcing relationship between criminal stigmatization of blacks and racial subordination: the criminal stigmatization of blacks perpetuates and justifies their subordination as a group, and the status of blacks as a segregated, subordinated group makes it easier to insist on ever-more-stringent stigmatizing measures in the criminal law. Cast as criminals, blacks deserve prison, not redress. The same is true of the poor, although with somewhat less vehemence because the lines between poor and rich are not so sharp.

But this downward spiral cannot go on forever. Unless we begin to think about what criminal justice policy would look like if we could not rely on double standards and disparate impacts, we will continue to be plagued by persistent crime. For pragmatic as well moral reasons, the future of criminal justice depends upon reducing the race and class disparities that society has thus far found so "useful."

ENDNOTES

1. Donald P. Baker, "Execution-Style Slaying in Richmond Spurs Gun Debate," *Wash. Post*, 12 January 1993, D1; Donald P. Baker, "Slaying Remains Unsolved Despite Crowd of Witnesses," *Wash. Post*, 25 January 1993, D3.
2. Tom Alex, "Why Case Against Two Cousins Unraveled," *Des Moines Reg.*, 5 April 1996, 1.
3. Benjamin A. Holden, Laurie P. Cohen, Eleena de Lisser, "Color Blinded? Race Seems to Play an Increasing Role in Many Jury Verdicts." *Wall Street J.*, 4 October 1995, A1.
4. Jeffrey Rosen, "One Angry Woman," *The New Yorker*, 28 February/3 March 1997, 54, 60.
5. Id.
6. Cheryl Corley, "Courts Attempt to Hike Number of Minorities on Juries," National Public Radio, Morning Edition, 12 July 1996 (transcript on Lexis).
7. *United States v. Berrios*, 501 F.2d 1207, 1209 (2d Cir. 1974).
8. George Gallup, Jr., *The Gallup Poll: Public Opinion* (1995) (reporting on a CNN/USA Today/Gallup Poll conducted 7/20/95-7/23/95); see also George Gallup, Jr., "The Gallup Poll Monthly, No. 339" (December 1993), reported in Bureau of Justice Statistics, *Sourcebook of Criminal Justice Statistics — 1993*, 171 (1994) (finding that 74 percent of blacks believe that blacks are treated more harshly than whites by the criminal justice system); see also Ruth Marcus, "Racial Bias Widely Seen in Criminal Justice System, Research Often Supports Black Perceptions," *Wash. Post*, 12 May 1992, A4 (reporting that 89 percent of blacks and 43 percent of whites think blacks do not receive equal treatment in the criminal justice system); "Black and White: A Newsweek Poll," *Newsweek*, 7 March 1988, 23 (reporting that 66 percent of blacks believe the criminal justice system treats black defendants more harshly than white defendants); Jon M. Van Dyke, *Jury Selection Procedure: Our Uncertain Commitment to Representative Panels*, 32 (Cambridge, MA: Beullinger Pub., 1977) ("Discrimination bred by prejudice has contributed to a widespread mistrust by black people of most of the institutions of power, and most particularly the agencies of law enforcement").
9. Byron P. White, "Austin Case a Trust Buster, Police Integrity on Trial With Community," *Chicago Tribune*, 13 January 1997, 1.
10. Clifford Kraus, "Poll Finds a Lack of Faith in Police," *N.Y. Times*, 19 June 1994, 1.
11. Bill Minutaglio, "Simpson Case Shows Races' Differing Views on Justice: Experi-

ence Has Taught Blacks to Mistrust the System, Experts Say," *Dallas Morn. News*, 6 August 1994, 1A.

12. Bureau of Justice Statistics, *Sourcebook of Criminal Justice Statistics — 1992*, Tables 2.18-2.20, 171–72 (1993).

13. Paul H. Robinson, *Fundamentals of Criminal Law*, 18–19 (Boston: Little, Brown, 2d ed. 1995).

14. See Paul H. Robinson, "Moral Credibility and Crime," *Atlantic Monthly*, March 1993, 72, 74.

15. Tom R. Tyler, *Why People Obey the Law*, 38 (New Haven: Yale Univ. Press, 1990).

16. Id. at 102.

17. See Tom R. Tyler & Kathleen M. McGraw, "Ideology and the Interpretation of Personal Experience: Procedural Justice and Political Quiescence," 42 J. of Social Issues 115 (1986); Tom R. Tyler & Robert Folger, "Distributional and Procedural Aspects of Satisfaction with Citizen-Police Encounters," 1 Basic & App. Soc. Psych. 281 (1980); E. Allan Lind & Tom R. Tyler, *The Social Pyschology of Procedural Justice* (New York: Plenum Press, 1988); J. Thibaut & L. Walker, *Procedural Justice: A Psychological Analysis* (Hillsdale, N.J.: L. Erlbaum Associates, 1975).

18. Austin Sarat, "Studying American Legal Culture: An Assessment of Survey Evidence," 11 Law & Soc. Rev. 427, 434 (1977).

19. Franklin E. Zimring & Gordon J. Hawkins, *Deterrence: The Legal Threat in Crime Control*, 192 (Chicago: Univ. of Chicago Press, 1973).

20. Robert Meier & Weldon Johnson, "Deterrence as Social Control: The Legal and Extralegal Production of Conformity," 42 Am. Socio. Rev. 292 (1977).

21. Charles Tittle, *Sanctions and Social Deviance: The Question of Deterrence*, 320 (New York: Praeger, 1980); see also Raymond Paternoster, Linda Saltzman, Gordon Waldo & Theodore Chiricos, "Perceived Risk and Social Control: Do Sanctions Really Deter?" 17 Law & Soc. Rev. 478 (1983) (fears that parents, friends, or lovers might disapprove were strong deterrent to drug use and theft among students, while risk of formal punishment played virtually no role); Harold G. Grasmick & Donald E. Green, "Legal Punishment, Social Disapproval and Internalization as Inhibitors of Illegal Behavior," 71 J. Crim. L. & Criminol. 325 (1980) (finding that the threat of legal sanctions, social disapproval of one's peer group, and personal morality each make significant, independent contributions to the decision to avoid criminal behavior).

22. John Braithwaite, *Crime, Shame, and Reintegration*, 90–97 (New York: Cambridge Univ. Press, 1989).

23. Carol Gilligan, *In a Different Voice: Psychological Theory and Women's Development* (Cambridge, MA: Harvard Univ. Press, 1982).

24. Robert J. Sampson & William Julius Wilson, "Toward a Theory of Race, Crime, and Urban Inequality," in John Hagan & Ruth D. Peterson, eds., *Crime and Inequality*, 37 (Stanford, CA: Stanford Univ. Press, 1995).

25. Robert J. Sampson, "The Community," in James Q. Wilson & Joan Petersilia, eds., *Crime*, 193, 195–98 (San Francisco, CA: ICS Press, 1995).

26. Sampson & Wilson, *supra* note 24 at 50.

27. Id. at 41–42.

28. Emile Durkheim, *Moral Education: A Study in the Theory and Application of the Sociology of Education*, 59 (tr. Everett K. Wilson) (New York: Free Press, 1961).

29. Id. at 233.

30. Elliott Currie, *Confronting Crime: An American Challenge*, 37 (New York: Pantheon Books, 1985).

31. Richard A. Cloward and Lloyd E. Ohlin, *Delinquency and Opportunity: A Theory of Delinquent Gangs*, 110–18 (Glencoe, IL.: Free Press, 1960).

32. See *supra* note 8; see also Michael H. Tonry, *Malign Neglect—Race, Crime and Punishment in America*, 49–80, 104–115 (New York: Oxford Univ. Press, 1995).

33. John Hagan & Ruth D. Peterson, "Criminal Inequality in America," in Hagan & Peterson, eds., *Crime and Inequality*, 15, 17 (1995).

7—Remedies

uppose one Justice had changed his or her vote, and Warren McCleskey, the death row inmate who challenged Georgia's discriminatory enforcement of the death penalty, had won. If the Court had concluded that a statistically significant racial disparity in death sentencing violated the Constitution, what would follow? McCleskey's death sentence would have been overturned, as would presumably all other death sentences Georgia had imposed for the murder of white victims. If McCleskey had prevailed under his equal protection theory that there was systemic discrimination against killers of white victims, those who had killed black victims might not be entitled to a remedy. But if the Court had adopted McCleskey's alternative theory that a constitutionally unacceptable risk of arbitrariness rendered Georgia's death penalty cruel and unusual punishment, all death sentences in the state would likely have been vacated. In either event, the remedy would have gone far beyond Warren McCleskey. If similar statistical showings could have been replicated in other states—and it is likely that they could have been—the death penalty would have been invalid elsewhere as well.

States intent on continuing to impose the death penalty would have been able to do so only as long as their results were racially neutral. One way of achieving that end would have been to direct prosecutors to seek the death penalty less often where victims were white and more often where victims were black. But such a response would entail explicit consideration of race in determining whether or not to seek the death penalty, and that in itself seems deeply problematic—and unconstitutional—for much the same reasons that the *McCleskey* data are troubling. If the problem revealed in *McCleskey* was that race appeared to play a role in deciding who lives or dies, how would it solve the problem to create a system in which race definitely and explicitly plays such a role?

This dilemma is by no means unique to the death penalty. Many of the disparities in criminal justice are not necessarily assignable to a conscious or intentional act of discrimination. In those circumstances, offsetting the disparity may require injecting an element of class or race consciousness into decisions that are not on their face race- or class-based. But any remedy that institutionalizes race- or class-conscious decisionmaking in criminal justice is deeply problematic, because here more than virtually anywhere else equality of opportunity and individual determinations of culpability are essential to the legitimacy of the enterprise.

This is only one of four major obstacles discussed below that confront efforts to redress race and class inequities in criminal justice. No remedy is without costs. But two imperatives require that we take remedial steps now: first, the moral dictate that criminal justice be administered equally, a promise we have failed to achieve; and second, the pragmatic reality that inequality in criminal justice encourages crime, impedes criminal law enforcement, and exacerbates racial divisions.

This chapter first addresses the obstacles to reform, and then moves on to propose directions for reform. A full-scale reform strategy would be another book in itself, so this chapter seeks merely to suggest directions for reform. Rather than propose a comprehensive program, my aim is to identify the general principles that must guide criminal justice reform if it is to address the problems created by the double standards I have outlined and critiqued above.

THE OBSTACLES TO REFORM

The first difficulty with remedying race and class disparities, illustrated by *McCleskey*, might be termed the "affirmative action" problem: to what extent can a solution that expressly takes race into account be a valid remedy for a wrong that consists in taking race into account? Although good arguments exist for adopting race-conscious measures to redress racial subordination in such settings as employment, contracting, and education, those arguments are ill-suited to most criminal justice questions. The criteria for who "deserves" admission to an elite school, a contract with a city, or a position on the police force are usually sufficiently debatable that adding affirmative action to the mix of connections, luck, merit, geography, and social class does not threaten the very enterprise. But while the criteria for criminal punishment are also contestable, the contest proceeds against a strong background assumption of individual responsibility. The notion that people should be arrested, convicted or sentenced because of racial considerations is repugnant to criminal justice in a way that is not true of college admissions or employment. Although affirmative action in admissions, contracting, and employment is itself controversial, it nonetheless has many defenders; support for affirmative action in enforcing criminal law is virtually nonexistent.[1] This point is reflected in federal law, which has long incorporated race- and class-based preferences in government contracting, but explicitly forbids any consideration of race, socioeconomic status, or economic hardship as a basis for criminal sentences.[2] The only criminal justice setting in which race consciousness is arguably permissible is in ensuring representative juries, and even there it is controversial.

A second obstacle to remedying the criminal justice system's disparate treatment of different social groups is that any solution implemented within the criminal justice system is likely to be constrained by forces beyond the system. If, for example, a significant factor in criminal behavior of the poor and minorities is the absence of meaningful employment opportunities in the inner city, rehabilitation efforts that fail to address that absence are certain to come up short. Similarly, the ability of wealthy defendants to purchase better legal assistance than poor defendants means that absolute equality of representation is not achievable absent radical redistribution of wealth or equally radical limits on what citizens can spend for their own defense.

Progressive critics frequently argue that as a result of the social determinants of crime, meaningful reform cannot be found within the criminal justice system, but requires redistribution of resources and economic opportunities in the society at large.[3] Only a redistribution of wealth can offset the socioeconomic disparities that underlie inequality in criminal justice. Community development projects, job training, economic incentives to businesses to locate and remain in disadvantaged neighborhoods, family planning counselling, housing programs, and improvement of public education are all likely to have substantial effects on the general character of community life, on socioeconomic inequality, and ultimately on crime. But such proposals are at once both too grand and insufficient—too grand because the sheer magnitude of the task is virtually certain to ensure that it will not be undertaken; insufficient because until we begin to attack inequality within the criminal justice system, we will not be able to heal the broader social divisions that impede efforts at socioeconomic reform. The criminal justice system as it is currently operated affirmatively contributes to and reinforces race and class inequality in complex ways. Thus, although broader societal remedies are undoubtedly necessary, we must also look for remedies within the criminal justice system, while recognizing that they will necessarily be partial.

Third, attempts to reduce disparities in treatment of criminal defendants may have the perverse effect of increasing disparities among crime victims. Most of us live in communities segregated by race and class, and as a result most crime is intra-race and intra-class. This can make furthering equality problematic. If, for example, black criminal defendants were treated more leniently to counteract their disproportionate presence in the nation's prisons and jails, their mostly black victims might complain that they are being deprived of equal protection of the laws. By the same token, efforts to respond to black citizens' victimization through increased law enforcement in the inner cities are likely to result in more incarcerated blacks. On these grounds, Professor Randall Kennedy has argued that the disparity in punishment between crack and powder cocaine possession should not be viewed as discrimination against blacks, but as a benefit to the law-abiding segment of the black community.[4] More broadly, *any* attempt to alter criminal justice policies to address racial disparities is likely to have double-edged effects on racial minorities. And because crime is also intra-class, the same paradox is presented by efforts to remedy class-based inequalities.[5]

The fourth obstacle to redressing race and class inequity is that rules that formally treat everyone the same—and thereby provide "formal equality"—are generally inadequate to achieve any real measure of equality, while reforms that seek to achieve "substantive equality" through more individualized treatment may reproduce the very inequality they seek to supplant. The inadequacy of formal equality is still best captured by Anatole France's remark about the "equality" of forbidding the rich and poor alike from sleeping under bridges; where the starting line is unequal, formally neutral rules will not create a fair race. But substantive equality is also problematic. It requires individual or group-based handicapping, but because there is no formal guide for setting appropriate handicaps, and doing so accurately would require endlessly nuanced and highly debatable adjustments, the handicapping process is susceptible to abuse. Traditional mechanisms for providing some measure of substantive justice, such as empowering judges to take individual defendants' circumstances into account in sentencing, may themselves invite race or class discrimination, for "the power to be lenient is the power to discriminate."[6]

On its surface, the criminal law is premised on formal equality: everyone is equal before the law, and punishment must be predicated on one's actions, not on one's status. In fact, however, the criminal law already incorporates significant mechanisms for considerations of substantive justice, because, paradoxically, assessments of individual responsibility are often impossible without them. In capital sentencing, for example, the jury must be able to consider any and all facts about an individual as "mitigating circumstances" that might weigh against a death sentence, because otherwise the defendant has not received individualized treatment.[7] Prosecutors are accorded discretion to "do justice" in individual cases by dropping a case or accepting a guilty plea. Police have substantial discretion not to arrest; they can issue formal or informal warnings, cite individuals for varying degrees of criminal behavior, or simply look the other way. And the doctrine of "jury nullification" recognizes that juries may acquit if they believe it is unjust to convict a defendant who has unquestionably committed a crime.

A criminal law without such points of discretion would be unimaginable. But this discretion coexists uneasily with the formal surface of the criminal law. The open-ended character of "substantive justice" mechanisms poses a constant threat to formal equality. Individuals who commit the same offense under the same circumstances may not be treated equally, and conscious or unconscious prejudices may affect outcomes. The criminal law has dealt with this tension principally by burying the operation of substantive justice. The formal surface of the criminal law—the laws themselves, trials, and the imposition of sentences—is open to the public. The substantive undercurrent of discretion is not. The jury is a black box. Prosecutorial discretion is exercised in secret, and discovery rules make it virtually impossible to gain access to the prosecutor's records. And the police by and large do not keep records of the countless discretionary decisions they make each day, most of which require no explanation or justification. We have screened off from public view the operation of substantive justice in criminal law.

The absence of public scrutiny associated with the exercise of discretion in today's system is troubling for two reasons. It allows race and class stereotypes to guide decisionmakers. And it fuels distrust and cynicism among the populace, who are asked to accept on blind faith that juries and law enforcement officials are using their discretion fairly, even as the system produces widely disparate results.

Thus, neither the criminal law's formal surface nor its discretionary underside is particularly well-suited to responding to race and class inequality. Both reproduce existing inequality—formal equality by doing nothing to respond to it, and substantive equality by relying largely on informal, unguided, and hidden discretion.

What unites these four obstacles to reform is that they stem in significant part from the race and class inequality that so pervades our culture: where inequality is so prevalent, it will often operate without our awareness; attempts to remedy its undesirable effects will necessarily be partial and insufficient; remedial interventions may have complicated negative side effects; formally equal measures will perpetuate preexisting inequality; and the discretion necessary to foster substantive equality will be subject to distortion by the very race and class inequities to which it is designed to respond. These problems make any effort to reform the criminal justice system extremely difficult. But they do not excuse us from trying.

SOLUTIONS

Responding to the problem of inequality in today's criminal justice system requires a three-fold response. First, we must acknowledge the problem by recognizing that we have built the current system on a fiction—that all are equal before the law. Second, we must seek to restore the legitimacy that the system's double standards have forfeited by adopting measures that extend the same rights and protections to all, even if that means reducing the rights now enjoyed by the privileged. And third, we must identify and develop community-based responses to crime, both at the preventive and punitive stages.

Acknowledging the Problem

The first and most basic step is to acknowledge that a problem exists. As I have demonstrated, the criminal justice system is premised on an assumption of formal equality, and as long as that assumption is accepted at face value, the criminal justice system's race and class disparities will likely be accepted as well. But the assumption of formal equality is a false one—in fact, we have answered virtually every hard choice in criminal justice policy and law by resorting to a double standard, which provides one level of protection and treatment for the privileged, and a very different level for minorities and the poor. Those double standards in turn contribute to the crime problems in disadvantaged communities. Until we acknowledge that we have built our criminal justice policy on an unjust edifice, we will not find real remedies for the crime problem.

The importance and difficulty of the initial step of recognition should not be minimized. Society has a lot at stake in denying the double standards, precisely because they have proved so "useful" in accommodating competing interests in the criminal justice system, and in maintaining both constitutional rights and a sense of security for the wealthy. Acknowledging that the double standards exist is thus deeply threatening to the status quo. Indeed, it was partly for that reason that the Supreme Court refused to attach constitutional significance to the stark racial disparities demonstrated in Warren McCleskey's death penalty case. As the Court candidly acknowledged, recognizing those disparities as constitutionally problematic would have required the Court to question the entire criminal justice system, because at nearly every level the system is characterized by racial disparities. It is largely to show that we have systematically relied on such double standards that I have written this book. Once we have acknowledged the problem, we must move on to consider ways to reform the criminal justice system to respond to the two principle "costs" of inequality—the law's loss of legitimacy, and the community's loss of cohesion.

Restoring Legitimacy

The key to restoring the criminal law's legitimacy is to eliminate or reduce the double standards. Unless all persons come to believe that they are truly equal before the law, and that the same rights apply to all, the criminal law will never regain the legitimacy it has lost among the disadvantaged. And restoring that legitimacy is critical to any further reforms within the criminal justice system. Thus, we should start by demanding that courts, legislatures, and police departments adopt measures that will reduce reliance on inequality in administering criminal justice. While much of my criticism in this book has been directed at the Supreme Court, the responsibility lies with all three branches of government, and we should call on all three to provide reform.

In each of the preceding chapters, I have suggested appropriate reforms. We need rules that more carefully circumscribe police discretion to detain and investigate citizens, and that require the police to inform suspects of their rights before seeking their "consent" to waive those rights. We should require public reporting of the racial character of police practices, and judicial monitoring of racial disparities under the civil rights laws. The right to counsel should be extended to all stages of the criminal justice process, and should be made meaningful by requiring government to appoint competent attorneys with the expertise and training necessary for their task.

Representative jury selection requires that we take race into account at one stage of the process, and prohibit its consideration at another. Jury venires should reflect the racial and ethnic makeup of the community, and that requires paying attention to race. But once a representative pool is created, we should demand that jury selection be race neutral, either by requiring much more persuasive explanations for peremptory strikes where a party has engaged in a racial pattern, or by eliminating the peremptory challenge altogether. And the courts should radically reduce the hurdles to bringing legal challenges to disparity and discrimination in the criminal justice setting. As long as we sweep these issues under the rug, the system will never regain the legitimacy it needs to be effective where it is needed most—in high-crime communities.

These measures would redress some of the most glaring disparities in criminal justice, and would provide avenues for airing and adjudicating charges of race discrimination. They would go far toward restoring the criminal justice system's legitimacy among disadvantaged communities. But these are not the only remedies available. Equality can also be achieved by reducing the rights that the privileged now enjoy to the level of those enjoyed by the disadvantaged. Indeed, I imagine that were the courts and legislatures to embark on a full-scale effort to create something approaching equality in criminal justice, the result would in some instances mean that the privileged would enjoy less expansive rights than they now have. For example, when the Minnesota Supreme Court ruled that the disparity in state sentencing guidelines between crack and powder cocaine penalties violated equal protection, the legislature responded not by reducing the penalties for crack to the levels for powder, but by increasing the penalties for powder to a level commensurate with those for crack.[8] Similarly, were we unable to discount the cost of Fourth Amendment protections by effectively coercing consent from primarily disadvantaged citizens, we might be less willing to grant some Fourth Amendment protections in the first place. Moving toward equality does not necessarily entail an expansion of constitutional rights for the criminally accused. It would simply require society to strike the balance more honestly and uniformly between law enforcement and constitutional freedoms. In the end, whether we expand or contract constitutional rights is less important than adhering to the principle that we draw one line for all.

Restoring Community

Even if all the reforms I have suggested were implemented immediately, they would be insufficient. In particular, they would not restore the communities that have been doubly ravaged, first by crime, and second by a criminal justice system that has locked up a substantial segment of a generation within those communities. As a result, they would do little to alter the stark disparities in incarceration. If current incarceration rates remain steady, one in four young black men born today will serve time in prison during his lifetime. This is an astounding figure, more troubling even than the more commonly reported fact that on any given day in 1996, one in three black men between the ages of twenty and twenty-nine was "under criminal justice supervision." The latter figure includes persons on probation or parole. But the one-in-four figure refers only to prison incarceration, which is reserved for those convicted and sentenced to more than a year of imprisonment. The damage that this mass incarceration has done and will do to the black community is incalculable.

Responding to these disparities presents all the remedial difficulties outlined above. Imposing more lenient punishment simply because of a defendant's race or class would violate the fundamental maxim of individual treatment, and would deny equal "protection" to the predominantly poor and minority victims of poor and minority offenders. Giving judges and juries discretion to tailor sentences to individual circumstances might ameliorate some disparities, but would also risk further discrimination based on unspoken and often unconscious race and class prejudice. And all remedies within the criminal justice system seem hopelessly insufficient in light of the multiple causes of criminal behavior among poor and minority populations.

If we are to respond to these disparities effectively, we must rethink our approach to criminal justice and develop what I will call a community-based criminal justice policy. Its first principle would be that all criminal justice decisions must take seriously the role that a cohesive community plays in deterring and preventing crime. A community-based criminal justice policy would adopt measures that support rather than destroy communities. Instead of building more prisons, imposing longer sentences, and incarcerating more criminals, it would focus on reinforcing the community ties that deter crime in the first place, encouraging community associations, involving the community in punishment and rehabilitation, using alternatives to incarceration wherever consistent with community safety, and reintegrating offenders into society. It is only by taking community seriously that we will break the vicious cycle in which both crime and criminal law enforcement disproportionately harm minorities and the poor.

Today's criminal justice philosophy is the antithesis of community-based. Our presumptive response to crime is incarceration, a process that radically severs ties between offenders and their communities and that places them in a setting where the only "communities" available are criminal subcultures. Yet virtually every time politicians return to the crime problem, it is to vote for longer prison sentences and more money to build and run prisons, even though we already boast the second highest per capita incarceration rate in the developed world. Parole and probation are seen as necessary evils in light of limited resources, rather than as a positive good. We do not take either probation or parole seriously. Probation officers' caseloads sometimes exceed 300 cases, and their contacts with probationers and parolees are infrequent, inconsistent, and highly formalized.[9] While "community policing" initiatives are a welcome reflection of the philosophical shift I advocate, the prevailing culture of policing is still far from community-based, and instead reflects and perpetuates an adversarial dynamic between the police and the communities they monitor rather than serve.[10] Programs designed to prevent crime by fostering community ties, such as recreational sports leagues in disadvantaged communities, are denounced as "pork."[11] Three-quarters of the federal government's drug-control budget is directed at apprehending and punishing drug dealers and users, while less than one-sixth is directed at treatment.[12] The 1997 federal drug-control budget spent more on prisons than prevention.[13]

Community-oriented measures are not unheard of in the criminal justice system. But today these programs are the rare exception to the rule, and they are superimposed on a system that for the most part pays little attention to the power of community. Community-based programs must become the linchpin of our criminal justice strategy.

Community-based initiatives begin with efforts to prevent

crime. Neighborhood watch committees, for example, encourage residents to take responsiblity for the quality of life in their neighborhoods, and encourage civic participation and interaction. Standing alone, they are likely to be ineffective, but in concert with other community initiatives, such committees can provide a base for community involvement in addressing crime. Organized youth activities, run by adults from the community, can also be important community-builders, providing an alternative to gangs, fostering positive associations between youth and adults within the community. In recent years politicians have derided such efforts as "pork," but nothing could be further from the truth. Particularly in areas where family supervision of children is lacking (because of one-parent families, working parents, etc.), these alternatives may be critical to keeping young people out of trouble.

We should also strengthen measures to keep children in school, which is the central locus of community life for most young people and the most important place for adult-youth contact outside the family. We should consider both positive incentives to stay in school—including monetary rewards—and punitive disincentives to truancy. A 1996 Rand Corporation study found that programs offering incentives to disadvantaged youth to finish high school were far more cost-effective in reducing crime than the more popular three-strikes-and-you're-out legislation.[14] The study estimated that, dollar for dollar, such incentive programs reduce crime three to four times as effectively as California's three-strikes legislation. By reinforcing a child's connection to school, and rewarding his or her successful completion of high school, these programs support one of the most important social networks an adolescent can have.

"Community policing" is another promising form of community-based crime prevention. This approach, already under way in many departments across the country, tries to make the police an integral part of the neighborhoods they serve through more decentralized police stations, more foot patrols, and regular meetings with citizens in the community. Where such programs develop effective channels for communication between the police and the community about their respective needs, the programs can play an important role in restoring community trust and overcoming the adversarial relationship too many police departments have with disadvantaged communities.

Boston, for example, instituted an intensive community policing program in 1990 in response to an all-time city record of 152 homicides, many of which were gang-related. Boston's program, named Operation Cease Fire, is credited with reducing violence in the city dramatically. From July 1995 to December 1997, Boston did not have a single juvenile gun homicide. By contrast, from June 1990 to October 1991, 66 people under the age of 24 were killed with firearms in Boston. Boston's program emphasizes strategically targeted prevention and enforcement programs, directed at problem areas and problem youth. On the prevention side, the Police Department has entered into partnerships with the Boys and Girls Club of Boston, schools, universities and churches to provide alternatives to gangs for youth. These include late-night sports programs, liaisons with college athletes, the creation of job opportunities for out-of-school youth, and counseling and mentoring.

In addition, the Boston police employ a targeted enforcement program used whenever gunfire flares in a neighborhood. The police immediately hold sit-down meetings with gang members and warn them that if the violence continues, the police will enforce a "no tolerance" policy, in which aggressive policing is combined with enforcement of minor quality-of-life offenses. The police also instituted a program that took probation more seriously, sending probation officers out with police on night patrol to identify probation violators before they got into worse trouble.[15]

San Diego provides another positive example of community policing. Its homicide rates fell by 54 percent from 1991 to 1996, matching New York City's more widely publicized drop. But where New York City achieved its results through aggressive "zero-tolerance" law enforcement, resulting in overloaded criminal courts, overcrowded jails, and a surge in complaints of police abuse, San Diego has stressed "problem-oriented community policing," in which the police seek to create mutual trust between police and neighborhood residents by including them in consultations and developing positive long-term relationships. From 1993 through 1996, New York's arrest rate for misdemeanors rose by 40 percent, while San Diego's rate dropped by 15 percent during the same period. Thus, by focusing on more constructive community interventions, San Diego achieved the same results as New York City without filling its jails and increasing animosity between the police and the citizenry.[16]

The Boston and San Diego experiences suggest that interventions designed to strengthen community can be very effective in reducing crime. A community-based criminal justice policy would favor such measures over the more common response of increasing criminal penalties. We must begin to see these initiatives not as "pork" or as isolated experiments, but as an integral part of our criminal justice policy.

Involving the Community in Punishment

The area most in need of community-based reform, however, is not prevention but punishment. Current punishment practices destroy community ties. We remove offenders from the law-abiding community and introduce them to a law-violating community in prison, and we have largely given up on rehabilitation.[17] We routinely impose severe "civil disabilities" on criminal defendants, which only serve to underscore further their ostracization. New York, for example, bars convicts from marrying while in prison,[18] even though married people commit far less crime than unmarried people. All but three states bar prisoners from voting while serving their time; fourteen states go further and disenfranchise ex-offenders for life.[19] All but four states bar felons from serving on juries; many make the bar permanent unless the individual is pardoned.[20] And convicted felons may not serve in the armed services.[21] Thus, as a routine matter of punishment we not only physically separate offenders from the community, but also exclude them from three of the most significant indicia of citizenship: voting, jury service, and military service. And on their release, we do little to reintegrate former prisoners into society, where they often find it difficult even to find gainful employment.[22]

These policies and practices isolate offenders from their communities in virtually every tangible and intangible way. Of course, someone who has committed a crime has by that very act already violated the bonds of community, and the penalty of incarceration is an understandable response: just as the offender rejects the community, so the community rejects the offender. But such a response is self-defeating because it further undermines the community ties that prevent crime in the first place.

A community-based criminal justice policy would seek appropriate ways to sanction criminal behavior without cutting off the offender from the community. One of the most potentially promising — and simultaneously frightening — developments along these lines in recent years is the growth of interest in "shaming" penalties. Shaming penalties substitute rituals of public opprobrium for incarceration. In their most simplistic form — for example, requiring an offender to display a sign outside his barn stating "A Violent Felon Lives Here. Travel At Your Own Risk" — shaming penalties seem almost barbaric.[23] But they are based on an important insight: shame can and should play a critical role in punishment. Shame is important from the perspective of both the offender and the community. Fear of being ashamed within one's community is a critical deterrent to crime. And the process of shaming allows the community to express its condemnation of the offending conduct. Shaming may also be a politically tenable alternative to imprisonment, because it meets the community's expressive needs and is less susceptible to being dismissed as soft on crime.[24] If we can achieve through shaming what we currently seek to achieve through incarceration — without incarceration's many costs — it could be a substantial improvement in fighting crime.

To be effective, however, shaming penalties must be more than an exercise in community outrage and offender humiliation. They must recognize and build on the important interrelationship between shaming and community. Australian criminologist John Braithwaite advocates "reintegrative shaming," a strategy expressly premised on reinforcing the community ties that prevent crime and make shaming work.[25] What distinguishes reintegrative shaming is that it stresses *both* shaming and reintegration, and insists that community involvement is critical to both. Braithwaite proposes that persons important to the offender's community — such as family members, employers, school officials, and members of the individual's voluntary associations (sports teams, churches, neighborhood organizations, etc.)—be brought into the courtroom to express their disapproval of the offender's conduct. At the same time, these community members must also take responsibility for reintegrating the offender into society. Thus, as they express their condemnation of the act, they simultaneously express their commitment to the individual as a member of the community. Victims might also be given a more significant role in this process, as they too are usually part of the community that needs to be repaired. Most importantly, a reintegrative approach would treat incarceration as a last resort, to be used for hard-core violent offenders who must be incapacitated for the safety of the community, *not* as the principal means of punishment.

All shaming is not alike, however, and some can be counterproductive, particularly in a multiracial society. Braithwaite contrasts reintegrative shaming with stigmatic shaming. Stigmatic shaming labels the offender as a criminal and outcast, sets him apart from society, and marginalizes him—paralleling incarceration's ill effects. Unfortunately, many of today's shaming advocates seem to focus on shaming without considering reintegration. In reintegrative shaming, by contrast, the community expresses its disapproval of the offending *conduct*, but at the same time affirmatively seeks to restore the offending *individual* to the social networks that are so critical to deterring criminal conduct. Reintegrative shaming recognizes that shaming only makes sense in relation to a community whose respect the offender wants to maintain, and therefore it recognizes that reintegration is inextricable from effective shaming.

Although reintegrative shaming is not a central mechanism in the American criminal justice system, it should not be unfamiliar to Americans, for it plays an important role in many other settings. Braithwaite's model is the good parent, who disciplines her misbehaving child by expressing clear disapproval and inciting shame, but simultaneously assures the child that she is a loved and integral part of the family. Another example of the phenomenon is Alcoholics Anonymous, which creates an environment in which individuals express shame at their own addiction, but do so within a group committed to helping the individual reform herself with peer support. The desire not to be ashamed in front of one's fellow AA members—not to "let them down"—can be a strong force against recidivism. Still another model is the Catholic Church, which develops in its adherents a profound sense of shame for their sins, but simultaneously offers a process of confession, expiation, and communion that reaffirms their ties to the religious community. The Catholic insistence that "we are all sinners" tempers the impulse to stigmatize and exclude sinners as outcasts. If we all require forgiveness and redemption for our sins, how can we deny forgiveness to others? These familiar models suggest that our culture has long understood the important role that group ties, shaming, and reintegration play in encouraging good conduct and discouraging bad conduct.

There is reason to believe that reintegrative shaming will be more successful than stigmatization and incarceration in deterring crime. The studies referred to in the previous chapter, for example, conclude that one of the most powerful deterrents to criminal conduct is the fear of being ashamed within one's community. In addition, several studies of juvenile and criminal justice systems have found that persons subjected to more rehabilitative and inclusive programs are less likely to engage in repeated criminal behavior than those subjected to more punitive and exclusionary measures, even after controlling for prior criminal acts and other factors that might explain the differences.[26]

Braithwaite points to Japan as a model for successful use of "reintegrative shaming." Japan is the *only* country with a crime rate lower today than it was during World War II.[27] It has one of the lowest crime rates in the world. In 1995, there were thirty-two gun murders in Japan, compared to 13,673 gun murders in the United States. Thus, with only twice Japan's population, the United States had more than 400 times as many gun murders.[28] Japan's detection of crime is also superior to our own; its 60 percent "clearance" rate, which reflects the percentage of reported crimes that are actually solved, is "among the highest in the world," and three times the United States's clearance rate.[29]

Japan's criminal justice system prefers informal processes of apology, confession, and forgiveness to formal conviction and incarceration. Only 5 percent of persons convicted of crime in Japan serve time, compared to 30 percent of those convicted in the United States.[30] While the average prison sentence has increased markedly in the United States since World War II, average sentences have decreased in Japan over the same time period.[31] The guiding notion in Japan is that the offender is not "a criminal," but a person who should be made to be ashamed of the offending part of himself, and then reintegrated into the community. The process, much of it effected quite informally, is reinforced by extensive voluntary community networks dedicated to participating in prevention and rehabilitation. In the 1970s and 1980s, Japan had 540,000 local crime prevention associations, 10,725 Vocational Unions for Crime Prevention, 126,000 volunteers engaged in street work with juveniles, 8,000 Big Brothers and Sisters for delinquents, 320,000 volunteers in the Women's Association for Rehabilitation, 80,000 volunteer probation officers, 1,640 volunteer prison visitors, 1,500 employers willing to provide jobs for probationers and parolees, and 2,028 Police-School Liaison Councils.[32]

At every stage of the Japanese criminal justice process, officials are encouraged to be lenient for the purpose of facilitating reintegration into the community. The police are permitted to close cases for so-called petty offenses (including assault, theft, fraud, and embezzlement) without referring them to prosecutors, and nearly 40 percent of cases are dealt with in this manner.[33] To close a case, police must counsel the defendant sternly, persuade the suspect to apologize and make restitution, keep a record of the closure of the case, and call in a family member, employer, or other responsible individual to undertake to watch over the suspect in the future. Prosecutors are similarly authorized to suspend prosecution where they conclude that notwithstanding strong evidence of guilt, "prosecution would not be in the interests of justice."[34] Prosecutors grant suspension of prosecution to about 40 percent of suspects referred to them.[35] And judges are given broad discretion to suspend sentences for all but a small number of crimes. Nearly 60 percent of those convicted are given suspended sentences.[36] For the few who actually receive prison time, short sentences are the rule. Less than 1 percent of prisoners receive — much less serve — terms of over ten years.[37] The object, achieved with remarkable success, is to return people to the community.

The philosophy behind Japan's avoidance of incarceration wherever possible is best reflected in a 1914 speech to police by the Procurator General:

> When one can achieve success through chastising, exhorting good behavior and admonishing against wrongdoing, without taking the step of imposing punishment, it is appropriate to do so. It is a mistake to say that punishment must be imposed on all offenders. . . . Some people say that the use of suspended prosecutions is for the purpose of reducing the number of prisoners and thereby cutting down on expenses. That is one benefit, but it is by no means the primary purpose of suspension of prosecution. Persons with prior convictions are likely to fall into despair; and for a person who has entered prison it is difficult to become a law-abiding person again following release . . . This is not only extremely sad for the individual in question . . . but also represents a very great loss for society as a whole.[38]

Our system could not be more different from Japan's. In part because we punish so many, we largely eschew criminal trials — the quintessential public drama of shame — for the more "efficient" process of plea bargains, in which the problem of crime is treated technocratically and administratively, substituting highly formalized and routinized acceptances of responsibility for genuine shaming rituals. While our system affords substantial discretion to police, prosecutors, and to some extent, judges, to divert violators from terms of imprisonment, we generally do so not as part of a practice and philosophy of reintegrative shaming, but for administrative convenience, efficiency, and cost control.

Nonetheless, there are some promising examples of reintegrative shaming already in place in the American criminal justice system. One is the "drug court." These courts offer nonviolent drug offenders an intensive and highly structured program of mandatory treatment and testing in lieu of a criminal sentence. Typically, drug court judges mete out plenty of shame, and demand signs of contrition, willingness to reform, and progress in treatment. The court closely monitors the defendant's progress, holding out the threat that failure to complete the treatment program will land the defendant in jail. These programs cost substantially less than warehousing an offender in prison, and preliminary results suggest that those who complete drug court treatment are less likely to be rearrested for drug offences than those who serve traditional prison sentences. By treating drug offenders in the community rather than banishing them to prison, society responds to the offender as a human being who has violated community norms and must be treated, not as someone whose ties with the community ought to be severed. The treatment programs themselves often rely on group-based counseling patterned on Alcoholics Anonymous and designed to provide a kind of community support for the painful process of curing drug addiction. Mandatory drug-treatment programs are an excellent example of a reintegrative shaming approach to crime. Their community-based aspects might be strengthened further by requiring the offender to be accompanied in court by a member of his community who would participate in the condemnatory process and commit to helping the offender return to a law-abiding, drug-free existence.

Other examples of reintegrative shaming currently used in the United States include community-based centers devoted to providing delinquent youth the structure and support of a law-abiding community. These institutions, such as the Centro Sister Isolina Ferre, a Catholic organization in La Playa, Puerto Rico, an urban ghetto, offer an alternative to gangs as a source of community. They are typically structured as an extended family and characterized by clear rules, strict discipline, and public shaming for infractions. At the same time, they also offer plenty of support and a group-based identity. Such groups often recruit former offenders from the community to serve as advocates and counselors on the theory that they will both command the respect of and be able to relate to troubled youth.

Although studies of the effectiveness of such projects are notoriously difficult to do—there are rarely adequate control groups, the activities are difficult to quantify, and it is virtually impossible to rule out other possible explanations for a project's results—most evaluations, even from conservative reviewers, are positive. For example, the American Enterprise Institute, a right-wing think tank, had this to say about the Centro Sister Isolina Ferre:

> Before Sister Isolina Ferre began her work, it was considered unsafe to walk in La Playa, at any time of the day or night. Now there is less stealing and less violence among Playeros involved with the center, and no homicide has occurred in La Playa in four years among the juvenile population. The schools continue to report some damage to school property, but there is much less vandalism at the program centers and in the neighborhood itself. La Playa, being a port, was once notorious for the sale and use of hard drugs, but the work of the center appears to have reduced their incidence. Little more than some marijuana and glue are now used among the youths, and few hard drugs are found in the area. Significantly, all categories of juvenile offenses recorded by police show a marked reduction in La Playa since the program has been in effect.[39]

These are all promising approaches to incorporating the community in the process of punishment. Community involvement can increase the power of shame and contribute to the goal of reintegration. Community ties can be fostered and harnessed to encourage rehabilitation and treatment. But in order to exploit the restorative power of community, we must reduce our reliance on incarceration, for that option deprives both the offender and society of the opportunities and strength that community can bring.

Overcoming Obstacles to Community-Based Criminal Justice

Despite its policy advantages, community-based criminal justice is likely to face two substantial obstacles—one political, the other cultural. The political problem is that some of its aspects, particularly its preventive and rehabilitative emphases, will be criticized as soft on crime, the kiss of death in today's politics of criminal justice. But there are limits to the unrelentingly "tough on crime" approach. One is economic. We live in a world of diminishing resources and growing debt, and politicians must operate in that setting. Incarceration is hideously expensive—it costs more to incarcerate an individual than it does to send him to Harvard. Some states are now spending more on prisons than on higher education.[40] We simply cannot afford to continue current incarceration rates. The prison population has increased five-fold since the early 1970s.[41] And since 1980, the proportion of nonviolent offenders in prison has jumped from one-half to more than two-thirds, and the proportion of drug offenders has increased from one-tenth to one-third. Opportunity costs will ultimately force even politicians to search for alternatives to incarceration for many of these nonviolent offenders.

At the same time, a growing number of law enforcement officials are questioning our current preference for incarceration. Former New York police commissioner and federal drug czar Lee Brown, reacting to a 1995 report that one in three young black men were under criminal justice supervision, stated, "You can't incarcerate your way out of the drug problem."[42] Current Drug Czar General Barry McCaffrey also favors alternatives to incarceration, especially for nonviolent drug offenders.[43] Connecticut Governor John G. Rowland, a Republican, has supported efforts in his state to keep nonviolent drug offenders out of jail.[44] Eventually, we will all be forced to confront the bankruptcy of our current approach, and these voices of experience and reason may finally be heard over the demagogues' din.

Community-based criminal justice is not soft on crime. The preventive elements of the policy—community policing, incentives to remain in school, youth activities—seek to stop crime before it happens. The reactive aspect of the policy stresses the importance of public, community-based shame. If studies about why people obey the law are to be credited, reintegrative shaming may be more effective than incarceration in deterring crime, and in that sense may be tougher on crime than current policies.

The second and more substantial objection to community-based criminal justice is that the United States lacks the social preconditions necessary for its implementation. Is community-based criminal justice possible in a society that prides itself on individualism, in which the very notion of "community" is threatened by race and class segregation, and in which the greatest crime problems are found in areas where the community has already been decimated by poverty, unemployment, and crime? Although each of these cultural obstacles is considerable, I think they can be overcome.

The first hurdle is the United States' fierce individualism, reflected, ironically enough, in our preoccupation with constitutional rights. Constitutional rights are predicated on an individualistic, libertarian distrust of collective intrusions on personal freedoms. By contrast, Japan's system relies heavily on confessions, imposes fewer limits on police investigations, and tightly restricts defense attorneys' ability to turn criminal proceedings into adversarial affairs.[45] Our preoccupation with individual rights may interfere with community-based criminal justice reform.

What's more, the United States may be more individualistic today than ever before. Alexis de Tocqueville once pointed to Americans' high degree of involvement in voluntary associations as a critical underpinning of our democratic tradition:

> Americans of all ages, all stations in life, and all types of disposition are forever forming associations. There are not only commercial and industrial associations in which all take part, but others of a thousand different types — religious, moral, serious, futile, very general and very limited, immensely large and very minute. . . . In every case, at the head of any new undertaking, where in France you would find the government or in England some territorial magnate, in the United States you are sure to find an association.[46]

In recent years, however, Americans' community involvement has been on the decline. Sociologist Robert Putnam has argued that Americans have drastically reduced their involvement in public life over the past twenty-five years.[47] From the early 1960s to 1990, voter turnout in national elections dropped by almost one-quarter. Participation in voluntary associations, from the Boy Scouts to the League of Women Voters, is down markedly from the 1960s and 1970s. The number of Americans who told a Roper poll that they had attended any "public meeting on town or school affairs" in the past year has dropped by more than one-third since 1973. And over the same period, Americans have become less trusting of their neighbors and government.[48]

If there is no community on which to base criminal justice policy, how can a community-based policy succeed? Some argue that such an approach, like communitarianism generally, represents an unrealistic and nostalgiac yearning for a period we cannot recover, a period of smaller towns, less anonymity, and more community spirit. But that view presupposes that there is some sort of evolutionary trajectory from communitarianism to individualism. In fact, the conflicting needs of the individual and the collective will always be with us. There are signs that the cultural pendulum on this issue may have reached its individualistic zenith. Americans from all points of view and in all walks of life are beginning to understand the limits of individualism, and are seeking to reinvigorate a sense of community in their lives. In the academy, a growing interest in civic republicanism, communitarianism, and civic engagement across many disciplines reflects an effort to move beyond individualism.[49] Ten years ago, Don Herzog proclaimed that "[t]he most dramatic revision [in the history of political thought] of the last 25 years or so is the discovery—and celebration—of civic humanism,"[50] a concept that stresses the importance of civic responsibility and engagement in the community. There has been a revival of interest in the views of political thinkers who stress the importance of community values, such as de Tocqueville and John Winthrop, first governor of Massachusetts, who said, "We must delight in each other, make others' conditions our own, rejoyce together, mourn together, labor and suffer together, always having before our eyes our community as members of the same body."[51]

The communitarian movement has extended beyond the university. In the political realm, communitarians favor local over national government on the ground that local government fosters civic participation.[52] That preference appears to be gaining ground. As Lamar Alexander explained after the 1994 congressional elections, in which Republicans gained a majority in Congress on a platform highly critical of federal power: "For the last 30 years, most of the talk about New Federalism has been intellectual—the kind of thing that one-tenth of one percent of the people were interested in. What happened on November 8 was just a huge scream from the gut about the arrogance of Washington, D.C."[53] In 1996, the Democratic Party sought to jump on the bandwagon, boasting in its platform that "For years, Republicans talked about shifting power back to states and communities—Democrats are doing it."[54]

Charitable foundations meanwhile are directing millions of dollars toward civic renewal and communitarian initiatives.[55] The

National Endowment for the Humanities is sponsoring a national "Conversation" to spark civic engagement.[56] The efforts are often bipartisan: retiring Democratic Senator Sam Nunn recently joined former Republican Education Secretary William J. Bennett in founding the National Commission on Civic Renewal.[57] Even the "family values" movement, claimed initially by conservatives but subsequently adopted by liberals as well (albeit in a more tolerant guise), signals a sense of the importance of reinforcing the informal ties and structures that make a community strong.[58] Thus, as individualistic as we are, we may be ready as a nation to accept more community-based solutions.

The second obstacle to community-based criminal justice is that we live in a racially polarized society. Although appeals to "community" can be unifying, they can also be divisive. Historically, appeals to community were often advanced to justify segregation and discrimination against blacks. Today, Louis Farrakhan, the leader of the Nation of Islam, stresses the importance of community and responsibility, but his appeals are also fundamentally separatist; they are about the importance of *black* community. How does one develop a community-based criminal justice system without promoting ethnic balkanization when we already live in divided communities?

More specifically, where minority populations distrust the criminal justice system, they are less likely to take part in the processes of crime prevention, shaming, and reintegration. As Professor Daniel Foote notes, "[i]n a criminal-justice system based on reintegration into the community, the presence of groups that have not been—or consciously choose not to be—assimilated presents a fundamental dilemma for authorities."[59] In Japan, for example, Koreans and day laborers, two "out groups" that have not been assimilated into mainstream culture, are substantially less satisfied with the criminal justice system because they believe that the system's informal discretion operates to their disadvantage.[60] In our society, far more heterogeneous and racially polarized than Japan's, these problems would be multiplied. For the reasons already identified in this book, community-based reforms would likely fail miserably without substantial efforts to restore faith in the criminal justice system's legitimacy among minority populations. Thus, community-based reforms must go hand in hand with elimination of the double standards that encourage class and race divisions. In particular, any efforts to implement shaming rituals as an alternative to incarceration must endeavor to involve minority community members in the shaming process, so that the shaming is not seen as—and is not—an edict from a foreign, already distrusted, community.

A final objection to community-based criminal justice is that the communities most harmed by crime and the criminal justice system also tend to be those least suited to community-based reforms. Evaluations of community-based responses to crime consistently find that they work least well in neighborhoods characterized by substantial disorder, transience, and crime. In other words, they are least effective where they are needed most.[61] This is hardly surprising. High-crime areas typically exhibit lower participation rates in community groups and more distrust among neighbors. Most studies have found that indigenous community groups are more successful in responding to crime than groups initiated from without, and that organizations with broad agendas are more effective than groups focused specifically on crime. These factors also work to the disadvantage of poorer communities, which are less likely to have such preexisting organizations in place.

Churches and religious groups, however, often play an important role in such areas, and some of the most productive anticrime and reintegrative ventures have been allied with religious institutions.[62] The first program of the Chicago Assistance Project, for example, which sought to address the problem of crime in a working-class Polish neighborhood in the 1930s, worked closely with the local church, which it identified as the strongest institution in the community.[63] The La Playa project is run by a Catholic organization. Boston's community-policing initiatives have been coordinated closely with religious ministers who provide faith-based counseling and education in their neighborhoods.[64] And some of the most prominent community-based anticrime and reintegrative efforts today are run by the Nation of Islam, which actively recruits converts in the prisons and offers a strong social network to help them stay straight after their release.[65] The Establishment

Clause places some constraints on the sorts of government assistance that can be provided to religious institutions, but if government money is made available equally to secular and religiously affiliated organizations, it may well be permissible.[66] In any event, attempts to foster community-based responses to crime must take into account the paucity of existing institutional structures and resources in poor urban settings, and disproportionately direct resources to those neighborhoods that need intervention most.

In the end, although the obstacles to community-based criminal justice are formidable, the alternative is worse. Continuing down the path we are now on will only further weaken the community ties so essential to fighting crime effectively. Race and class divisions must be carefully considered in constructing community-based reforms, but nothing is likely to lead to greater division on this issue than more of the same. We cannot wait for communities to rebuild themselves before seeking community-based change in criminal justice, because the inequities in the criminal justice system have themselves contributed to the division and destruction that we see today. A divided society is not fertile ground for communitarianism, but more of the same will only deepen our society's divide. If we are to reform the criminal justice system, we must seek to reinvigorate community networks across race and class lines, within and beyond criminal law enforcement.

All the remedies in this book I have suggested are necessarily partial, and many are subject to the criticism that they fail to address racial and socioeconomic inequality directly. Acknowledging the problem is only a first step; restoring legitimacy by extending rights protections equally to all will not address much of the disparity in incarceration; and community-based criminal justice policies will be hampered by social forces beyond their control. But while such criticisms are valid, they must not prove debilitating. If the crime problem cannot be solved without first achieving racial and economic justice, the temptation is to give up on solving problems within the criminal justice system. But we must make choices every day about how we structure the criminal justice system, and about how we allocate resources toward preventing crime. Those choices should be informed by an understanding of the values of legitimacy and community in preventing crime, and the effects of different types of interventions and sanctions on those values. That criminal justice remedies are incomplete does not mean that they are futile. As is always the case in social reform, the solution, like the problem, extends far beyond one institution. But the synergy between inequality within and beyond the criminal justice system demands that we begin to look within the criminal justice system for alternatives to our current reliance on race and class disparities. We must stop using inequality to avoid difficult choices, and we must work to repair the damage our past uses have done.

ENDNOTES

1. But see Paul Butler, "Racially Based Jury Nullification: Black Power in the Criminal Justice System," 105 Yale L.J. 677 (1995) (advocating that black juries should acquit factually guilty black defendants of certain nonviolent crimes on the ground that they are black and that there are too many blacks in prison already).

2. U. S. Sentencing Commission, *Guidelines Manual*, §5H1.10, §5K2.12 (Nov. 1995).

3. See, e.g., Elliott Currie, *Crime and Punishment in America* (New York: Metropolitan Books, 1998).

4. Kennedy, "The State, Criminal Law, and Racial Discrimination: A Comment," 107 Harv. L. Rev. 1255 (1994); Randall Kennedy, *Race, Crime, and the Law* (New York: Pantheon, 1997). For a detailed response, see David Cole, "The Paradox of Race and Crime: A Comment on Randall Kennedy's 'Politics of Distinction'", 83 Geo. L.J. 2547 (1995).

5. "[I]n regard to crimes against the person, . . . the offender and the victim are usually of the same race, the same economic class, and also of the same neighborhood." Edwin H. Sutherland, *Principles of Criminology*, 44 (Philadelphia: Lippincott, 1939); see also Ronald Barri Flowers, *Demographics and Criminality: The Characteristics of Crime in America*, 105–11 (New York: Greenwood Press, 1989) (violent crime victims and perpetrators are predominantly poor); James F. Short, Jr., *Poverty, Ethnicity and Violent Crime*, 20–27 (Boulder, CO: Westview Press, 1997) (same).

6. *McCleskey v. Kemp*, 481 U.S. at 312 (quoting Kenneth Culp Davis, *Discretionary Justice: A Preliminary Inquiry*, 170 (Westport, CT: Greenwood Press, 1973)).

7. *Roberts v. Louisiana*, 431 U.S. 633, 636–37 (1977) (striking down mandatory death penalty because it precluded individualized consisderation of capital defendants).

8. See *State v. Russell*, 477 N.W.2d 886, 891 (Minn. 1991); Minn. Stat. §§ 152.023-152.025 (Supp. 1993).

9. Bill Leukhardt, "Probation Officers: Measuring Success in Increments," *Hartford Courant*, 13 April 1997, C1; Mark Braykovich & Cameron McWhirter, "California Offers Prime Example of How a Parole System Can Go Awry," *Gannett News Service*, 17 December 1995; Charles Linder & Robert L. Bonn, "Probation Officer Victimization and Fieldwork Practices: Results of a National Field Study," 60 Fed. Probation 16, 20 (June 1996).

10. See, e.g., *United States of America — Police Brutality in Los Angeles, California* (Amnesty Int'l Pub., 1992); Selwyn Raab, "Charges of Brutality: The Force," *N.Y. Times*, 17 August 1997, 41.

11. See, e.g., Janet Hook, "Crime Drop a Boost for Clinton, a Challenge for GOP," *L.A. Times*, 7 May 1996, A4 (Republican platform labeled Democratic crime bill as a "pork laden excuse for a crime bill").

12. Peter Reuter, "Punishing Without Reflection," 2 Drug Policy Analysis Bull. 1 (May 1997).

13. *Keeping Score*, 32 (Washington, D.C.: Drug Strategies, 1997).

14. Peter W. Greenwood, Karyn E. Model, C. Peter Rydell, & James Chiesa, *Diverting Children from a Life of Crime: Measuring Costs and Benefits* (Santa Monica, CA: Rand, 1996).

15. Prepared Testimony of Paul F. Evans, Commissioner, Boston Police Dep't, Before the Senate Judiciary Committee, Subcommittee on Youth Violence, Nov. 15, 1997 (Federal News Service, available on NEXIS); Blaine Harden, "Boston's Approach to Juvenile Crime Encircles Youths, Reduces Slayings," *Wash. Post*, 23 October 1997, A3.

16. Judith Greene, "Rudy's Crime-Rate Claims Seem Hollow," *Newsday*, 16 July 1998, A48.

17. Francis A. Allen, *The Decline of the Rehabilatative Ideal: Penal Policy and Social Purpose* (New Haven: Yale U. Press, 1981); Stephen D. Sowle, "A Resume of Social Death: Criminal Punishment in the Age of Prisons," 21 N.Y.U. Rev. of L. & Soc. Change 497 (1994); Elliott Currie, *Confronting Crime: An American Challenge*, 236–241 (New York: Pantheon, 1985) (arguing that conclusion that rehabilitation doesn't work may well be based on rehabilitation programs that failed to devote sufficient resources to the task); Neal Peirce, "Prison System in Georgia is an Olympic Tragedy," *New Orleans Times-Picayune*, 15 July 1996, B7 (detailing Georgia's reduction in rehabilitation and substance abuse programs in prisons).

18. N.Y. Civ. Rts. Law § 79-a.

19. Andrew L. Shapiro, "Challenging Criminal Disenfranchisement Under the Voting Rights Act: A New Strategy," 103 Yale L.J. 537, 538–39 (1993).

20. U.S. Dept of Justice, Office of the Pardon Attorney, *Civil Disabilities of Convicted Felons: A State-by-State Survey*, Appendix A (Oct. 1996).

21. 10 U.S.C. § 504.

22. Wendy Zentz, "Rough Road to a New Life: Ex-Cons Face High Hurdles," *Northern New Jersey Record*, 24 April 1991, A1. A recent survey of American employers found that about two-thirds are unwilling to hire former prisoners. Sherwood Ross, "Job Seeking Ex-Convicts Face Big Barriers," *Calgary Herald*, 2 March 1996, H10; see also Henry J. Patrick, "Eleven Myths About Hiring Ex-offenders," 66 *Personnel* 27 (Feb. 1989) (discussing employers' fears of hiring ex-prisoners); Clay Robison, "Jobs for Ex-Offenders a Crime Issue, Too," *Houston Chron.*, 17 July 1994, 21.

23. Jan Hoffman, "Crime and Punishment: Shame Gains Popularity," *N.Y. Times*, 16 January 1997, A1.

24. Dan M. Kahan, "What Do Alternative Sanctions Mean?," 63 U.Chi. L.Rev. 591, 630–53 (1996).

25. John Braithwaite, *Crime, Shame, and Reintegration* (New York: Cambridge Univ. Press, 1989).

26. For example, Theodore Ferdinand found in a study of juvenile justice programs that children subjected to "inclusionary," or rehabilitative, programs were less likely to engage in future criminal behavior than children subjected to "exclusionary," or punitive, measures. Theodore Ferdinand, "Juvenile Delinquency or Juvenile Justice: Which Came First," 27 Criminology 79, 103 (1989). See also Stevens H. Clarke and Anita L. Harrison, *Recidivism of Criminal Offenders Assigned to Community Correctional Programs or Released from Prisons in North Carolina in 1989,* 29–30 (Prepared for the North Carolina Sentencing and Policy Advisory Comm., 1992) (after controlling for other factors, finding that increase in severity of sanctions does not reduce recidivism in adults, and may increase it); Marvin E. Wolfgang, Robert M. Figlio, and Thorsten Sellin, *Delinquency in a Birth Cohort,* 25 (Chicago: Univ. of Chicago Press, 1972) (finding that the greater the punishment they received, the more likely children were to engage in criminal activity later); D.M. Hamparian, R. Schuster, S. Dinitz, and J.P. Conrad, *The Violent Few: A Study of Dangerous Juvenile Offenders,* 119 (Lexington, MA: Lexington Books, 1978) (finding, after controlling for type of offense, race, and economic status, that youth subjected to the least intrusive sanction were least likely to engage in subsequent criminal behavior, and those subject to the most severe sanction were most likely to do so).

27. Braithwaite, *supra* note 25 at 61.

28. Nicholas D. Kristoff, "In Japan, Nothing to Fear but Fear Itself," *N.Y. Times,* 19 May 1996, E4; Federal Bureau of Investigation, *Uniform Crime Reports for the United States, 1995,* tbl. 2.10 (1996).

29. Daniel H. Foote, "The Benevolent Paternalism of Japanese Criminal Justice," 80 Cal. L.Rev. 317, 318, 345 n. 174 (1992); Federal Bureau of Investigation, U.S. Dept. of Justice, *Uniform Crime Reports for the United States,* 163, tbl. 20 (1990).

30. Foote, *supra* note 29 at 318.

31. Braithwaite, *supra* note 25 at 61.

32. Id. at 63–64.

33. Foote, *supra* note 29 at 342.

34. Id. at 347.

35. Id. at 350.

36. Id. at 353.

37. Id. at 355.

38. Id. at 348, quoting Speech of Procurator General Hiranuma (1914). That philosophy continues to inform the today's criminal justice system. Id. at 348–50. In describing the goals of suspension in Japan today, five Ministry of Justice researchers wrote:

> Japanese prosecutors have two primary missions. One is that of the strict prosecutor who does not let the evil sleep and who cries along with the victims. The other is that of the prosecutor who devotes efforts to the reform of offenders so that they will not return to crime, a role that at time entails crying along with the offfenders . . . Suspension of prosecution is a key tool for prosecutors in achieving this [latter] mission.

Id. at 349 (quoting Takeo Momose et al., *Study on the Actual Administration of the System of Suspended Prosecution after World War II (Following the Enactment of the Current Code of Criminal Procedure) and Recidivism by Those Whose Prosecution was Suspended*).

39. Robert L. Woodson, ed., *Youth Crime and Urban Policy: A View From the Inner City* 95 (Washington: American Enterprise Institute, 1981).

40. *Keeping Score, supra* note 13 at 34 (reporting that Florida and California now spend more on prison systems than on public universities).

41. "Crime in America: Violent and Irrational — and That's Just the Policy," *The Economist*, June 8, 1996, 23, 24.

42. Fox Butterfield, "More Blacks in Their 20's Have Trouble With the Law," *N.Y. Times*, 5 October 1995, A18.

43. Statement of General Barry R. McCaffrey, Director, Office of National Drug Control Policy, Before the Subcommittee on National Security, International Affairs, and Criminal Justice of the House Committee on Government Reform and Oversight, 28 February 1997, 8.

44. Christopher S. Wren, "Hartford Mulls an Overhaul of Drug Laws," *N.Y. Times*, 21 April 1997, B5.

45. Foote, *supra* note 29 at 380–81.

46. Alexis de Tocqueville, *Democracy in America*, 523 (trans. George Lawrence, ed. J.P. Mayer) (New York: Harper & Row, 1969).

47. Robert D. Putnam, "Bowling Alone: America's Declining Social Capital," 6 J. of Democracy 65 (Jan. 1995).

48. Id. at 67–73.

49. See, e.g., Frank Michelman, "The Supreme Court, 1985 Term — Foreword: Traces of Self-Government," 100 Harv. L. Rev. 4 (1986) (republicanism); Cass R. Sunstein, "Beyond the Republican Revival," 97 Yale L. J. 1713 (1988) (same); Amitai Etzioni, *The Spirit of Community: Rights, Responsibilities, and the Communitarian Agenda* (New York: Crown Pub., 1993)(communitarianism); Robert D. Putnam, *Making Democracy Work: Civic Traditions in Modern Italy* (Princeton, N.J.: Princeton Univ. Press, 1993) (civic society); see also Robert N. Bellah, Richard Madsen, William M. Sullivan, Ann Swidler & Steven M. Tipton, *Habits of the Heart: Individualism and Commitment in American Life* (Berkeley, CA: Univ. of California Press, 1985) (arguing that individualism has overtaken Americans' commitment to community, and threatens democracy).

50. Don Herzog, "Some Questions for Republicans," 14 Pol. Theory 473 (1986).

51. John Winthrop, "A Model of Christian Charity," in Edmund S. Morgan, ed., *Puritan Political Ideas, 1558–1794*, 92 (Indianapolis: Bobbs-Merrill, 1965).

52. See, e.g., Andrzej Rapaczynski, "From Sovereignty to Process: The Jurisprudence of Federalism After Garcia," 1985 Sup. Ct. Rev. 341, 389.

53. Rochelle L. Stanfield, "The New Federalism," 27 Natl. Journal 226 (January 1995).

54. Richard L. Berke, "Forget Washington: Social Issues Shift to the States," *N.Y. Times*, 19 October 1997, sec. 4, p.5.

55. Melissa Healy, "Civic Renewal: New Money, Old Values: The US Is Awash with National Commissions Being Set Up to Promote 'Active Citizenship,'" *The Guardian*, 8 January 1997.

56. Jacqueline Trescott, "Hackney: Can We Talk?," *Wash. Post*, 11 November 1993, C11.

57. Healy, *supra* note 54.

58. See, e.g., William Bennett, *The Book of Virtues: A Treasury of Great Moral Stories* (New York: Simon & Schuster, 1993); William Bennett, *Moral Poverty . . . And*

How to Win America's War Against Crime & Drugs (New York: Simon & Schuster, 1996).

59. Foote, *supra* note 29 at 376.

60. Id. at 369, 375.

61. See Wesley G. Skogan, "Community Organizations and Crime," in Michael Tonry & Norval Morris, eds., 10 *Crime and Justice: A Review of Research* 39, 42 (1988).

62. Diane Cohen & Robert Jaeger, *Sacred Places at Risk* (Philadelphia: Partners for Sacred Places, 1998).

63. Robert J. Bursick, Jr. & Harold G. Grasmick, *Neighborhoods and Crime: The Dimensions of Effective Community Control*, 160–66 (New York: Lexington Books, 1993) and Stephen Schlossman, et al., *Delinquency Prevention in South Chicago: A Fifty Year Assessment of the Chicago Area Project* (Santa Monica, CA: Rand Corp., 1984).

64. John J. DiIulio, Jr., "How Faith Fights Crime: Fixing Stained-Glass Windows," *Pittsburgh Post-Gazette*, 30 November 1997, B1.

65. See, e.g., See, e.g., Ann Kaslow, "Nation of Islam Extends Its Reach Behind Prison Walls," *Christian Science Mon.*, 20 May 1996, 9; James Brooke, "Million Man March Inspires Action in Denver Neighborhoods," *Dallas Morn. News*, 31 March 1996, 4A. As noted above, although the Nation of Islam understands the importance of community, its efforts are compromised by its reliance on separatism to foster community spirit.

66. See *Bowen v. Kendrick*, 487 U.S. 589 (1988) (rejecting constitutional challenge to Adolescent Family Life Act, which authorized federal grants to public and private organizations, including organizations tied to religious institutions, on ground that purpose and effect of program was not to further religion).

—Index

Please remember that this is a library book,
and that it belongs only temporarily to each
person who uses it. Be considerate. Do
not write in this, or any, library book.

DATE DUE

DE 12 '03			

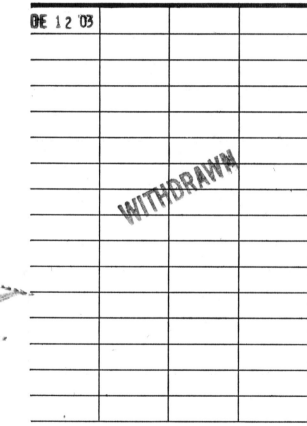